Dancing with GIs

Dancing with GIs

A Red Cross Club Worker
in India, World War II

Libby Chitwood Appel

ISBN 1-886057-52-4
Library of Congress Control Number: 2004106157

Library of Congress Cataloging in Publication Data.
Appel, Libby. Dancing with GIs. Summary: A memoir of
the adventures of a Red Cross club worker in India
during World War II. 1. WWII 2. India 3. Red Cross
4. Memoir 5. U.S.A.F. 6. The Hump 7. CBI.

Manufactured in the United States of America
First Edition

To

J.C.

My favorite GI

"The dancing foot,
the sound of tinkling bells—
Find these within yourself, then
shall your fetters fall away."
The Dance of Shiva

Assignments and Stopovers
(Follow the numbers)

Foreword

"A true war story is never moral. It does not instruct, nor encourage virtue, nor suggest models of proper human behavior, nor restrain men from doing the things they have always done."

Tim O'Brien in "*How to Tell a True War Story.*"

This is a happy story about the lighter side of WWII. It tells of close shaves and scary encounters, but not of combat or casualties.

In November 1943 I was part of a motley crew of Red Cross, military, and civilian personnel, along with 10,000 GIs, that left from Santa Ana, California on the refurbished liner *Uruguay*, headed for the Far East.

We Red Cross girls, attached to SAF (Services to the Armed Forces), served as adjunct personnel to the military in cities and remote field stations all over the CBI (China Burma India) theatre. I was assigned to a jungle base in Assam, then to the city club in Karachi. Two glamorous leaves fulfilled childhood dreams: three weeks aboard a houseboat in Kashmir and a fabulous week as guest of an Indian prince, The Nawab of Palanpur.

As staff assistants and club directors we served coffee, doughnuts, and entertainment, plus lots of loving listening, to bored GIs who lounged about the Red Cross canteens. Homesick soldiers treated us variously as pals, servants, or special angels.

My main job was to play piano for dancing, singing, and just plain listening to the wonderful tunes of the '20s through the '40s. But I also wore other hats: program director, house manager, accountant, hostess to celebrities, counselor, and sympathetic hand-holder for troubled GIs.

This is a memoir, not history. Memory lapsed on some details, so creative reconstruction filled in the gaps. Told in anecdotes, vignettes, letters, local color, and social comments, it chronicles the sometimes fearful and often amusing interplay of male-female relationships in an exotic wartime setting. The final chapters carry through my courtship and elopement in India with my GI husband, J.C. Appel.

Contents

Part Six: We Visit the Prince

Prologue

"Be careful what you set your heart on, for some day it
may be yours."

Agnes Cady Chitwood

Cross Nurse Girl

On a sunny summer afternoon in 1917 one of my
mother's friends stopped by for a chat on the front
porch of our buff brick house in Morgantown, West Virginia. Mom was reading in the wicker rocker while I played
doctor with my dolls on the grass rug. Mrs. Carlin plunked
down on the wooden swing, asked the names of my dolls
and the status of their health. Satisfied that Henrietta
and Sarah Jane were receiving adequate medical care,
she said, "What do you want to be when you grow up,
Elizabeth Anne?"

"I'm gonna be a Cross nurse girl," came the instant
reply. "And take care of sick soldiers and fix bandages on
their broken arms. My Mommy's gonna make me a white
cap with a big red cross on it."

At age three I was deep into the glamour of World War
I, though protected from the horrors of combat in our quiet
university town, where young lieutenants in the ROTC
practiced their drills on Main Street and danced with campus beauties at the military balls.

Florence Nightingale, in her nun-like white hood, was
the idol of good little girls everywhere. The Red Cross nurse
symbolized compassion, service, beauty, and adventure.
Newspapers, magazines and billboards all over town depicted American nurses, with big red crosses on their
starched white uniforms, ministering to bandaged and
bleeding casualties. Olive drab ambulances with red
crosses on sides and tops, sirens screaming, drove through
downtown alerted all to help out in the war effort.

By the time I was six and the war over my attraction to the medical field ended. Though the nurse part of my childhood ambition never did come true, the Cross part was fulfilled twenty-five years later, when I volunteered for duty in 1943 as an American Red Cross overseas recreation worker. For eighteen happy months I was a dedicated Red Cross staff assistant, serving coffee and doughnuts and lots of loving attention to GIs in India—proud to be a part of that great organization.

Part One
Washington Training and Pacific Cruise

"Ship me somewhere east of Suez
where the flying fishes play."

Rudyard Kipling

The Crucial Question

"Can you hold your own in that morass of sex?"
Mrs. Kinsolving's beady eyes bored into mine. Her thunderbolt question, shot at me in a cold, clipped New England voice, momentarily stymied my response.

It was the last question at the end of a hot, grueling day. On my reply depended my biggest life-changing moment—acceptance or rejection by the American Red Cross for their exclusive overseas club service.

Riveted to her steely stare, I dared not wince or turn away. But I needed to collect my thoughts.

How should I answer? What could I say? What did she expect—literal truth or a hedged reply, innocence or a working knowledge? Should I come right out and admit to fifteen years' experience in warding off predatory males? Should I appear hardened or softly Southern? What was she looking for—a business type or a butterfly, a career girl or a deb? How about a naive-sophisticate?

A booming repetition of the question interrupted my musing.

"CAN YOU HOLD YOUR OWN IN THAT MORASS OF SEX?"

Suddenly, from out of the blue, a single forceful word escaped my lips, surprising both of us. Unflinching before her forbidding presence, I shouted "Yes!" and then lowered my glance to await her reply.

Mrs. K. eased back in her leather swivel chair. "You'll do," she said. "Pick up your orders in the office next door and report back here in two weeks."

After a pause and a smile, she concluded, "And by the way, welcome to the Red Cross."

That scorching summer day marked the culmination of nine months of dreaming and scheming. The "big boss" had sealed my fate for the next two years and, indirectly, my destiny for the next forty-seven.

The Mrs. Miniver Hat

It all began in the fall of 1942, when I was working on my doctorate in French at the University of Wisconsin. Casting about for some way to help in the war effort, I applied for officers' training in the WAVES, hoping for assignment in Europe or North Africa, where my spoken French would come in handy.

For the next six months I haunted the post office in vain for a reply. Fifteen months later in India a letter from the Navy arrived, commanding me to report for ensign training.

In the meantime I had heard about the Red Cross overseas club service and, in the spring of 1943, wrote them for an interview. This job, I reasoned, was right up my alley, tailor-made for an enthusiastic, adventure-loving, socially inclined Southern gal, who loved male company and could dance, sing, and play the swing tunes of the 20s, 30s, and 40s on the piano by ear.

Ten days before I was due to walk up the aisle in cap and gown to collect my graduate degree, a letter from ARC summoned me to Washington. Right away I dashed into Dean Fred's Bascom Hall office in my usual class outfit— shorts, sneakers, bobby socks, and two long plaits with red end-ribbons hanging down my back—not exactly the most appropriate attire for a serious interview.

Looking me up and down, Dean Fred greeted me first with a frown, then with a wide grin. Breathless before him, I blurted out, "Oh, Dean Fred, I've got to report to Washington in two weeks, so I can't stay for commencement. Could you please send my degree later on to my home?"

"Wa-a-it just a minute!" came his surprised reply. "Why can't you pick up your degree in person? I'll need some explanation to give my committee."

All in a burst I described my situation and my need for a few last days at home to pack up, get a perm, do some shopping, and say my goodbyes.

He gave me a look of mock seriousness. "Well, young lady, we'll have to bend the rules a bit, but I guess that can be arranged. But be informed: it will be the first time the University of Wisconsin has ever awarded a Ph.D to a candidate in pigtails!"

Euphoria set in. I felt like a preacher, called to minister fun and games to lonely GIs. A glow of joyful anticipation transformed me. I could hardly wait to fulfill my girlhood dreams of high adventure.

A week later, dressed in a beige suit, and wearing a big, brown Mrs. Miniver hat, I boarded the train for home. Within a half-hour a tall handsome colonel invited me to join him for a drink and chat during the stopover in Chicago—the perfect prelude to what was to follow during the next two years.

Getting to Know Us

A fitting start of the Great Adventure for this small-
town girl was my first overnight ride in a Pullman,
from Shenandoah Junction to Washington, D.C. in midsummer 1943. From the moment a white-coated porter
tossed my bags into an upper berth, I experienced a happy
exhilaration that lasted throughout my Red Cross career.

On arrival at Union Station I was whisked off to the
Eye Street headquarters for check-in, then ferried over to
American University for registration and orientation. Ini-
tially my living quarters were the Hotel Benedict, close to
the main Red Cross office. Then I was transferred to the
Burlington on Thomas Circle, a hostelry already known
to me from childhood, when I was taken across the mountains to have my teeth straightened by Dr. Stephen C.
Hopkins, whose office was in that hotel.

Washington itself was like a second hometown to me.
All through the 1920s I had spent summers and my father's
sabbaticals at our second home in Herndon, Virginia, then
thirty miles from Georgetown but now a part of greater
D.C. We used to ride the "milk train" into Roslyn, and
then hop on the trolley to the Smithsonian, the Library of
Congress, Capitol Hill, Woodward and Lothrup's, and the
little shops along F Street. I learned to drive in Washington during the summer of 1930.

By 1943, however, "the city," as Dad called it, had
greatly changed. The trolley was gone. The downtown
streets had become boulevards, though the pesky traffic
circles remained. The little shops had moved uptown to
posh Connecticut Avenue. And Woodward and Lothrop's
now bowed to Garfinkel's for preeminence in ladies' fash-
ions. Expensive restaurants had sprung up all over to serve
the sudden influx of wartime personnel and their families.

Red Cross training was a far cry from the learned
lectures of my ivory-tower years. Our instructors

indoctrinated us with pride in our chosen career and loyalty to the philosophy of the American Red Cross. I wrote home:

> *They make us feel like we are part of a big organization about which we should know everything. They make us feel equal—no one is above anyone else in the opportunity of rendering service. We keep so constantly thrilled that we wear ourselves out.*

> *For the first three days we learned about Red Cross involvement overseas, its set-up, operation, and general expectations, as well as details of our association with and dependence on the military and government agencies. After that we got down to the serious business of how to staff and run canteens and clubs, with hands-on training in Washington and coastal Virginia.*

> *As overseas workers our raison d'etre was to boost the morale of homesick GIs and attached civilian personnel. Some years later my husband told me, "You were sent over there to keep us GIs out of the beer halls."*

From the very beginning I was hooked on this job and could hardly wait to go overseas.

This is the Life!

*M*aking thatched panels of finger-pricking straw and attaching them to a rough wooden frame was hard on lily-white hands and manicured nails. "Hands-on training" was a good name for this project. But we didn't mind scratched fingers and sunburned faces or even the broiling Washington heat. It was all for the good of the cause and a new adventure for us. Our job was to build a rustic canteen for the "Back the Attack" campaign in downtown DC, where we were to sell war bonds and refreshments.

For this huge army show, set up around the Washington Monument, twenty girls were chosen from us Red Cross trainees, the New York office, and nearby training camps. We served GIs, Red Cross personnel, and luminaries in the military and theatrical worlds, as well as war bond buyers who needed refreshment. A carnival atmosphere prevailed as we worked like gas meters to meet the construction deadline for setting up a basha like those in far Eastern stations. We called it The Hut. Just before we opened for business I wrote home:

> *Under ordinary circumstances I would be nicely dressed and sitting before a table laden with delicious food, but now as the clock says 6:30 I'm as dirty as a pig and sitting in a hot clubmobile, typing on my knees. All day long, except for an hour for lunch, I've been down here at The Hut doing all kinds of work, from shoveling sand to keeping the accounts in my little office.*
>
> *We are working hard but we love it. The construction work is all done. Beginning tomorrow we administrative assistants in this rustic office will be working on six-hour shifts. Now our real duties begin.*

Attracting bond buyers to The Hut was our first challenge as canteen staff. With the help of the military and public-spirited civilian volunteers, we provided entertainment and a temporary respite from the glaring sun. For those who watched the troops, tanks, and stage shows parading down Pennsylvania Avenue, we served the usual Red Cross fare: coffee, doughnuts, and cold drinks.

From our ringside seats inside The Hut we had a good view of the performers' stand and the taped-off street. We waved to celebrity Lucille Ball, resplendent in a frilly pink satin frock and golden curls, as she threw kisses from her open limo to the cheering crowds. On another day a young Victor Borge stumbled through his hilarious routine, enchanting the audience with his antics and artistry. Other movie stars: Greer Garson, Paul Henreid, Judy Garland, James Cagney, and Fred Astaire thrilled the throngs as they sang and danced and did their routines on the flag-draped outdoor stage.

In the last week of the show, a nice camaraderie developed between the Red Cross girls and the military men who frequented the canteen. I wrote:

> *My, what a three days this has been! Last night I talked with three very interesting men: a Jewish private who was a writer before being drafted; a big burly Wisconsin lieutenant who couldn't read a word of music, but beat us all playing piano by ear; and a corporal who got so interested in clay modeling that he forgot to go to work.*

During the last week four Signal Corps men became our regular visitors and buddies. Two were professional writers; one was a photographer, and one an artist. All worked on scripts and skits for army propaganda films. They hailed most recently from Astoria, New York, where William Saroyan and other writers were still stationed.

Sympathetic listening, spirited conversation, and exchanged confidences became our stock-in-trade with these interesting GIs.

The artist, a short fat fellow, made caricatures of us Red Cross girls. His pencil portrait exaggerated my square, jutting jaw. As I tore up the unflattering sketch, I commented, "Now I understand Bobby Burns's 'seeing oursel's as ithers see us.' I didn't know I looked that bossy. Next time, please sketch me below the knees."

Lester Cooper, most quiet of the four, had sold a story the week before and was supporting the other boys until that payment ran out. One day he and I got into a serious personal conversation. He told me he had been engaged to Kathie Thompson, a lovely girl whom I had met at the Embassy Club in Washington. Somehow I reminded him of her.

Lester loved hearing me play on the little console piano in the canteen. One day when I was playing a Chopin nocturne, Harold came by to unload his problems. We talked for the rest of that day. Over in a corner Kermit, the youngest and handsomest of the four, was creating a lovely lady of clay. I wondered if his imagined model was Nancy Sprague, a Red Cross girl to whom he was attracted. Kermit was married.

I hated to say goodbye to these great guys, knowing I probably would never see them again and that some of them might not come back from their assignments. They made me feel good about my mission as a Red Cross worker.

As the last week wore on, the morale of workers and visitors deteriorated, with changes in personnel at The Hut and many of our GI regulars called to duty. The life seemed to have gone out of the project. Only a handful of us builders were left and the new girls didn't share the affection for the place that we had. It was time to move on to new adventures.

At Camp Patrick Henry near Newport News, Virginia. we had our first taste of living with the troops.

For two weeks we were privileged to bunk in unheated, unpainted wood barracks. We slept on army cots sans sheets, with steel lockers at the foot for storing gear and personal items. A single chair was the occasional resting place for thirty girls, for the footlocker tops, though just the right height for sitting, were cluttered with cosmetic paraphernalia. A smelly, unheated outdoor latrine, with shower and two washbasins, prepared us for primitive facilities in the field.

In mid-October 1943 I wrote home from this training station:

> *This life is so full, exciting, and wonderful that I have to pinch myself every once in a while to see if it is real. I wouldn't have missed the experience of being in this camp for all the money in the world. We're working like dogs, and loving every minute of it.*
>
> *We plan all the entertainment for the men (GIs, not officers) and are on duty all day long until 10:00 PM. At that time we usually walk back to the barracks with enlisted men, then go out until 11:00 or 12:00 to the officers' club. Keeping the men off is our biggest problem. They all love us and want dates.*
>
> *In the morning we serve coffee and doughnuts, which means a lot of KP, plus sweeping, mopping, and straightening the rec halls. We do everything from emptying the garbage pails to running the cash register.*

Afternoons usually found me trying to cheer up the soldiers in Rec Hall 2 where most of the black GIs hung out. My main job was to dance with these men. Their great good humor and hearty laughter were refreshing after the eternal GI gripe. And oh, how they could "swing and sway with Sammy Kaye!" I was good at the two-step, rumba, tango, waltz, and Charleston, but never did get the hang of the jitterbug. To the youngsters who tried to teach me that tricky routine I tried to teach the Charleston, both with signal unsuccess.

Whenever my dancing partners, white or black, got a little too chummy, I turned the conversation to "book larnin." As soon as I mentioned graduate degrees, the cheek-to-cheek clutch relaxed. If they persisted in a too close embrace, I'd say, "Loosen up, friend. You're strangling me and my legs won't work."

My favorite duties at Camp Patrick Henry, pure pleasure, always involved music and art. There I began playing by ear the hit tunes for dancing and singing. Favorite songs were "It Had to be You," "Sweet Sue," "Stardust," and "Shine on Harvest Moon." When I wasn't providing the music, we used records and radio. Occasionally we could gather together a four-piece combo or quartet from among the GIs and hornswoggle a few officers to help out. Often I served as vocal soloist or jazz accompanist for these groups.

My letter continued:

> There are a good many first-rate musicians here. Yesterday, we had a grand time singing the last scene from La Bohème, with a tenor, a baritone, a pianist, and me. And there are also some grand artists here. I'm starting an art club tonight after the library closes. We are to meet three times a week and draw portraits. Tonight I am the model.

> We're going to offer prizes for the best artwork, as a part of the county fair planned for this weekend.

Army chow at any post always comes in for gripes and jokes. The men lucked out at Camp Patrick Henry, where hamburgers, fried chicken, spaghetti and meatballs, and even occasional steaks topped the menus. Cakes and pies, plus Hershey bars, satisfied my sweet tooth and chocolate addiction. I wrote to my family:

> I love Army life and don't mind the food. We do not dine in the mess hall with officers, but "mess" in a rough barracks with the enlisted WACs, most of whom are truck drivers and rather rough. But we have our own tables and like the WACs on the whole.

> Originally there were 19 girls in our group, distributed between two service clubs with attached rec. halls. Now our group has dwindled to 11 or 12 and gets smaller almost daily, as some are called to active duty, or replaced by new trainees.

> The other night, when we were coming back from supper, we saw a strange sight. A big, tall oak tree,

tired of living, had keeled over and died, smashing the barracks two doors down from ours. We all figured out what would have happened if it had been our barracks. I would have been flattened and Anna Lou would have got quite a bump on the head.

Within ten days, call-to-duty had lowered our numbers, leaving barracks space for visitors. We shared quarters with two attractive black staff assistants who came to help out in Red Hall 2. Later a troupe of USO girls lived with us for a few days. These transient female attractions provided a temporary boon to a few officers, but luckily did not cut into our nightly dates with our special beaux.

Throughout our training and field duty the "man problem" was the greatest concern of our supervisors. Control of dating was everywhere a losing proposition, which explains Mrs. K's interview question about sexual forbearance. Some supervisors insisted on our dating only enlisted men. Others forbade off-duty socializing with GIs. A few scheduled our work hours to preclude nighttime dating. But at each station most of us soon settled down to a steady, who usually survived as best friend only a few months after we arrived at our next station.

But before I had a chance to get too embroiled with the CPH troops, I was shipped back to Washington to await a long delayed voyage across the Pacific.

Betty

At Camp Patrick Henry we lower-echelon Red Cross girls ran into a problem prevalent throughout the service— our personal relationships with group leaders and our distaste for taking orders from our peers. Betty was a case in point.

We were fifteen eager, rebellious staff assistants from all over the US and from varied professional, business, and social backgrounds. Betty, our group leader, was a tall, slender, dedicated former high-school teacher from Michigan, in training to be a club director. On her footlocker reposed the only personal photo in the barracks— a handsome blond corporal in dress uniform, obviously her true love. She dated no one at camp. We others dated officers nightly and sometimes "walked out" in the daytime or after work with GIs.

Betty's duties were to schedule our assignments and keep us in tow. To these she added two others; to monitor our off-duty behavior and to set an example, in which roles she was unappreciated. While we staff assistants bent the rules and sneaked out for nighttime fun, Betty, who opposed evening dates, especially with officers, stuck to her guns and spent her evenings in the post library or played cards with GIs. We chafed against her strict leadership.

None of us really cottoned to Betty and she had no special buddy. Her aloof manner turned us off. We excluded her from our mealtime confabs and nightly bull sessions. Though she never pulled rank, we made snide remarks as she sauntered by, ramrod straight, head held high in perfect self-control.

"Why can't she smile once in a while?" we complained. "And why does she have to be so damned righteous about everything?"

So Betty became a loner. It never occurred to us that she was simply doing her job and getting no help from us. Only years later did I realize how lonely she must have been and how totally bitchy we had been to her.

One night at dinner in the mess hall Stella Reichert said, "I'm fed to the teeth with Her Highness' rules." To which Mary Marshall added, "I can't stand her smug air of superiority. Why can't she loosen up a bit and join in the fun?"

Back at the barracks a dozen disgruntled females ganged up on her and let her have it. A startled Betty was invited into the only chair, in the middle of the room, while we staff assistants squatted on the bare floor in a circle around her.

"We're tired of being treated like children," Jenny Johnson said. "We're old enough to know how to behave. We can make our own decisions."

"Why don't you have a date once in a while?" Susan Sontag chimed in. "Your true love can't watch you from overseas."

"It would be nice if you would occasionally help to clean the latrines. And your corporal surely wouldn't object to your dancing in the rec halls. We all know you're a good dancer. You need to keep in practice. Officers aren't off limits, you know." And so it went for a quarter-hour.

As we spouted off our complaints, Betty sat there, a solemn silent defendant before the prejudiced jury of her peers. She offered no defense or apologies; she showed no anger or evidence of guilt. She took it, as they say, like a trooper. And down deep, then and later, we admired her for her stance.

In the hectic days after that I forgot all about Betty. She was shipped off right away to North Africa and I, after a month's wait in Washington, was transported across the country to California and departure for India.

A year later, in 1944, Betty showed up again in my life, not in person, but by association with the handsome GI, whose photo had graced her footlocker at Camp Patrick Henry.

One day in late December a GI whom I had met at a dance the week before came into my canteen for the first time. He looked vaguely familiar. We started talking about home and the friends we had left behind. He told me about his long-term love, who was now with the Red Cross somewhere in North Africa. It had been months since he had heard from her and he was really hurting for a letter. In fact, he had given up on her.

"What's her name?" I asked, just to make conversation.

"Betty Dehn," he answered. "We went together for four years in Michigan. But I haven't heard from her in six months, so I suppose she has found an officer to take back home."

"Oh, I know her," I said. "She was my group leader back at Camp Patrick Henry in 1943." I refrained from further comment, except to say, "I know she is doing a good job as club director wherever she is."

Fifty-five years later Betty popped up in my life unexpectedly at the retirement complex where I now reside. One Sunday in 1998 I spotted Robbie Ross, elegant wheelchair resident from the nursing wing, having dinner in our main dining room with a handsome non-resident couple. Happy to see her outside her confined quarters, I went over to welcome her with a hug.

"Do sit down and join us," she said. "I want you to meet my guests from Charlotte."

To her left was a tall slim woman, of what the French call uncertain age, the epitome of style in her beige Montaldo's suit and Ferragamos. To her right lounged a handsome hunk with thick wavy salt-and-pepper hair.

"This," Robbie said, "is my young friend Betty Graham and her Jim, who was my late husband's protégé so many years ago."

Then turning to me, Robbie said, "And this is Libby Appel, who often comes to see me and plays the piano for us in Health Care."

The usual exchange of social chitchat soon revealed that Betty had grown up in Michigan and had been a Red Cross club director during the war. On learning that I had served in India as a Red Cross staff assistant, Betty looked at me quizzically and said, "Did you say your name is Libby Appel?"

Before I had a chance to answer she blurted out, "Oh, I remember you from Camp Patrick Henry. You must be Libby Anne Chitwood."

"And you must be Betty Dehn," I responded. Wherewith we got up from the table and embraced each other.

Then began a fun-filled exchange of illuminating accounts of our association with the same man. When Betty protested a simple friendship with J.C. Appel over their four years of going-together before the war, I could not refrain from remarking, "But I found your clothes still in J.C.'s hunting cabin when we went back there for a belated honeymoon."

"Yes, but it was purely a platonic relationship," she said. "We were best friends and respected each other too much to become involved in the way you imply."

Her Jim, off to one side, sat back in his chair, chuckled, and said, "Just wait 'til I get you home tonight."

Betty and I promised to get together again to hash over old times. This we did, and still do, and we have become good friends. Betty had found her handsome Captain on a second Red Cross tour in Italy. Now with five attentive children and their families nearby, she carries on alone without her Jim, who died soon after that meeting here at The Pines.

Our GI corporal, after thirty years as a wildlife refuge manager, died in 1992 at age seventy-three, but still lives in the memories of the two women who loved him.

The Blue Panties

The WAVES had it all over us, with their stylish navy twills, dress whites, and perky little hats with turned-up brims. Even the WACS in their khakis looked more trim and alluring than we Red Cross girls in our summer uniforms. Our light gray seersucker suits with their narrow knee-length skirts always hiked up when we climbed in and out of jeeps and weapons carriers, not to mention gharrys and tongas, which required a big step up.

Once in Karachi (now Pakistan) I had reason to curse the tight skirt as I dismounted from a jeep outside KGA Hall, our Red Cross city club. The usual quorum of GIs, hanging around outside, ogled my every move. I heard a ripple of laughter and mild catcalls from the onlookers.

"What's the matter, fellows?" I demanded. "Something on your mind?"

"We like your blue panties," one intrepid GI answered. The others chorused, "We sure do!" I was shocked, mildly.

"How do you know they are blue?"

"Saw them when you climbed into the jeep," the GI confessed. "Why do you think we're standing here?"

"Glad to know you are observant," I said. "But how about allowing a girl some privacy. Can't you stand back a little?"

Thereafter, I was careful to pull down my skirt and mount all vehicles on the side away from the line-up, though it did seem a shame to deprive homesick GIs of such a simple pleasure.

Our winter uniforms were a cut above the skimpy seersuckers, both in comfort and fit. Dark blue wool twill suits with white broadcloth shirts were trim and almost wrinkle-proof. For really cold weather we were issued heavy overcoats. When Karachi's three-week winter swooped down on us without warning, we were grateful for the ugly, bulky outerwear. Our year-round work shoes were low-heeled black oxfords. High-heeled pumps were only allowed on off duty.

Looking pretty was essential to keeping up our morale and to brightening up that of downcast GIs. Though we wore our uniforms for most official duties, luckily we had sartorial leeway for the rest of the time. Sweaters, tailored slacks, shorts, and even drab army fatigues were acceptable for daytime wear at field stations and some outlying city clubs. Colorful, casual short afternoon dresses or long evening gowns were de rigueur for post entertainments and dates on the town.

We girls were generous in lending one another clothes. We even gave them to newcomers whose baggage was lost. When Nancy Hemingway arrived at our outpost in Assam in early 1944, with literally only the clothes on her back, we four staff assistants pitched in to provide dresses and sweaters for her. The new plaid cotton that my mother had sent me just a few days before looked better on her than on me. It became her favorite day dress for the next few weeks.

Like the college girls we had been, we traded clothes and jewelry as we tired of them. The long pink lace gown that my mom had worn, as mother of the groom at my brother's wedding in 1938, was still in style five years later, and it looked great on Esther Pfennig, a gorgeous blonde former model for *Life.*

I combed the native bazaars for exotic fabrics to take home with me: bright cotton Indian prints, Benares silks, and embroidered satins in vivid red, teal blue, sunlight yellow, lime green, hot pink, purple, and black. A local durzi was kept busy stitching up perfectly fitted shorts and skirts for me.

My favorite out-of-uniform attire in Kashmir was an Indian animal-print shorts and halter, with sheepskin Russian style hat. In Karachi, a satin paisley housecoat in bright blue and red, created for at-home wear but elegant enough to wear to a GI dance, was the eye-catcher that attracted the corporal who beat out all officers for my attention.

Only a few of these glamorous outfits eventually made it back to the States, graciously shipped home by the army in early 1945. All the rest, along with well worn uniforms, shoes, treasured jewelry, artifacts, and personal items, were stolen from my overstuffed B-4 bag in Tripoli, during the long return trip by air across North Africa in June 1945. I arrived in Miami with only the clothes I was wearing, minus a shoe, left behind somewhere in the bowels of the huge, overcrowded C-87 that brought me back to the States.

Belles and Beaux

Readers of this generation may find it hard to understand the male-female relationships of my youth in the '30s and '40s, before the term "sexual harassment" was invented. It was a comfortable, happy, easy time of inter-gender comradeship that occasionally developed into love. A casual arm on the shoulder was a friendly gesture. A hug was not a proposition. Innuendo was often considered a compliment. The wolf whistle brought smiles to our faces. When the whistles stopped we were considered "over the hill."

Guys were "cute, darling, and swell." Gals were "sweet, sexy, and fast." "Gay" described a happy, fun person and was the given name of many lovely girls. "Cool" was how you felt on a hot summer's day after a dip in the pool. Four-letter words covered school lavatory walls, but never passed the mouths of nice girls.

As a college freshman in 1930 I was "sweet sixteen and never been kissed." By 1943, however, a more lenient wartime moral code prevailed among us females attached to the military, and the man-problem became a major concern of our Red Cross supervisors. Repelling the advances of homesick, lonesome officers and GIs, who played on our vulnerability and compassion, became the toughest part of our job.

Holding our own in "that morass of sex" was not the only challenge faced by us Red Cross girls overseas. We had a hard time staying untouched by the coarse and often obscene talk heard all around us. We rubbed shoulders with men we never would have known in civilian life. We played cards with thugs, learned how to deal with drunks, laughed off propositions, and endured jibes and insults with equanimity. We became adept at resisting the pawing advances of men of all ranks and ages. And all the time we held our tempers and practiced patience.

While we gained a great deal in human understanding, tolerance, and experience, we hardened a bit to stay afloat in the male military environment. Inevitably we lost some of the sweetness, femininity, and refinement of the hometown girl—the very virtues that helped get us into the club service.

At the beginning of my training I was enchanted with so much male attention. For the most part, my Washington dates were of the "good guys" variety—non-threatening, non-binding, and lots of fun. As the weeks passed and I heard the same old "lines," I learned to turn a deaf ear to the proposals and propositions. Experience soon taught me to tighten my heartstrings until "the right one comes along."

At Camp Patrick Henry, my heart for a while got the better of my head and I made the mistake of confiding my schoolgirl affections to my family. These exuberant letter-excerpts, about the short-term attentions of a handsome young officer, sent them into a real tizzy:

> *Now for the big thing. I've met a darling first lieutenant who will be leaving tomorrow. His name is Bert Cole; he is six feet tall, sandy-haired, slim, straight as an arrow, a darling person, good looking, refined, cute, sweet, smart, and as "good American" as they come—in fact, he is half Sioux Indian and looks it, with his high cheek bones and ruddy complexion. He is just about perfect except for one thing: he has no education and feels overawed in the presence of so-called sophisticates. He has never even been to high school, but has picked up a good vocabulary and expresses himself well.*

How that last paragraph must have upset my professor father and Phi Bete mother, who wanted the best for their three-degreed daughter! The letter continued:

> *Bert has been in the army six years, having enlisted at the age of 18, worked up through sergeant, and gone to Officers' Candidate School because he had an IQ of over 110. He is an army man and plans to be a career army man after the war and is well liked by the enlisted men. As for principles, he is*

*entirely good, sincere, honest, and fine. In fact, he's
your type of man and I know you will like him. If he
comes back from the war I may marry him someday.*

*He is very attractive, just about the cutest person
on the post. Gee, I wish I had a picture of him.*

Surprising was my WASP mother's reaction to the fact
of Bert's ancestry. Apparently she forgot about Dad's "one
drop of Indian blood," inherited from Pocahontas in our
proud Randolph ancestry. Mom's return letter revealed a
prejudice unknown to me before then. Here is my answer
to her protest:

*I am amused at your concern about Bert. In the
first place, I haven't decided yet to marry him, for a
number of reasons, but his color isn't one of them.
In the first place, he may not come back from the
war, for as you guessed, he did go over. In the second
place, I may find someone who suits me better. In
the third place, I'm not sure I'd be satisfied with
someone who has as little education as he.*

*But as for his being half Indian, I can't see that
argument for a number of reasons. There isn't any
social stigma that I've ever heard of in this country
against American Indians. For example, Mrs. Major Fletcher was half Indian and Mrs. Cassidy too,
and both were well considered. We have Indian blood
in our veins and I'm proud of it. Moreover, as far as
I can see, there are no racial characteristics in Bert
of the Indian except his ruddy complexion, his
straight hair and his straight stature, all of which
are good characteristics.*

*However, we don't have to worry, because I'm not
planning to get married anytime soon. Maybe it
would be best for me not to write home about my
dates and the people I like, because the family always gets upset; and from past experience, you
know that I don't marry them all. But I understand and appreciate your concern and will take*

into consideration all the things you say when the time does come for me to settle down to a husband.

Twenty months later when I did choose a mate, none of the family preference played in their daughter's selection.

Secrecy—was a way of life in World War II, especially in overseas service. Long before embarkation we were cautioned to hazard no guesses about when, how, or from where we might leave or where we might be heading. All letters were carefully censored for leaks about troop locations and movements. Though actual censorship of my mail did not begin until I was on board ship out of California, we were under strict orders even at Camp Patrick Henry and Camp Santa Ana not to reveal our location.

After our initial training some of us had a long wait in Washington for overseas assignments. Since I was fairly fluent in French, my logical destination would have been North Africa, where French was the official language. But the African contingent pulled out without me. I then hoped to be sent to India, but rumor had it that all Pacific tours were temporarily suspended because of stepped up Japanese activity in the air and ocean. Subs had been sighted in the Bay of Bengal and indeed an assault on Calcutta was made soon after that. So I settled back to boring makeshift clerical duties at American University.

We really lived it up while waiting to leave. Fine food became such a part of our daily life that it's a wonder we didn't lose our slim figures before we went overseas. A generous per diem permitted us to dine at the best restaurants, where for $3 to $4 per entree we enjoyed gourmet fare at Maxim's, Ruby Foo's, and the Mayflower dining room. Pre-dinner cocktails cost a dollar. (From champagne cocktails at the Statler, I progressed through Australian beer in Tasmania to army-rationed Seagram's VO overseas.)

In August 1943 we began getting clues about our final destinations, but the clues changed as the weeks wore on. We repacked our luggage from summer to winter clothing as our guesses shifted from North Africa to India to China. Our families pinned maps on kitchen bulletin boards and moved colorful thumbtacks around the globe as we relayed our hopes back home.

From Washington, I wrote:

I don't know how long I'll be here.

Whenever I do go, nothing must be said. And above all we must not discuss rumors and hunches. I do hope Gram didn't mention to that taxi driver the possibility of my going to India.

These things have to be kept quiet because the lives of thousands of soldiers may be involved. The only thing we can know for sure is that when I send a suitcase home with my clothes, I'll be on my way to a port of embarkation. But when we will sail no ones knows.

Things really are stirring around here now. My roommate cleared this AM and Marge Boulter just received notice this afternoon. The rest of us are on pins and needles, expecting to move on a moment's notice any time now, maybe before the week is up.

During my time in the field I lived with security uppermost in my mind, trying to curb the enthusiastic big mouth in my voluminous letters. But a few black smudges from the censors' felt pens dirtied my V-mails and sharp scissors snipped whole sentences out of my typewritten epistles.

Not all the snippings, however, were from military censors. A self-appointed home censor sought to protect my dad and grandmother from knowing the full truth about my activities. Mom gathered the morning mail while Dad was at the university, read it quickly, then sometimes mutilated, with fine sewing scissors, my masterpieces meant for posterity. Her aim was not security inspired, but a well intentioned, if unnecessary, means of keeping Dad ignorant of some of my escapades. Mom was easily shocked. Dad, who was fifteen years her senior, was more broad-minded and forgiving, and would have enjoyed the account of my visit in Calcutta with a famous prostitute, and the subsequent beautiful performance of the nautch dancers.

Though V-mail was our speediest means of communication with family and friends, it was hard for recipients to decipher. To save weight and space my originals were photocopied and reduced to one-fourth size, making the copies often unreadable even with a magnifying glass.

Here is a sample of V-mail as received:

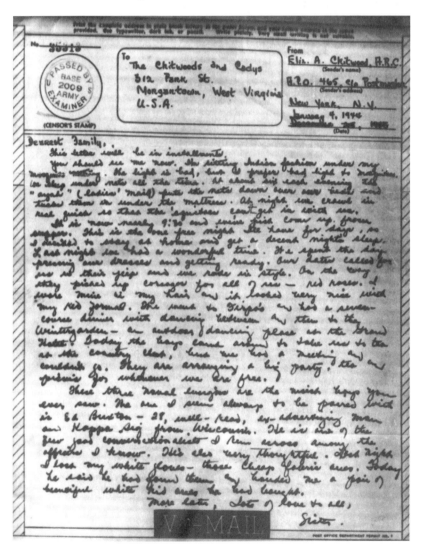

Troopers All

Finally the great day arrived, bringing to an end our days of high living. In early November we were trundled off to the West Coast on a crowded troop train, destination California. On our way at last to the greatest adventure of our lives, we were ready and eager to get on with it.

Staging at Camp Santa Ana was no joy ride. We were not tourists. All we saw of the great state of California was the grim inside of a huge fenced-in army installation, then the bustling docks of nearby Los Angeles where we boarded our "cruise ship" for the Far East.

Put through tough military paces every day, our bodies, exercised-to-the-limit, became sore and our spirits deflated. But we stuck it out literally like troopers.

That introduction to California was exhilarating to me, as indicated in this letter home on November 15, 1943:

> What a climate this is! It was 90° in the shade all day and gets as cold as Christmas at night. But I like it.
>
> You should see us in our olive-drab fatigues. They fit like sacks. And our field shoes, which come up over our ankles, weigh about a ton. Altogether we make a very funny picture.
>
> They are keeping us so busy here that we haven't even had a chance to go to the officers' club. Last night we packed bed rolls until 3:00 AM and got up at 6:30 today as usual for chow.
>
> Incidentally, we have the best chow I've ever eaten in an army camp.
>
> These barracks are palatial, compared to those at Patrick Henry. We sleep in hospital beds, with sheets, and have two latrines right in the barracks. The barracks are well built and cheery, as barracks go, and convenient to the PX, where we can buy delicious Cokes, milk shakes, etc.

We are being put through all the regular army paces.

Today we went through the gas chamber as a test for our gas masks. We learned how to put them on, clear them of gas, etc. The gas chamber was filled with tear gas and they made us get a whiff of it as we went out. My gas mask works fine.

They also gave us a whole outfit of gas-protective clothing, which is sticky and smelly, not to mention great stacks of special garments and drugs. The army certainly leaves nothing undone for the welfare of the people going into the service.

The hard work, exercise, good meals, good sleep, and wonderful weather certainly combine to make us healthy. I feel fine, energetic and alert.

It is amazing how smoothly we all get along together. An unbelievably large number of girls live in one room and we haven't had a single personality conflict.

Gas-mask drill was "a gas" compared to what followed the next day. The real test of my fortitude and determination came in the abandon—ship procedure—the most terrifying maneuver I ever had to perform. I had a lifetime fear of high places so I always avoided mountain lookouts and the edges of overhangs, even those protected with fences. Hence, when I had to descend the 60-foot concave simulated side of a ship, backwards, down a rope ladder in full military regalia—30 pounds of clothing, gas mask, helmet, bedroll, and other equipment—I was sure my Red Cross dreams were over.

"Hallelujah!" I shouted when my feet touched solid ground. I knew that anything to follow would be a piece of cake.

The Good Ship Uruguay

Our last day in the United States was, as they say, something else again. We had breakfast at 4:30, then donned our glad rags (uniform, topcoat, and raincoat) and added helmet, pistol belt with canteen, gas mask, and army musette bag loaded with cosmetics, plus a B4 bag bulging with shoes and clothing. Decked out in this garb we walked a mile to the tracks where we waited forever to board the train that ferried us out of Camp Santa and eventually dumped us at the port of departure near Los Angeles.

With all these trappings we could hardly sit down. By the time we reached the docks we were suffering temporary curvature of the spine. But, thanks to Red Cross volunteers who fed us coffee, sandwiches, and cookies, we recovered enough energy to walk up the gangplank into the huge steamer awaiting us. Hundreds of GIs hung over the six deck-railings to noisily welcome us aboard.

That first night in port we stayed outside on deck and watched the harbor lights until bedtime. The next morning our ship dallied around in the harbor for several hours, and then pulled out into the bay. We wouldn't see land again for another four weeks.

The smooth Pacific had a soothing effect on our frazzled nerves. The past faded into a limbo of forgetfulness. It was a glorious dream from which I didn't want to awaken. I understood why the lotus-eaters of mythology never went back home. We were all so happy and carefree; it didn't seem possible that we were involved in a war to kill people. Yet underneath those calm blue waters lurked submarines waiting to throw torpedoes at us.

Our ship was a big, fast, former luxury liner, the *Uruguay*. Now stripped bare, she carried about 8,000 American troops, plus some 400 officers, Red Cross workers, civilian personnel, and her regular crew. The GIs were crammed like cordwood into the four lower decks. We enjoyed the luxury of triple-decker bunks in a tiny stateroom, nine to a cabin designed for two. We shared a tiny bath with the nine people in the adjoining cabin. It wasn't like home, but we didn't complain. What a beautiful introduction to the Pacific, so different from my peacetime crossing of the Atlantic in 1937 on the Bremen, with four non-English-speaking German matrons crowded with me in a miniscule third class cabin!

Surprisingly, we on the top two decks had some unexpected comforts: clean sheets and towels once a week; a steward to make up our beds daily and clean the room weekly; a valet to wash and iron our clothes (at a good high price); fresh water for shampooing, laundering, and bathing; plenty of castile soap for showers; and ice water for canteens. Though our inside recreation space was limited to a tiny library-lounge for meetings, poker, and bridge, we had plenty of deck space with only one restriction: we girls had to be off the deck by 11:00 pm so that the GIs could sleep out there, to relieve congestion in their three-decker, ten-man, side-by-side bunks.

During the day we wore slacks and fatigues, both inside and on the dirty deck, where we had to sit on the floor. Slacks were just the thing for this leisurely life where the wind would flip skirts and expose panties. For dinner inside we wore our skirted uniforms.

Drills, drills, drills kept us on the alert for any eventuality. Abandon-ship every three days taught us to evacuate in an orderly fashion. Gun drills were exciting. Fire and air raid warnings sent us straight to our assigned posts in lifeboats. Two doctors and several hardened sailors offered good company and skilled help in my lifeboat, in case of a sudden "dunking in the drink."

Still run by a private company, the *Uruguay* provided excellent chow for two sit-down meals, served on white tablecloths by waiters in black pants and white shirts. At 8:30 we had a full breakfast and at 5:30 a four-course dinner. In the meantime and after dinner we got pretty hungry, but with candy, cookies, and crackers from the PX, plus fruit and hard-boiled eggs sneaked out from the dining room, we managed to maintain our weight.

Life aboard our luxury-liner-turned-troopship was easier and more fun for us girls than for the GIs. We had all day for fun and games, while the poor GIs had to stand in line most of the day for two meals slopped onto their tin trays. We played lots of bridge, wrote letters in the tiny library, danced on deck, and put on skits and shows for everyone. On Thanksgiving eve we had a little skit in which I played Priscilla to a GI John Alden and sang a silly song called "How Come You Do Me like You Do, Do, Do?"

For most of us on the top decks, dates with officers were our main source of recreation. With only the crowded open deck and the wee rec room for dating, we didn't indulge in heavy necking. Lacking privacy, most of us made do with simple Coke-and-chatter, though a few who dated the ship's civilian crew in their quarters had ample opportunity for entertainment beyond just playing bridge. One beautiful Powers model managed to get pregnant on board and was shipped home on arrival in Bombay.

Early in the voyage I wrote home:

> *I'm having a wonderful time on board, too good a time in fact. Most of the men are married, but they are all interested in having a good time. Lots of them won't come back and they know it, so they want as much fun as possible. We probably won't see any of these men again, or even care if we see them, but on board everyone is friendly and gay.*

> *I have a date every night. Some of the girls have settled down to going steady, but not me. Four of the men I've dated have wanted to date me up for the rest of the voyage, but I'm not going to be tied down to any of them, so I've been dating eight different ones. It works much better that way, as far as I'm concerned, because none is attractive enough to keep me interested all day long for as long as we will be on this boat.*

> *Until today the sea has been calm and few have been sick. Today she is heaving a little. I like it better this way, because it feels more like I am really on*

the ocean. After the war I'm going to take my vacations on an ocean liner. This really is the life!

After our first shore leave, the dating situation changed, when Lieutenant Jack Hyman became my shipboard steady. I wrote:

Yesterday I spent half the afternoon writing you a long newsy letter. Then, as I got up to dress for supper, it blew into the sea. Today I am at it again, sitting just where I was yesterday—on an orange crate on the deck with Jack. Funny how much an orange crate can mean. For weeks we sat on the dirty floor until our legs went to sleep and our derriéres ached. Then one day we found an empty orange crate in the kitchen trash and now we are much happier.

Little things mean so much to us—things like a mason jar to put our jam in and a spoon smuggled from the dining-room, hard boiled eggs for lunch, and peanut butter for our midnight snacks. All these things Jack has brought me, as well as a beautiful ring fashioned from a florin (which he made himself) and salt tablets to keep me feeling well in this tropical heat.

The sea is calm and smooth as glass. The flying fish make clear little paths against the waves as they come up out of the water. The ocean is always so beautiful. We've seen every kind of cloud formation, every kind of sunset, all planets and constellations. Saturn is the brightest star in these heavens and we've also seen the Southern Cross.

The men are having boxing bouts out on the deck this afternoon and seem to be enjoying it immensely. The morale on board this ship now is high in spite of the heat, because the GIs have some sort of entertainment nearly every day and all day deck privileges.

Jack is sitting beside me as usual. He's the best looking officer aboard and very sweet. He's a

Second Lt. in the Air Corps (not a flyer), is 27, has dancing blue eyes, black curly hair and a fine physique, even though he is small. He is always happy and just vibrates with life all the time. None of the dreamer, he is 100% practical, and smart to boot (154 on the Army IQ test).

This trip is so much fun, I'll be sorry, in a way, when it's over. But our work will be just as much fun, I know, and will be even more satisfying. I certainly did choose the right work. I wouldn't have missed this for anything—not even for marriage and a family."

Champagne and Cow's Milk

Two shore leaves in the last quarter of the voyage broke the monotony of blue-water vistas and revitalized us all. In Hobart, Tasmania, and Perth, Australia, we were delighted to exercise our land legs and to stock up on a few supplies.

Coming into Tasmania we observed strange rock islands that jutted up out of the sea—little stratified peaks at first, then clusters of larger irregular formations like something out of *The Wizard of Oz*. Bare of vegetation and obviously uninhabited, they might have been stalagmites rising out of ocean caves. Then the mainland appeared— fertile farmland with green pastures and soft rolling hills. Goats and cattle feeding on the slopes and an occasional pink farmhouse, with bright blue roof and vivid flower garden, announced our approach to civilization. Then the beautiful seaport of Hobart, against a lush green mountain rising to the clouds, greeted us.

The large island of Tasmania lies southeast of Australia, with many small adjacent uninhabited islands. The population was largely concentrated in Hobart, though hundreds of small villages in the forests housed native aborigines, many of whom came into the city to work on the docks and in the homes and businesses. English and Dutch settlers had felled the forests to build this modern city. English was the official language in Hobart, but back in the jungle villages, dark-skinned aborigines clung to about 250 strange, prehistoric dialects.

Late in the afternoon the *Uruguay* docked without the aid of tugs. Thrilled to set foot on land at last and intoxicated with the beauty before us, we needed no artificial stimulant to raise our spirits as we descended the gangplank. Dockside was a large jam factory, where we bought jars of plum, apple, and peach to take back on board for our evening snacks.

Hobart was a picture postcard of riotous color, with gaily-painted wooden houses and a patchwork of gardens.

Everywhere our eyes feasted on window boxes, hanging baskets, postage-stamp vegetable and flower plots, and grass and wildflowers poking up to the sun through thatched roofs. Bougainvillea draped over porches. Potted geraniums and hydrangeas in red, pink, white, and blue decorated patios. Daylilies, begonias, roses, and exotic tropicals lined driveways. Everything about the city was clean and neat—no trash on the streets, no peeling paint on buildings, no apparent poverty anywhere.

Jack and I hailed a taxi, drove through the town for a cursory tour, then headed for the resort hotel on the beach, where we spent the rest of the evening dining and dancing. Curfew for return to the *Uruguay* was 11:00 PM.

We had hoped to spend the next morning shopping and walking around the town, but to our surprise and chagrin the ship's orders were changed after midnight. We awoke in a moving vessel far out to sea.

Staving off boredom was a major problem for all of us aboard ship. The GIs spent most daytime hours waiting in line for their two daily meals, with only a few minutes in between for exercise or reading. We Red Cross girls offered nighttime entertainment in the form of skits, shows, meetings, choir practice, and community sings. But depression was endemic among the men and even plagued some of the officers and us as well.

It was a great blessing when, from that first shore leave in Hobart the men came back on board with Australian florins. From then on they busily pounded the silver quarter-size coins into rings for us girls, and for wives and girlfriends back home. The happy tap-tapping of the jewelry makers lifted our spirits and theirs too.

Two imaginative GIs, a corporal and a buck sergeant, found another means of relieving boredom while recouping their earlier gambling losses. Clarence and Charlie, experienced con men, pooled their meager resources and started a lucrative on-board business. At the first shore leave they bought several dozen long bars of old fashioned Octagon soap. In a chemist's shop they bought a hundred flour pills, big as nickels, for $2. Disposal of the harsh smelly laundry soap and the horse-size tablets was a really slick scam.

Back on board, Charlie and his confederate cut each long soap-bar crosswise into ten thin rectangles. Careful to avoid any accusation of fraud, they made no claims for the efficacy of either product. They did no advertising. They simply laid out samples of their wares on an orange crate and "allowed" gullible officers and others to snap them up from the "limited supply." The word soon got around that Charlie and Clarence were selling saltwater soap and seasick pills for a mere pittance—seventy-five cents each for the soap bars and fifty cents for the pills. Shipboard scuttlebutt touted the effectiveness of both items.

One day when the supply was getting low, an officer approached Charlie. "I hear you've got the very thing for salt water," he said. "How about letting me have five bars."

"Sorry old man," Charlie said. "Our supply has almost run out. We have to ration the remainder to one bar per person. But I can let you have a larger end bar for a dollar and you can share it with your buddies."

"Guess that'll have to do," the officer said, as he reached into his pocket. "Can you change a fifty? It's all I have."

"It just so happens that I can," said Charlie, as he whipped out a wad of cash and peeled off the change in ones and fives.

"Thanks, soldier."

"Happy showering, sir!"

The net profit from these and other imaginative enterprises allowed the two men to pay off their shipboard debts and to replenish their stock on the next shore leave in Perth. By arrival in Bombay they had recovered enough for a day on the town, with lunch at the elegant Taj Mahal Hotel and the purchase of trinkets to send back home.

Later, when I questioned Charlie about the ethics of such transactions, he said, "We didn't tell them it was salt water soap. We just didn't tell them it wasn't. And who were we to deny a poor officer the chance of swallowing a harmless pill when his seasickness was all in his head anyway?"

Our second port of call in Perth, Australia, gave us shopping time and even an invitation to tea in a local home. But there was little of interest in this commercial city and nothing we wanted to buy. So we spent most of our day there holed up in a bar drinking the champagne for which Australia is noted.

A sad episode ruined this last leave in Perth for one unlucky GI. Though officers and civilians were permitted to bring alcoholic beverages back to the boat, GIs were strictly forbidden this luxury. The same MPs who handed out condoms to all men leaving the ship were on duty as they came back, to check on undeclared purchases.

As one GI started to board, with a large bulbous something under his coat, the MP grabbed him by the shoulder and said, "Whatcha got there, soldier? Enough for your whole platoon?"

"Milk," replied the GI. "Two gallons of good fresh milk."

"Don't give me that crap," the sergeant bellowed. "You can't hide champagne from me. No one pulls a fast one on this MP."

With that the MP struck a heavy blow with his night-stick against the covered bundle. A stream of beautiful white Australian milk poured down the GI's legs into the water. A saddened GI stepped away from the broken glass, his coat a soggy mess.

That night we steamed away from Perth on the last lap to Calcutta. In the pre-dawn, we Red Cross girls in Cabin 20 were awakened as the troopship swerved, then cut through the rough sea at increased speed.

"Gracious! What was that?" Lou called out from the middle bunk. "Wonder if a sub is on our tail."

"Almost knocked me from my perch," Margot cried from the top bunk across the way.

"Don't fall on me," cautioned Milly, who was hanging halfway out of her lower bunk in aisle 3.

"Must not be anything very dangerous," I said from the lower in aisle 2, "or we'd have heard the alarm bell. Goodnight, all. I'm going to catch a few more winks."

At breakfast the next day we learned the cause of the ship's sudden change of direction. Japanese activity in the Bay of Bengal, we were told, made landing in Calcutta unsafe. So Bombay, on the west coast, would be our port of entry into India.

Christmas came upon us while we were still docked in Bombay. We Red Cross girls tried to make it a happy one for all onboard. On December 25, 1943 I wrote home:

> *Today is Christmas and it is quite the most unusual Christmas I've ever spent. The girls have decorated the whole boat with Christmas trees, evergreen, Santas, angels, and everything imaginable, so that everyone has had the spirit for several days. It is amazing what can be done with a minimum of supplies.*
>
> *Thursday night the officers had their Christmas dance and it was loads of fun. The dining room was arranged cabaret-style and decorated in red and green streamers. At 9:30 a very good floorshow was put on, with a jitterbugging couple, a mime, a French chanteuse (me), and a magician.*
>
> *Yesterday afternoon we sang carols in the enlisted men's mess hall. Several quartets, trios, and larger singing groups participated. My group was made up of about a dozen enlisted men and four girls. We were the best group of singers and the men really enjoyed it. In the evening we had a Christmas exchange in the officers' dining room, with a big tree and a live Santa Claus. I got two decks of cards, which I gave to some enlisted men. The Red Cross chipped in with shaving stuff, small clothing items, and board games for all the GIs, and commercial companies donated cigarettes and Hershey bars.*

At eleven we celebrated an ecumenical communion. Though the merry-making went on until the wee hours, I came back to my cabin before midnight and went to bed.

The winter uniform.

The corporal on
Betty's footlocker.

The Hut
ARC War Bond Center
in Washington 1943.

The Mrs. Miniver Hat.

Libby's Room

Red Cross quarters in Washington, DC. Summer 1943.

Part Two

India at Last: Bombay and Calcutta

How long ago was that?
Then, reckless I
ran headlong into life
grabbing and tasting each delight.
How long ago was that?
When did words of grace first
find my downed heart?
Who was I then?
A stranger I hardly remember.

Author Unknown

Porthole Panorama

"Lib, Lib, wake up! We're coming into port." Lucia's words cut into my slumber. To my unwilling ears her sharp voice was a clanging cymbal; its metallic tone vibrated the thin membrane of my consciousness.

So we're coming into port, I thought. So what! Please go away and let me sleep.

Lou's hand, still damp from her shower, shook my reluctant shoulder. Wearily I opened one eye, saw that a roommate was using the washbowl, and dozed off again.

Lou was adamant. For thirty-nine days she had made it her thankless task to rouse me each morning in time for the second breakfast sitting. She wasn't about to let me sleep through this last and most important morning of our cruise across the Pacific. Knowing that my apathy was not due to a lack of interest, but rather to a long established aversion to getting out of bed, she realized that if she did not wake me up in time for the landing festivities, there would be no living with me afterward. Weeks ago, experience had taught her that a dash of cold water on my face and a cup of hot coffee beside my bunk usually changed the grumbling bear into a docile lamb.

"Get out of that bunk this minute, you lazy lummox," Lou scolded, tightening her grip on my shoulder. "Do you want to sleep through all the fun? It's a circus out there. We're coming into Bombay."

The word Bombay hit like a cannonball. In a single motion I threw back the sheet, cleared my bunk, and groped my way to the washbowl. Lou settled herself on a suitcase and waited for me to finish my toilette.

Though she was only two years my senior, Lucia treated me and everyone else like children. Recently divorced, but still in love with her ex, she prided herself on keeping her emotions corseted. The corset pinched her natural ebullience, simmering below the surface, into a straight-laced demeanor. Luckily she had a great sense of humor, laughing more at herself than at anyone else.

A few minutes later, as I ran a comb through my page-boy bob, Lou jumped to her feet, dashed into the narrow aisle between the bunks and stood as though transfixed. Pointing to the open porthole, she said, "For goodness sake, Lib, look at that sky. I've never seen anything like it in my life."

Picking my way through the mounds of life belts, helmets, gas masks, and luggage strewn on the cabin floor, I stumbled to the porthole to see what was happening below. Someone had pushed an empty orange crate against the wall to use as a step up to hook our arms over the opening.

Directly in front of me, like a patch of Day-Glo paper pasted on the dull gray cabin wall, was a flaming red disc—the Bombay sunrise framed by our porthole. A little chill tickled my fourth vertebra; my heart thumped strangely. I wanted to fix forever in my memory the sensation produced by this first glimpse of India, the blazing Indian sunrise seen through a soft haze. It was as though the Creator had made that vision to my special order, for it was just as I had imagined an Indian sunrise to be. I never again saw the morning sky so vividly red-gold.

We took turns leaning out the narrow opening. In the dim light of dawn I could distinguish nothing below. Lou, who had the vision of a lynx, watched with interest the landing process. Where Lou saw ant-like human activity below, I saw only dark smudges moving about on the quay.

"Now that the she-wolf has been lured from her lair," I said dryly, "how about handing over the bait. Where is the circus you were talking about? I can't make out a darned thing in this light."

"Oh, damn!" Lucia said, as I pulled myself up again to the porthole. "You're too late! It's gone now."

"What's gone?"

"The circus. The elephant. I saw him way over there toward the city. He was huge, with shiny armor all over his body and a turret on his back. Do you suppose it could have been a maharajah out taking his morning constitutional?"

I groaned. "So that's what you got me up to see, just another invention of your over-productive imagination. The only decorated elephant you've ever seen outside the big top was a pink one last night and I'm sure he didn't look like that. Did you have more champagne than the rest of us?"

"I'm sure it was an elephant."

After a long silence Lou said, "Hurry up and get dressed. Anything might happen now. We don't want to miss anything. I'll keep watch while you finish dressing and let you know if anything exciting happens. But for heaven's sake, make it snappy. We need to go up on A-deck to get a decent view of the land."

My toilette required little attention, so my thoughts could go off on little excursions of their own. Who was this strange paradox of a cabin mate, Lucia Carter Cortlandt?

Lou was a strange combination of the sophisticated and the naïve. She looked like a Charles-of-the-Ritz ad, with short black curls swept up in a mass on her forehead, full round lips naturally turned down at the corners, large eyes with Garbo lids, delicate mother-of-pearl complexion, and a racehorse figure. Most of the time she talked as she looked, with that I-know-what-I'm-talking-about-because-I-have-lived air. Her voice carried a tone of conviction, often misconstrued as that of authority. But every once in a while she would come out with something completely unexpected, like the elephant business, and you realized that underneath her reserve still lurked the child who sees elves in tree crotches and dwarfs in coal bins.

Lou was amazingly creative. Take for instance that time we were steaming into port at Hobart, Tasmania, and first sighted those strange stratified rock islands rising up out of the sea, for all the world straight out of a Grimm's fairy tale. Any normal person could tell that those barren crags were incapable of sustaining animal life. Yet Lou maintained that she spotted a mountain goat, with long curling horns, on one of those hillsides. We tried to reason with her, but I finally gave up. It was more fun to go along with her and enjoy the fruits of her fertile imagination.

Ready at last, we dashed into the narrow passageway outside our cabin. As we made our way up to the top deck we realized that the great turbines below had stopped and that the *Uruguay* was quietly and smoothly moving forward without the aid of steam. Intermittent jerks and low boastful whistles announced that we were being helped toward the dock. Two tiny tugs bustled around our stern like fussy bantams around a Dominicker rooster.

In peacetime Bombay, passenger vessels and merchant ships were berthed in slips at the end of narrow channels that meandered between high cobblestone quays for several hundred yards into the city. For an hour the *Uruguay* was towed between these rough-edged walls. We had no sensation of the boat's motion. Only the changing scene around us indicated our forward movement.

On the wide brick walks on top of the quays, lines of olive-drab army trucks and jeeps abutted stacks of huge plywood crates containing airplane parts, firearms, and ammunition. Beyond the piled boxes gleamed the red-tiled roofs of harbor warehouses. In the distance minaretted buildings cut stagy silhouettes against the backdrop of low, green hills.

By 9:30, after much pulling and tugging of derricks and hoists, the *Uruguay* came to a standstill. On that late December morning Bombay harbor was jammed with ships of all sizes and shapes. Nearby we recognized the Navy destroyer *Hermitage* that had escorted us from Australia. Smaller corvettes, destroyers, and LST's, as well as antiquated tankers, found resting space farther out. Tiny creatures swarming over the docks like termites were unloading tankers and merchant ships flying the flags of the Allied Nations. From all directions came the clanking of hoisting chains, the screech of giant cranes, and the singsong hum of human voices.

For every Western ship we saw at least ten native sailing craft, their lopsided sails motionless in the morning sunlight. Fishing sloops with tall masts loomed over moored pleasure dinghies and tiny junks. Weaving in and out among the vessels at anchor, like water fleas around pond lilies, were countless flat-bottomed skiffs manned by sleek, mahogany men wearing floppy white gauze turbans and scanty loincloths.

We had been warned about the stench—a heavy mixture of cow dung, human sweat, machine oil, decayed meat, gunpowder, animal and human urine, and wet fur, plus spicy cooking aromas, musk, and the delicate distant fragrance of bougainvillea. We whipped out perfumed hankies and covered our faces like Muslim women.

Hundreds of natives swarmed over the dock to view the unloading of the American ship. We watched open-mouthed as lithe landlubbers in loincloths and dirty turbans balanced heavy barrels and iron beams on their heads. Uniformed policemen in yellow bellboy hats stood regally erect along the dock. Peddlers in draped cheese-cloth trousers and black silk European jackets hawked a white paste wrapped in leaves. Ubiquitous beggars, some maimed or blind or without feet, cried their needs. An occasional low-caste woman, in bright full-skirted calico with a yellow gauze scarf thrown over her head, suckled a baby slung across one hip. At the edge of the quay, an Indian in a fez withdrew a little from the crowd, turned his back, squatted low, and unabashedly urinated on the dock.

Once the *Uruguay* was moored, a great chattering dialogue went up between the natives on the shore and the Americans crowding the decks and portholes. We caught snatches of Hindustani, British English, and American slang. Chants of "Bakshish, sahib," "Hello, Joe," and "Gimme cigarette" rose to our top-deck aerie. The soldiers on board started a game of throwing pennies and cigarettes down to the Indian bystanders. Half-naked natives dived into the filthy bilge water to retrieve the pennies, while others scrambled for the cigarettes that landed on the quay.

At ten o'clock the penny game was interrupted by the scream of the ship's siren, the signal to go ashore. Waiting for the crowds to thin out, we watched as the bulging *Uruguay* delivered her human burden. Three lowered gangplanks began to swell with pushing masses of chattering, laughing, khaki-clad Americans, eager to set foot again on solid ground.

From our peanut gallery lookout the streams of soldiers appeared as so many long wriggling worms, writhing in and out on the dock, then finally disappearing in the distance. Finally Lou and I went below to join the fantastic centipedes.

A Good Eating House

You and I had made no definite plans for our first day in India, other than to fill our eyes with exotic sights and our tummies with decent food. There had been no time for breakfast, so we set out through the streets of Bombay to locate a good restaurant.

As we pushed our way through the sweating, stinking crowds I suggested that we try out our Hindustani on a native. "Good idea," Lou said. "It'll give us a chance to check on the Army method." Lou referred to the daily Hindustani lessons broadcast over the loudspeakers aboard ship. Though we had made no special effort to memorize the phrases thrown at us, a few expressions stuck in our minds and now we hoped to put them to use.

"There's a likely looking chap over there," Lou said, pointing to an Indian dockworker standing apart from the crowd in apparent meditation. "Why don't you ask him where the nearest restaurant is? I'm sure your Hindustani is better than mine."

We approached the turbaned Indian, who salaamed as we came up to him.

"Na-mas-tay, ba-ha-i!" I said, enunciating each syllable clearly. "Restaurant ke-han-hay?" (This was the way the Indian words sounded to me.) The man looked at me with a blank expression.

Then I added gestures and spoke with exaggerated clarity. "Na-mas-tay, ba-ha-i! Restaurant ke-han-hay?"

Still looking nonplussed, the Indian bowed again and replied, "Jes' Christ, memsahib, no unnerstan' Inglis."

We decided to pursue the matter no further.

"Stupid fool," Lou said, as we continued our walk. "Can't even understand his own language."

"Maybe he's not the only stupid person around here," I countered. "There could be something wrong with our accents, you know. Or maybe literary Hindustani is not the dialect he speaks."

"Or there might be a flaw in our training. I'll bet the army has dished out a bunch of highfalutin' expressions that the run-of-the-mill Indian never heard of."

"Could be. Just imagine a well-educated Indian coming to the United States and saying to a hardened New York dockhand, 'How do you do, my good man. Will you please be so kind as to direct me to the nearest eating house?'"

From that moment on we made no attempt to learn Hindustani, for it was not the language of the man in the street. We had no time to learn dialects. Later we picked up a few choice phrases from our bearers and canteen workers, not all of them ladylike.

Bombay's harbor streets were clogged with peddlers and beggars who thrust goods and grasping palms at us from all sides—gurkha knives and pseudo-antique sabers, plus shoddy swagger sticks still flaunted by some Britishers. Our shouted rejections of their wares had about as much effect on the mob as a Flit gun on a swarm of healthy June bugs.

Finally Lou tossed a quarter-pack of cigarettes to a little boy and grabbed one of the leather-covered sticks he was selling. With a wide swing of the stick and the loud utterance of a recently learned Indian expletive, Lucia dispersed the swirling mob. Her "Jaldi jao!" (Get the hell out of here!) scattered the urchins so that we had a short spell of relative peace.

At the end of the dock all sorts of conveyances waited to carry sightseers around the city. We had a choice of large open taxis, vintage early 30s, driven by tall, sinister looking bearded chauffeurs in pink turbans; box-like closed coaches pulled by thin mangy horses; or open victories, manned by floppy-turbaned coachmen. We had been warned against riding in taxis or closed coaches. Rumor had it that some of the Sikh taxi drivers tampered with the meters and were known to bodily attack passengers who refused to pay exorbitant charges. A few of the closed-coach drivers were reputed to be members of a gang that did a thriving business in fleecing Europeans and

Americans in out-of-the-way quarters of Bombay. So instead, we chose to ride in an open victoria or, as it is called in India, a gharry.

"Taj Mahal Hotel," Lucia said to the driver, as we settled back comfortably on the padded seats facing each other.

The Indian gharry is the last word in comfortable leisurely transport. I felt like Mrs. Astor whenever I stepped into a coach and gave orders to the driver. The slow dogtrot of the horses, bedecked with fresh flowers on their silvered harnesses, allowed us to catch a glimpse of a shopkeeper wrapping betel paste in a plantain leaf and of a low-caste woman brewing tea on the street over a tiny charcoal brasier. With the sun streaming down upon us we mingled with the cows and goats and oxen in our path. We could almost reach out and pat them. Our ears tingled with the nasal chatter of the bargaining shopkeepers. For land travel in India I always preferred the gharry to the tonga, the rickshaw, or the bicycle, though it meant suffering the flatulence of the ill-fed horses.

A few minutes later our Cinderella coach drew up before a huge elegant hotel facing Bombay harbor. We gave the driver the regular two-rupee fare plus a generous half-rupee tip, which seemed to please him. After making reservations for lunch in the formal dining room, we spent the intervening hour sipping lime squash and chatting with boat friends in the cocktail lounge.

Our first meal in India was quite a celebration for Lou and me. From our briefing and experience aboard ship we had learned something about how to command good service. A few strategically placed rupees (about 30 cents each) soon brought a retinue of obsequious bearers prancing around our table. Lou ordered a four-course meal of soup, salad, sizzling steak, and ice cream. I opted for something more exotic: rice, lamb curry, mango chutney, and fresh papaya with almond cookies for dessert.

Apart from the liveried waiters there was little local color in that dining room. The décor was nineteenth century English; the clientele largely English and American, plus a sprinkling of upper-caste Indian men in European attire and their "Anglo" (Indo-European) wives in gold-embroidered Benares silk saris. The tables were set with plain white linen, English bone china, and Waterford crystal. Over in a corner the instruments of a small string orchestra and a drum leaned against straight chairs, waiting for the dinner hour when musicians in tuxedos would play American hit tunes.

The waiters and their service were right out of the Arabian Nights. Over white duck jodhpurs they wore long, crisp white tunics buttoned up to a narrow round collar and belted with green webbing caught into a great brass buckle over their flat bellies. A wide strip of green silk crossed their chests from left shoulder to right hip. A narrow green stripe accented the front of their white turbans, setting off the beautiful dark chocolate color of their foreheads. The dark skin tone shone also where slim naked feet peeped out below the white jodhpurs.

These storybook characters, always hovering nearby, pulled out our chairs, spread yard-square napkins across our laps, filled our water glasses each time we took a sip, and answered requests with alacrity and deep respectful salaams. The elegant service lured Lou and me back to the Taj that evening for dinner and dancing.

The Turquoise Bracelet

The Bombay bazaar, like most Indian marketplaces, occupied several blocks in the center of town. Little sheds, set several feet above the ground, and enclosed at night by folding grillwork gates, opened directly onto the dirt sidewalks. Most shops sold a single specialty, such as silver jewelry, brassware, earthenware pots, saris, hardware, or sweets.

Several large brick and tile buildings housed more elegant shops along inner alleys. Lou and I hoped to find here the heavily carved silver bands we had seen circling the ankles of women in the streets. We could wear them as bracelets and take them back home for gifts, along with delicate filigree necklaces—perfect accessories for that "little black dress."

For all our searching and garbled inquiry, we found no jeweler who had the anklets in stock. Several offered to make them to order, but we hadn't time to wait. So we substituted something that took our fancy and was much less expensive. Under a glass case in one of the big buildings we found crude, but beautiful bracelets hand-fashioned of what we assumed to be turquoise set in gray plaster on a silver base.

A dark Indian wearing a silk European jacket reached into the case and laid two bracelets and a necklace on a square of black velvet for our approval. Lucia picked up a bracelet and tried it on.

"Ver' beautiful piece," the man said. "Genuine turquoise. Ver' fine jewelry. I sell it you cheap."

Not wanting to rush into buying on our first day, we stalled.

"Where is this sort of jewelry made?" I inquired.

"Bracelet made in Tibet, memsahib. Ver' fine work and ver' rare."

The man was a smooth talker, obviously used to gullible buyers. But we weren't about to be taken in, though we wanted some memento from Bombay.

Still undecided about a selection, we moseyed over to the Chinese jade and sandalwood counter. Several well-dressed Indian men were drinking tea and smoking their hookahs in a back corner of the shop. Our host, who had left us for a few minutes, returned shortly bearing a tray with two steaming cups of tea and a small plate of "biscuits." Directing us to two chairs at a small round table, he set down the tray and said, "Memsahibs, please to sit down and have tea. Best Darjeeling and sweets from England. Please, to sit down."

"Oh, thank you very much," I replied hastily. "That is most kind of you, but we can't accept your hospitality. You see, some friends are coming right away to take us to tea at the Taj. We don't want to keep them waiting." Our tea-drinking friends were mythical, of course, but we dared not expose ourselves to dysentery this early in the game.

The merchant left the tray on the table, then went back behind the glass counter. Silently he got out the turquoise bracelet again and laid it on the velvet pad. Lucia picked it up and examined it carefully,

"How much do you ask for the bracelet?" she said.

"Ver' cheap, memsahib. I make you special price so you tell American friends about my shop." Then he hesitated.

"Precisely how much is that special price?"

The dark man made a pretense of reading the illegible price tag. "Regular price thirty rupees. I give it you for twenty-five."

"That's a ridiculous price for this junk," Lou said.

"No, no, memsahib, is not high price," the jeweler said as though offended. "Bracelet not junk. Is genuine turquoise with silver lining."

"OK, but twenty-five rupees is too much money. We're in a hurry and haven't time to bargain. We'll give you thirty rupees for the bracelet and the necklace together. You're jolly lucky to get that much."

"Price of bracelet twenty-five rupees, memsahib. Necklace I give you for fifteen rupees." The Indian did not take his eye from Lucia.

With a flick of her wrist, Lou flung three ten-rupee notes on the counter, coldly picked up the bracelet and necklace, looked the Indian full in the face, and strode out of the shop, confident of having "dealt with these people properly" and gotten a good bargain to boot. As I followed her outside, I thought I heard a low laugh from behind the glass showcase.

Later I was sure that the merchant had chuckled, for it did not take long to find out that Lou had been royally gypped. The "genuine turquoise" turned out to be bits of white stone colored with non-permanent ink, set in cow-dung plaster on a silver-washed brass base. The color soon wore off and the bracelet came apart. Like so many things in India intended for sale to visitors, it was beautiful to look at but poorly made underneath. Much later I learned to rummage around in the back of the shops for mer-chandise intended for their own people, where I found some real treasures to bring back home.

Bakshish, Memsahib!

After lunch Lou and I decided to explore Bombay. We walked the few blocks to the native quarter. From the moment we left the hotel we were plagued by the usual bands of begging children, wailing their sorrowful "Bakshish, memsahib." We felt like beating them off with Lou's new swagger stick, but dared not disobey the army order against molesting Indians in any way. As quickly as one little group was disbursed by a vociferous "Jaldi jao!" another whining bunch took up the pursuit.

All about us in the street sat mendicants, some blind, some without hands or feet, some with hideous diseases—all crying for us to drop coins into their bowls. Sickened by the sight of an old man with elephantiasis, his genitals filling the whole wide area between his spread-eagle legs, we quickly turned and ran.

With the sun streaming down on our bare heads, Lou said, "Now I understand why Englishmen buy pith helmets the minute they step off the boat. I suppose we'll be regarded as Noel Coward's Mad Dogs and Englishmen." But neither of us suffered any ill effects from the bright sun, for nearly six weeks of lounging on deck had prepared us for the Indian noonday.

Picking our way around ubiquitous piles of manure, alive with swarming blue flies and crawling insects, we walked to the bazaar, trailed by a band of young beggars. Along the way we nearly stumbled over a pretty little girl of about six, dressed in headscarf, dirty yellow blouse, calico skirt, and tinkling ankle bracelets. She squatted in the street, sweeping up trash with her bundle of dried grass. She performed with serene acceptance the task that the caste system designated as her life's work, a lowly duty, which an American child would have found unthinkable.

We marveled at how fastidious the little girl was in guiding the animal droppings into a neat mound. Just as she was about to gather the mound into her bare hands and put it into a straw basket, she suddenly stepped back, out of the path of an oncoming bicycle. Without even a frown she watched a high-caste Indian boy, wearing immaculate Western clothes and a look of disdain, deliberately direct his bicycle through the neat mound. The little girl politely salaamed as he cycled on. Her face showed no malice as she began sweeping the scattered refuse again, no flickering shadow of anger or hurt—only a blank look of acceptance.

Lou was outraged. "I'd like to get my hands on that little whippersnapper and rub his nose in it," she said. "It wasn't any accident. I'll bet he does it every day just to show his rank."

"A sweeper hasn't a chance in this society, much less a female child." I said. "She doesn't even consider any other way of life. But what can we do about it? Even the British sanction it with their own class system."

As we walked through the bazaar we found ample proof of three generalities often stated about India: India is a land of burden bearers; India is a nation of animal lovers, or more accurately, animal toleraters; India is a place where time is of little importance.

Everywhere we were struck by the natural grace of the people. Even the begging gestures of the alms seekers and the namaste hand greetings were almost like a dancer's gestures. Doubtless the beauty of body movement came from the habit, learned in earliest childhood, of balancing objects, large and small, on their heads.

American charm schools would do well to teach the graceful carriage of the Indian woman we saw carrying a large brass jar of water on her head. One hand balanced the jar, the other swung freely at her side. Her head was held high, her thin lithe body, straight and firm. On a side street a dhobin (laundress) walked briskly with a huge bulky, sheet-wrapped load atop her slicked-back hair. Beside her a tot of two balanced a tiny terra cotta jar on her curly black pate. It appeared that low-caste Indians carried nothing in their hands if they could possibly manage it on their heads.

"Look over there," Lou said, bursting into laughter. "There's a free spirit if I ever saw one." She pointed to a young woman swinging her arms as she walked briskly in the road, a tiny bundle on her head that would fit easily in one hand.

The funniest sight I saw in all India was a group of swarthy, sweating native men, clad only in loin cloths, racing madly down Calcutta's crowded Chowringhee Road, a grand piano on their turbaned heads. Later the sight of Assamese women, toting heavy baskets of bricks on their heads to male masons, brought us closer to tears than to laughter.

Seldom did we see anyone using his hands for portage. Indian men seemed to rely on their sturdy shoulders for pulling and pushing. The bheesti (water carrier) slung his pair of bulging, dripping goatskin water bags over his shoulders, while coolies with ordinary buckets usually suspended them on the ends of a pole balanced on their upper backs.

Bombay's animal population seemed as large as its human population. In the streets all manner of domestic creatures had the right of way over vehicles and people: humpbacked Brahmin cattle, donkeys with pack sacks, oxen pulling two-wheeled carts, gharry horses, herds of goats and long-haired sheep, cats and dogs, and an occasional water buffalo.

In rural areas the water buffaloes used for farming appeared about as friendly as a tethered pasture bull. I never saw one in a rage, but in the provinces the water buffalo has been known to charge and gore a native to death. In one northern state, we were told, these rampaging beasts were brought before a public tribunal, tried as criminals, and sentenced to prison (strong cages) for disturbing the peace.

In this whole street scene Lou and I were the only pedestrians who hurried. People and animals moved only when necessary and then with apparent reluctance. Little groups of Indians and animals congregated in the middle of the filthy streets. Many squatted on their heels chatting, while animals chewed their cuds, barked, bellowed, or shook their harness bells, as taxis honked past them. Despite the pandemonium, Bombay was a refreshing change from the speeding traffic of American cities.

As we continued through the winding alleys of the Bombay bazaar, the little band of beggars kept us company, their strident demands increasing as we plunged deeper into the native section. A woman carrying a naked baby accosted us. Weeping and wailing, she cried, "Bakshish, memsahibs. Balshish for baby. Baby sick. Baby need medicine. Bakshish for baby."

We found it easy enough to steel our hearts to the pleas of the predatory children and even the maimed grownups, but the sight of the weeping mother made us feel uncomfortable and cruel. We did not have the heart to shout "Jaldi, jao!" at her. Lou put on her severest scowl and tried to shoo her away, but this pretense did not work. The woman was a better student of human psychology than we.

"Maybe if we give her a little something she'll leave us alone." I suggested, rummaging in my bag for change. Lou agreed that it was a good idea. I could find no change. In desperation I pulled out a crisp five-rupee note, a fabulous sum to a beggar, and thrust it into her outstretched hand.

Before I realized what was happening, the Indian woman threw the baby toward me. Instinctively I put out my arms to catch it. In a flash the woman scampered away into the crowd, leaving me with a squalling dirty infant in my arms.

Hordes of beggars, lured by my show of generosity, closed in around us. I tried to push them back, to run after the fleeing woman. But she was long gone from sight and we were penned in by the mob.

We tried to palm off the baby to the beggars, but they would have none of the noisy infant. I never felt more helpless in my life. Lou thought that whole situation immensely funny and even threatened to snap my picture with "Lib's Indian offspring."

"Just think, Lib," she said pleasantly, "what a wonderful spread it would make in your hometown paper. Can't you see your father picking up the *Post Gazette* and reading the caption under the touching shot: 'Local Girl Has A Baby in India.' Wow! Would that ever make the professor sit up and take notice!"

I failed to see the humor in the situation. "A lot of help you are," I said. "Just what do you propose we do with the papoose? He's likely to give me a shower any minute now and I must say I can think of a pleasanter way of getting my afternoon bath."

"Why don't you adopt him, Lib? I'm sure the Red Cross would be happy to put you up in a nice bungalow and buy a layette. And think what you'd be doing for humanity. Why, you might even start a fad adopting Indian babies. And think of the publicity!"

I was ready to choke my roommate. "Oh, for heaven's sake, Lou. Can't you be serious for a minute? This problem calls for immediate action."

"OK, little mother. I have an idea. Let's take him to the jewelry store and ask our Indian friend to get rid of him for us."

Ten minutes later we laid the now docile infant on the glass counter where we had bought the turquoise baubles. The man behind the showcase smiled knowingly as Lucia told him our tale of woe.

"Now listen here, my good man, this baby was palmed off on us by one of your people. We'd appreciate it very much if you would turn it over to the proper authorities."

"But, madame," replied the suave Indian," we deal in jewelry, not babies. However, for a consideration I might convince a gendarme to take it off your hands." All this was said in perfect, even elegant English.

A gendarme, of course! Why hadn't we thought of that ourselves? But we had no time to hunt one up now. Lucia handed the man a five-rupee note as I gently put the baby on the counter. The Indian shook his head.

Fumbling in my purse, I got out two silver coins and threw them on the counter. Then Lucia and I turned on our heels and quickly left the store. As we went out the door I thought I heard a low chuckle behind us and realized that once again we had been taken.

Later we learned that the baby changed hands several times daily and brought in rajah-rupees to the woman and her accomplices. Sometimes a dead baby was thrust into the arms of a shy GI and that posed a real problem of disposal.

After this early "baptism by fire" we quickly caught on to the tourist snares and managed to avoid them at later stations.

Taxi, Taxi!

Transport in India offered both thrills and exasperation to the visitor. Even a simple taxi ride could raise one's blood pressure and lighten the pocketbook, as Lou and I discovered in Bombay.

By five o'clock that first day we still hadn't seen the sights. With only a few hours before dinner we had to rustle up something faster than a gharry or rickshaw. Our only alternative was to hire a taxi and hope that we wouldn't get skewered. From the many vehicles waiting outside the Taj Hotel we selected a later model among the mobile antiques lined up—a tan touring car of unknown make with the lines of a Chevrolet circa 1934. Like all Indian taxis it boasted a hollow-honking squeezehorn, which the driver used incessantly, scattering cows and chickens and people right and left as we hurtled through the streets.

Our driver was a large bearded Sikh dressed in white dhoti (draped diaper-like trousers), tan military-style cotton coat, and the traditional big pink turban of his sect. His thick beard, covering most of his face, gave him a formidable appearance. But his eyes were kind, so we felt secure with him. He spoke adequate English and promised us a running commentary on Bombay's points of interest. We called him Joe, a name he obviously had heard before.

Before I left the States two Parsi friends had told me what I must see if I ever got to Bombay. "Be sure to drive along the Marine Drive," Sherie Doongaji said. "My cousin lives there in a lovely pink house. It will change your mind about all Indians being poor."

The other Parsi friend Uma said, "Don't miss the Towers of Silence. That's where our dead bodies are put out for the vultures to dispose of."

"Seems barbaric," I said to Uma. "Burial or cremation are much more civilized."

"Not necessarily," Uma replied. "In that hot country, with no refrigeration or morgues or even embalming except for royalty, we have to get rid of bodies quickly to prevent the spread of disease."

At the outset of our tour in Calcutta we made sure that the driver understood and agreed to the stops and the sum he was to receive for the round trip. Lou was our negotiator.

"We know what the British pay you for these tours," she said, 'but we haven't time to bargain. We'll settle for ten rupees. Take it or leave it!"

The driver pondered a moment, knowing it was twice the usual fare, then said, "OK! I take you for ten rupees to see Hanging Gardens, Marine Drive, and Towers of Silence."

"Agreed," Lou said. "Let's get going."

Our tour started along the Marine Drive, an asphalt boulevard skirting the circular inlet of Bombay harbor. On one side of the drive the blue bay rolled up on a white sand beach; on the other side the door plates of modern town houses and apartments bore the names of Bombay's socially elite. Most of these two and three story structures were of white, light blue, or pink stucco, with wide windows, balconies, and flat tiled roofs. Each house had a tiny enclosed yard, immaculately tended and tastefully landscaped with bougainvillea, palm trees, and flowering tropical bushes.

As our taxi whizzed along, the driver bragged about what a fine car he had. When we started up the little hill to the Hanging Gardens, however, the vehicle coughed and sputtered and blew steam from her rusty radiator.

"We stop here a few minutes, memsahibs," he said, as he pulled the puffing vehicle to a stop off the road under a shade tree. Lucia took this opportunity to have a smoke. Joe fussed around the motor, tapping here and there with feigned authority.

"What seems to be the matter, Joe?" I said. "Won't this old crate make it up the hill?"

"Oh, yes, memsahib. My taxi goes up hill all the time, but she is like a lady. I cannot always know what she will do. Perhaps she is hot and tired. We'll rest a few minutes."

Seeing Lucia smoking, his eyes flashed. "You smoke American cigarettes? I like American cigarettes. Too expensive in India. I cannot buy them."

Lou took the hint and handed him two, which he snatched from her as fast as an opium smoker grabs the little pills after a week's abstinence.

"If it means that much to you," Lou said, "take the rest of the pack."

Joe bowed deeply and smiled his thanks. A few minutes later he stepped on the starter and the motor engaged with a rattle.

At the top of the hill we got out to inspect the Hanging Gardens, expecting to see an eleventh Wonder of the World. But Bombay's gardens were a far cry from those of ancient Babylon. They were ill kept and shabby. A low brick wall enclosed a simple, small plot of badly landscaped ground, with only a few scraggly marigolds peeping through the weeds. There were no hanging flowerbeds or even pots of tropical greenery. We didn't bother to explore.

Nor were we enticed to get out and inspect the Towers of Silence as we drove down the hill to the native quarter. On these brick monoliths the bodies of dead Parsis were laid out to be consumed by carrion eaters. Dozens of vultures circled the towers and scanned the landscape. We dared not venture outside the car for fear they might take us for the walking dead and start pecking at our pale faces.

It was still light when we reached the most interesting part of our tour—the red light district of Bombay, at this hour almost deserted. Tiny box-like rooms with iron-barred fronts, raised several feet off the ground, lined the filthy alleys. Aptly called "the cages," they reminded us of circus-animal quarters. Behind the iron gates of each cell we saw a small bed with embroidered coverlet, piled with bright velvet cushions. A pull curtain offered privacy when the room was in use.

After dark this district would present a totally different aspect. Indian nighttime enchantment would blot out the filth, as lanterns and red door-lights cast a soft welcoming glow. Charcoal brasiers would waft savory odors of spicy evening meals. Sensuous incense, a strong enticement for wandering, randy military men from the ships at anchor in the harbor, would mask the stench of sewage and spittle.

At eight o'clock Joe delivered us back to the Taj for a late dinner with our friends. We paid the ten rupees agreed upon, plus a two-rupee tip—a sum probably three times as much as Joe would have collected from another Indian and twice the sum that an Englishman would have given him. But he was not satisfied.

"Memsahibs," he protested, lapsing back into his servile lingo. "My taxi she eat up much petrol and I take you on long, long ride. Petrol very expensive. Give me ten rupees more, please."

"My dear fellow," Lucia answered in the voice she reserved exclusively for children and servants, "we agreed on a certain sum—a sum far too large to begin with. We have paid you that sum, plus an ample tip, not to mention that pack of cigarettes. We do not propose to pay you one anna more. Good day!"

We started up the steps to the hotel, but Lou's frigid words had not dissuaded Joe. He followed us, tugged at Lou's sleeve, and babbled, "But memsahib, you rich. You rajah memsahib. I poor taxi driver. I use five gallons petrol and you no pay me enough. Ten rupees? No? Then five rupees. Please, memsahib, gimme four rupees... three..."

Joe had not reckoned on Lou's resolution. When she made up her mind she could not be dissuaded. As we entered the Taj Hotel's wide front portals that no lower class Indian would dare step through, we heard Joe still calling. "Three rupees memsahib ... two rupees, just two rupees and I go away."

After a wonderful six-course dinner and dancing, we returned to the ship in an open gharry. With the canvas top pushed back, convertible style, we jogged along leisurely in the warm night air. Except for a few cafes still open for foreign trade, the city was now asleep. Occasionally a single candle or a dying charcoal fire lighted the tiny stalls where merchants, still wearing their daytime attire, slept on the counters. Motionless bundles of people wrapped in their dhotis and cheesecloth shawls lay on the streets, their only home. No moon, no street lights— only a million tiny stars pierced the canopy overhead.

The next day we left by cross-country train for ARC headquarters in Calcutta, which was to be our home base for the rest of our Indian sojourn.

The Bengal Famine

In late December of 1943 our Red Cross contingent arrived in Calcutta just as the great Bengal famine was winding down. Dead and dying bodies littered the sidewalk. Emaciated Brahmin cattle roamed the filthy streets. Skeletal, half-naked mothers pacified simpering babies from dried-up pendulous breasts. Bone-thin, barefoot rickshaw drivers in loincloths pulled fat memsahibs decked out in fine silk saris and gold bracelets.

Picking a footpath around manure piles and betel-juice spittle, we healthy Americans shielded our noses against the stench as we carefully side-stepped sick, prone bodies covered only by thin gauze dhotis. Hordes of sad-faced children tugged at our uniforms, chanting "Gimme anna, memsahib. Gimme cigarette!"

Saddened by the street scene, we momentarily took heart when we first saw great mounds of wheat stashed in a city park. Dozens of rhesus monkeys played on the cloth-covered stacks, molding in the humid air. Green shoots of sprouting wheat pierced through the white cloth covers.

Back at our quarters in Park Circus, we queried Mrs. Scott, our housekeeper. Why this great waste while millions starved? Surely, we reasoned, the famine could be alleviated if the wheat, ground into flour, were made into a nourishing gruel or fried into chapattis. Why hadn't the British done more for their starving subjects? This is what she told us:

For centuries under local rule, famine (along with foreign invasion) had been an accepted means of keeping the population stable. In the 1920's the British tried an experiment known as The Bengal Plan in the rice-growing area north of Calcutta. A rudimentary farming plan was set up. The land was irrigated; agricultural agents came from Britain and the US to train the people in better methods of rice cultivation; and dispensaries for free medical care and medicines were set up for the local people. In a few years, thanks to this plan, the province of Bengal became self-sustaining and her people were fatter and healthier than ever before.

But with the increase in food and improvement in health, the birth rate rose and infant mortality soared to such an astonishing degree that within a single generation the province could no longer provide enough food for its burgeoning population and had to seek elsewhere for rice. The plan that worked so well for twenty years was a failure in the long run. Drought and floods decimated the crops as the population exploded.

Before the war Japan, Burma, and China had supplied most of Bengal's extra rice. After the war began, British ships brought rice for a time from other parts of the world. But for months now, the Japanese had successfully prevented Allied merchant ships from entering Calcutta harbor, so Bengal's rice supply was cut off. The attack on Calcutta Harbor in December of that year, just before we arrived in Bombay was a continuation of the blockade. We were told that the great Bengal famine of 1942-43 was a result of this action.

The British tried to alleviate the suffering by giving the people daily rations of wheat, to replace the rice rations so long exhausted. Setting up distribution centers throughout the city, they spread the word that free food was available for the asking. But only a handful of natives came. For generations the native people subsisted on a daily ration of a cupful of rice and a few fish. Now their weakened digestive systems could not sustain the change of diet and many became sick. Others did not like the taste of wheat and refused to change their habits even to preserve life. The majority, however, were devout Hindus, whose religious beliefs prevented them from eating anything unblessed or improperly prepared. Thus, many more languished and died.

We wished we could help, but all we could do was mourn for those whose lives were unimaginably sad. As temporary residents we were helpless to do anything about the situation. The wheat piles continued to mold in the sun and the monkeys kept on playing tag on top of the mounds. So we turned our energies toward relieving the loneliness and boredom of our troops.

A week later our Calcutta experience was over and we were hard at work in Assam, making a difference in the lives of American GIs.

Cross Country to Calcutta

After the overcrowded quarters aboard ship, the European-style Indian train from Bombay to Calcutta across India's wide central plains was a luxury ride, though all cars were filled to capacity. No first class cars were available, so we Red Cross girls rode second-class, four to a compartment. For recreation en route we played lots of bridge, drank lots of Cokes, wrote letters to our families, and visited back and forth the length of the long train.

Toward the end of the first day, as the sun was setting behind us, the train slowed down as we approached Ahmenabad.

"Wonder what the problem is now," Lou said. "I thought we were supposed to go straight through."

"Maybe there's been an accident aboard," I said. "I saw a bunch of medics running by our compartment."

As the train squeaked to a stop, the four of us gathered at the compartment window. Outside, a small crowd of inquisitive locals clustered around an olive-drab truck. Presently a pair of GI medical corpsmen, bearing a loaded stretcher, rushed off the train to the waiting ambulance.

Immediately we recognized a familiar figure on the stretcher, now cuddling a healthy newborn.

"Oh, no! It can't be! But it is. It's Hannah from Boston. I wondered why she was so overweight."

"And I marveled at her agility as she hopped up and down from the top bunk."

"No wonder she had nothing to do with the rest of us and spent all her time in the Captain's cabin playing bridge."

"What a bunch of dummies we are, not to have suspected it!"

At dusk on New Year's Eve we arrived—hot, dirty, and tired—at Howrah Station in Calcutta. Barefoot porters in bright red tunics and floppy red turbans pounced on our luggage, each grabbing one item and immediately tossing it onto his head. The rule apparently was one item per man. The size of the item made no difference: a steamer trunk weighing a hundred pounds, a bulky bedroll, a musette bag packed with cosmetics and sundries, a portable typewriter, or a tiny box that had escaped from an overstuffed B-4 bag.

Lucia burst into a gale of laughter. "I can't believe it. Red caps in India with turbans falling down over their eyes and numbers on their tunics!"

What a sight we were as we filed in a line to the waiting Army trucks—a platoon of Red Cross girls followed by a retinue of turbaned porters, regally carrying all our worldly possessions on their heads!

From the station, Army trucks carried us to Red Cross hostels throughout Calcutta. Lucia and I were taken across town to a small hostel in the native quarter on Park Circus, where we lived for three glorious, glamorous weeks. Some of the girls landed in downtown hotels, the Great Eastern and the Grand. Others were billeted in apartment houses in the British quarter. Though not as elegant as the big hotels, our modest quarters on Park Circus in downtown Calcutta were, we thought, the choicest spot for seeing the real, exotic India.

Our hostel was a square, two-story white cement building surrounded by a high iron wall with fancy grillwork gate, the latter presided over by a durwan in floppy turban and European suitcoat over his dhoti. The ground floor housed our living room, dining, and serving areas, as well as the housekeeper's quarters. On the second floor our bedrooms, though clean and comfortable, were each meagerly furnished, with mosquito-netted single bed, one straight chair, and a table with drawers for writing and storing stuff.

Archways hung with dark green baize served as doors. Large unscreened upstairs windows opened onto a back sundeck and veranda overlooking the street. Through these windows and doors came in almost anything alive: winged, crawling, or wee furry critters, and occasionally a servant or thief. Pilfering crows sneaked into our bedrooms and made off with small jewelry and trinkets. We quickly learned to put everything away.

Our hostel boasted five bathrooms with washbasins and running cold water. We crouched in skimpy galvanized steel tubs, with hot water heated on the kitchen's charcoal stove and toted up by paniwallahs to our tiled facilities. Since these were the first hot baths we had had in weeks, we considered the tin tubs a real luxury.

Mrs. Scott, an Englishwoman past middle age, ran the house. A resident of India for over thirty years, she had no desire to return home. She was an agreeable and efficient house manager under whose direction the staff of fifteen servants kept everything running smoothly.

Heading the list of household servants was a tall thin ascetic-looking head bearer with white hair and a long thin white beard. He resembled the Hollywood version of a Tibetan monk, his countenance serious, his manner dignified, his watchful eyes missing nothing. The Indian counterpart of an English butler, he served the table, managed the servants, and ruled with a tyrant's hand. We often heard his angry babble rising from the cooking quarters as he castigated an underling.

Below him in the servant hierarchy were several second bearers, water-carriers (paniwallahs), gardeners (mahlis), the gate keeper (durwan) who invariably went to sleep at his post, two little sweepers, and several personal maids (ayahs) who made our beds and took care of our laundry. The ayah assigned to Lucia and me was a little Hindu woman with two small diamonds set permanently in her nose.

We quickly settled into the easy Eastern way of life as practiced by the British, with emphasis on fine food served often and a highly organized social life, with as little physical exertion as possible. The daily menu called for five meals: chota hazri brought to us in bed at 7:00, consisting of hot tea, a banana, and a slice of buttered bread; a regular breakfast of bacon and eggs, hot cereal, toast, and coffee at 8:30; a three-course luncheon at 1:00; tea and cakes at 5:00; and a five-course dinner at 8:00. Later in the evening, after bridge or dancing, we were offered a light supper. We soon learned to dispense with chota hazri and the midnight snack. The other meals satisfied our hunger and soon filled out our lean bodies.

Lou and I spent our days sunning on the veranda, writing letters to family and friends, riding through the bazaar in rickshaw or gharry, haggling with peddlers and nearby shop owners, then soaking in the tub before the evening's festivities. Nighttime found us out dining and dancing with officers we had met on the boat and also British officers. In the weeks after our arrival we took in most of the famous night spots: Firpo's, Christie's, the Wintergarden, the Great Eastern, the Grand Hotel, and our favorite, the popular B and A (British and American) Club. None of these establishments had the flavor of the East except in the garb of the waiters. I'd have to wait for months to get my first taste of a real Indian curry.

Park Circus, appropriately named in the nineteenth century by an Englishman, was a circular space where many streets came together. From our upstairs porch we observed the activities of four converging streets. Just the sounds told us we were in a different world: hollow tong-tong of rickshaw bells, screeching of the tram, honks from taxis, lowing of cattle and bullocks, occasional distant beat of drums, and cries of peddlers hawking their wares.

Children played in bare feet among the manure piles. A little girl cupped her hands and drank from the filthy gutter. A lad in loincloth balanced a flat tray of oranges on his head. A coolie pulled a potbellied Englishman in a rickshaw. Two other coolies, yoked like oxen, pulled a cartload of wood. A small herd of goats snuffled at three coolies wrestling a load of rawhide. An English soldier in shorts rode his bicycle too close to a little girl with a baby on her hip. The tram, jammed with Indian men wearing white shirts with shirttails hanging to their knees, stopped to pick up three Muslim women in spook-like hoods.

Down the street we saw a funeral procession. Two coolies carried the body of a poor Hindu laid out on a stretcher with a thin red canopy. A handful of mourners trailed behind. A veritable menagerie completed the procession: a pack of "jungli" dogs, three nonchalant Brahmin cows; and a two-beast two-wheel oxcart with the driver seated forward on the long tongue between. He guided the oxen by pulling their ears. Life and death walked side by side and seemed of equal importance, or more accurately, of no importance at all.

Though it was late December when we arrived in Bombay, Calcutta was so hot and muggy that we slowed down to sheer indolence. With servants to do all our chores and taxis and military transport to take us everywhere, we fluffed off on strenuous exercise. How would we ever be able to handle the work awaiting us in the field? Now we understood why Englishmen, longtime in the East, often did not want to go back to their homeland.

A Chic Chapeau

Our long rests in Washington, on the Pacific, in Bombay and in Calcutta, seemed like mindless, exaggerated laziness, which was certainly not of our choice, for from the start we were anxious to get our teeth into the job and be of some real use in the war effort. By the time we finally did make it into the field, six months after first coming on board, we had become veritable bums. I wrote home on January 4, 1944:

> *Today we got up enough energy to go downtown and look around a bit. Having lived a lazy sedentary life for so long, the exertion nearly killed us. After seeing lepers and half-dead dogs and thin beggars all morning, we've been scratching ever since. But actually, we're as healthy as hogs. I'm sure that I've gained five pounds in the few days I've been here.*

> *We had lunch at Christie's, then came home to take a nap. Twice I had just gotten into bed when callers came. I also had to entertain two other batches of enlisted men, so I finally gave up on the nap idea. We've given up sleeping for the duration.*

> *Today our training lectures began. We had one on censorship. Saturday night Peggy and I are going out with the Lt. who gave the lectures and a friend of his—i.e., if the Red Cross doesn't require us to go elsewhere. Tomorrow we have interviews all day, then go to the enlisted men's dance at one of the nearby camps—20 miles away. Thursday we start a short orientation course; go to a party from 5:00–7:00 and then to the Navy officers' dinner party afterwards. Friday—more classes and a clubmobile trip in the evening. Saturday—a picnic or tea with the Navy (unless more duties turn up) and evening dates with G2s (Army Intelligence officers). Beyond that we can't plan, for we don't know when we will be assigned, but surely we will go to the enlisted men's dance Sunday night.*

Such is life—all gaiety, with more dates than we can take care of. When work starts, though, we'll be working at night and that will cut down on the dates. We've gotten so spoiled, we won't know how to work.

After all-day classes the following Friday I bowed out of a clubmobile jaunt and stayed at the hostel to shampoo my hair and catch up on sleep. It was, of course, the night that everyone I knew in Calcutta had asked me for a date. But I stuck to my guns and went resolutely upstairs to get the pesky chore done.

In the midst of the last rinse, the bearer came up from below, tapped on the flimsy bathroom door, with a message for Memsahib Chitwood. "Navy sahib here," he announced. "He bring you these flowers." A bunch of deep red roses stuck their heads through the half-open bathroom door as I drew back the shower curtain.

That was just like Ed—never would take no for an answer. And here he was trying to soften me up with the very gift no female can resist. I was a little provoked with him. After all, we weren't well enough acquainted for him to issue commands, even with roses.

"Please tell him I'm busy and cannot see him," I told the bearer. "Tell him memsahib has her hair all sopping wet."

A moment later I heard the gentle tap-tap again. "Memsahib, Navy sahib say he in no hurry. He say he wait."

Ed's soft sell began to work. "All right, bearer," I said. "Please put the flowers in my bedroom and tell the sahib I'll be down in a minute."

Slipping into my red and black civilian suit, I hurriedly tied a big white bath towel around my head, turban fashion, and went down to reason with the persistent ensign. After all, if he insisted on calling at such a time, he'd have to take me as I was.

Instead of gasping when he saw me, he smiled approval of my new chapeau. "That's the best looking hat I've seen in Calcutta," he said in all seriousness.

"Don't be silly, Ed. It's just a plain old bath towel. After all, I could hardly come downstairs with water streaming onto my shoulders."

"No, I mean it. That turban is a knockout on you. It does something for you, which is more than can be said for most women's hats."

"OK, Ed, I'll take your word for it, but let's not spend the whole evening talking about it. What have you been doing the last two days while we've been tied up with training?"

"The usual thing that a guy does in a strange town when he's broke—staying at home in my bunk reading."

"But what about tonight—the flowers? They're beautiful, Ed! You shouldn't have done it."

"Oh, that's OK. Paul wasn't quite as broke and he lent me 50 rupees. Come on, Lib, don't you want to go to the club?"

I loved the B and A Club, but tonight I wasn't really tempted. "Of course I like the club, but I told you three times I'm not going out tonight. What does it take to convince you?"

"There's a gorgeous moon out there. Let's not waste it. You'll be leaving soon, then where will I be? Please, Lib, don't be stuffy. After all, you've already finished your evening chore."

"Even so, I couldn't possibly go with a wet head. I'd catch my death of cold in this hot climate." I was testing his persistence, knowing I eventually would capitulate. "No, I won't go out with you tonight."

"If you wear that turban you won't catch cold." Now he was calling my bluff.

"And suppose I should wear this turban. You wouldn't be caught dead with me in a Red Cross bath towel, even one tied around my head."

"That's just where you're mistaken. I'd even be happy to take you in your GI bathrobe. So, hurry up and let's get going, just as you are."

"At least let me put on a scarf and concoct a respectable headgear."

"Nope. Don't want you to change a thing. Damn it, Lib, you're beautiful just as you are."

Who could resist this smooth-tongued Navy man? I weakened, then relented. "Well, if you can take it, I guess I can. Come on, Ed, what are we waiting for?"

As we walked out to the jeep, the night watchman stared at me in utter amazement, fingering his own turban thoughtfully, probably thinking, "What will the memsahib do next?"

In the dim light of the club no one seemed to notice my turban until I got up to dance. I recognized three or four Red Cross girls from the boat. When we danced close to Sally Clark, she looked at me in horror.

"My God," she exclaimed in a stage whisper. "What is that thing you've got on your head? No, it can't be! Good heavens, it is! A bath towel! What next?" Then her partner whisked her out of earshot, sparing me her further scrutiny.

More self-conscious than my date, I bore the stares of a few other properly attired females until I reasoned to myself: Why wouldn't a bath towel turban, carefully draped with the knot on top, be as chic as a cloche or beret? I'd have to send a suggestion with picture to *Harper's Bazaar*. Maybe it would start a fad.

That night in Calcutta, as I danced away the night with a handsome navy ensign, I added another "best time I ever had in my life" to an already long list.

Seeing the Sights

One day in early January 1944, Lou and I went sightseeing in Calcutta with about thirty American soldiers, sailors, and Red Cross girls—all piled into an antiquated Indian bus with seats facing a center aisle.

Two very young Navy recruits attached themselves to us like leeches, entertaining us with sweet nothings and marshalling us protectively in and out of the bus all along our route. Before the day was over Lou and I received the usual proposals, with impassioned hugs when we said goodbye.

At every stop Sven, a hefty six-footer from Min-ne-so-ta, insisted on lifting me down the three-foot drop to the ground.

"You make me feel like a featherweight," I said, as my black uniform shoes touched earth. "I'm glad to have such a healthy protector. But please don't squeeze me quite so hard."

"Sorry, sweetie, I couldn't resist a free hug."

"OK," I said, "just lighten up a bit. I don't want a broken rib."

Lou's eager self-appointed squire was an undersized seaman from South Carolina. Much to her annoyance, Charlie C., in true Southern fashion, took her arm as they dodged street filth.

"Ma'am," he would say, "watch out for that betel gob. I don't want you to mess up your shoes."

"So what if I do?" she countered. "I'm perfectly capable of walking without assistance. You make me feel like an old lady."

"But Sugar, I only wanted to touch some beautiful soft female flesh. Surely you can understand that."

Lou softened a bit. "It's OK," she said. "You can take my hand and lead me around the next mound of manure." Charlie C. beamed.

At our first stop—the infamous Black Hole of Calcutta—our two young escorts were Johnny-on-the-spot to help us. As we all crowded into a dank, windowless 14'x18' subterranean box, Charlie C. said, "So what's to see? Looks like a hell hole to me."

"That's just what it was," Lou said.

"Read what it says on that marker over there on the wall," I chimed in.

Charlie C. obliged as the room emptied quickly of the other GIs. When we all got back in the bus, he told us the sad story of the Black Hole of Calcutta:

In 1757, during the Seven Years War in Europe that spread to skirmishes in India, the Indian leader Minorca imprisoned hundreds of British soldiers in this hot humid airless cell where they died of suffocation. Subsequently the British took over all of Bengal and established the British East India Company, whose political, economic, and social domination lasted for nearly 200 years.

Luckily we stayed only a half-hour at our next stop. At the burning ghats on the banks of the sacred Hoogly River, the sight and stench of human bodies on open pyres turned our stomachs.

"Gosh," said Lou. "This is worse than the Towers of Silence in Bombay. Give me the vultures picking my carcass any day to doing a Joan d'Arc on my husband's bier." Here Lou was referring to the centuries-old Hindu custom of sutee, still practiced in the 1940's, where a healthy wife lies down on the funeral pyre to join her husband in death in the cremation rite.

Remembering the beauty, the silence, and the sacredness of American cemeteries, where Dad and I had walked many happy paths, I was repelled by this sandy, barren, unlovely Hindu burial ground. A narrow passageway between a row of tawdry native dwellings brought us to a little rise above the river, with forty or fifty pits dug into the ground. Smoke still rose from the smoldering ashes in some of the pits. No mausoleum, no markers, no temple, no shrine—just the flat, parched earth.

As we stood there, a procession of Hindus entered the area by the same passageway that we had used. On a stretcher carried by four men lay a flower-bedecked corpse.

A few men carried bundles of wood; others came along to watch the ceremony. The number of flowers and the size of the wood bundles indicated the financial status of the family, for wood was scarce and costly in Calcutta. This was a middle-caste family in mourning today.

The stretcher was set on the ground. Two men laid a bundle of sticks in one of the pits. Two other men lifted the corpse from the stretcher onto the sticks. Two more men piled the rest of the wood on top of and around the body. The dead man was the father. His dry-eyed son lit the fire. As flames licked at the body, no one wept. Bystanders carried on conversations. It seemed like the most natural thing in the world to them. To us, it was unthinkably barbaric. We turned away in sadness from the scene.

A short while later we walked into a veritable paradise. After a wandering route through the narrow alleys of the native quarter, the bus stopped before a grillwork enclosure and we alighted at the fabulous Jain temples. Even the GI's joined Lou and me in "oh's" and "ah's" as we gazed upon a pod of glittering, jeweled temples set in exquisite gardens with mosaic walkways and gushing fountains. Every exterior inch of the temples, masterpieces of hand craftsmanship, was covered with carvings, metal work, and fine mosaics.

The Jains, mostly merchants and businessmen, are a small sect then found only in India—the first of many reform offshoots of Hinduism. Jainism advocates nonviolence, humility, and striving for perfection through meditation, forgiveness, patience, and sincerity.

The main Jain temple (of three), dedicated to their 10th prophet Sithal Nathi, and built in 1867, is a mass of arches, minarets, and tall spires rising above a wide marble stairway leading up to the interior of the temple. Inside, beads of silver mixed with tiny rubies, emeralds, and pearls covered the walls. In little open mosaic houses in the front yard, dedicated to minor prophets, some of the prophets were depicted riding on caparisoned elephants. Only one thing marred the beauty of this spot: the water in the pools was stagnant and stinking.

The next day two Navy ensigns, officers on LCTs (military landing craft) based in Calcutta, finagled a Jeep and took us on an outing to the beautiful botanical gardens about fifteen miles outside the city.

Through some wheedling and the offer of a healthy tip, Lou persuaded the hostel cook to fix us an elegant picnic supper, complete with beef sandwiches, rosette deviled eggs, and decorated sugar cookies. We dressed in slacks and took along wool jackets for the breezy return in the cool night air.

Once out in the suburbs, Lou, sitting in the back seat of the Jeep with Paul, tapped the driver on the back and said, "Slow down a bit, Ed. I just want to prove to Lib that the circus has come to town. Take a look at those jumping jacks up there in those trees. If those aren't real live bona fide monkeys, then I'm a Dutchman."

"Hi ya, Dutchie," said Paul, who was looking in the wrong direction.

We drove by slowly. I spotted the monkeys—hundreds of them jumping about in the trees. Some sat in little groups along the road. Some played on the canvas-covered mountains of stacked wheat moldering in the hot sun. One of the monkeys took a shine to Lou and tried to jump into the Jeep.

"Step on the gas," I shouted, "before Lou has a monkey in her lap! They bite and scratch, you know. I don't want to have to use up my Band Aid supply this early in our tour." Ed gunned the engine.

Our next stop was at the botanical gardens, which were much like those of any nation: Rock Creek Park in Washington, the Bois de Boulogne in Paris, or the Wintergarten in Munich. We walked down macadam roads in and out of a semi-landscaped park, across little streams and over little knolls. We sauntered through a large greenhouse with tropical trees and flowers in hanging pots, glad to rest at last on the concrete benches inside.

Nearby we found the giant banyan tree, reputed to be the largest in the world. For a moment we stood transfixed before its network of exposed roots spreading over several acres. Under its canopy I felt as though I were in an endless pillared hall. It scared me just a bit.

"It's like being in a cathedral," Lou said, awe-struck.

"Yes," I said, equally moved. "Maybe we should say a prayer of thanks."

We enjoyed our picnic on a little knoll overlooking a pretty pool. Nearby, dozens of monkeys offered diversion as we devoured our supper and talked over the day's tour. Then we climbed back into the bus and sang old-time songs all the way back to the city.

Calcutta coolies in turbans and dhotis.

Mosque architecture. Victoria Memorial, Calcutta.

Park Circus street corner
in Calcutta late 1943,
Note gharry on far right.

Jain temple in Calcutta.

Calcutta: Libby with
friends late 1943

Part Three
On the Job in Assam

"This is a great moment when you see,
however distant, the goal of your wandering.
The thing that has been living in your imagination
suddenly becomes a part of the tangible world.
It matters not how many ranges, rivers
or parching dusty ways may lie between you;
it is yours now forever."

Freya Stark, writing from Persia.

The Tea Plantation Bungalow

In January 1944, a large group of Red Cross club workers climbed into a C-47 at Dum Dum airport in Calcutta and headed north to Assam, assigned to small ATC (Air Transport Command) bases between Calcutta and the Ledo Road. In addition to its human cargo, the plane, already heavily loaded with military supplies, carried all our worldly possessions. Limited to 120 lbs. each, our basic luggage included a bedroll, small steamer trunk, suitcase, musette bag, and an overnight bag slung over a shoulder. Add to this the extra boxes and sacks, sneaked by feminine wiles past the baggage men, and you will appreciate the size of the ceiling-high mound strapped in the center of the plane.

We passengers picked our way around the luggage to squeeze into the steel "buckets" where regular seats had been removed. As we surveyed the pile of parachutes in front of the washroom door in the back of the plane, Lou said, "Let's hope our bladders hold out to the first stop."

"And let's pray we don't have to bail out in an emergency," I added. Luckily we had an easy ride and no one got sick.

At each stop along the way several girls got off at military bases and the rest of us stretched our legs. Soon we had breathing space and could move about the plane. At the fifth stop Lucia and I alighted at Jorhat airbase where a Red Cross field director whisked us away in an old Chevy station wagon to our quarters on a British tea plantation in the jungle.

Jorhat air base, a concrete runway flanked by taxi strips, hangars, and service buildings, served as way station for planes carrying oil and supplies across the Hump into China. From 1943 to 1945 Jorhat was home to several hundred American and British former commercial pilots and their crews, as well as a small squadron of British fighter pilots (for protection against Japanese activity in nearby Burma), a staff of mechanics and maintenance personnel, plus two canteens for six Red Cross workers who lived off the post.

I loved this first assignment from the moment I first set foot on the runway, where monster C-87's crouched like giant condors, awaiting flight across the Himalayas. One of the newer installations in the Brahmaputra valley, the air base had literally been carved out of the jungle. Rice paddies had been drained and the bush uprooted to clear land for the airport, supply and maintenance buildings, and quarters for military personnel. Thousands of local coolies had been hired to build the runways and roads by hand, to crush and carry huge stones to underlay the concrete. The quantity rather than the quality of the local labor had accomplished this task in a record six months.

Across the river in the jungle, the Burma hills were visible from the airstrip on a clear day. Beyond this enemy-infested territory small units of British soldiers reputedly routed smaller units of Japanese in almost daily confrontation. Gains were measured in feet-of-front taken or lost each day. Losses lately apparently had outnumbered gains.

On the other side of Jorhat lay the Naga hills, about thirty miles into the bush. For centuries headhunting savages had inhabited these wild reaches. Currently, however, the Nagas were friendly, partly because of long-term missionary influence and gifts from the British. A few American and English soldiers were stationed here in remote one-man radio stations. These hills also were infested with snipers, some of whom were said to have violated Naga women. We were unable to substantiate these rumors, but they added to our sense of dangerous living that spring of 1944.

Two Red Cross canteens were already serving the base when we arrived. Lou drew the strip canteen, a stop-off point near the runway for both GIs and pilots. Here she and a native helper served coffee and doughnuts in an army tent sparsely furnished with a few straight chairs and a card table. In this modest cafe the men found a little bit of home as an American girl served their coffee and listened to their gripes. The favorite sweetener, however, was not the white stuff. Every day some GI would chant, "Hold off on the sugar, pretty lady. Just put your finger in my cup and I won't need any."

I was assigned to the base canteen, a recreation center for enlisted men only, located about a half-mile from the runway in the living area of the post. Across the road was the Area 3 mess hall. We did a good deal of moonlight requisitioning from there. Around the corner was the open-air theater, aptly called the Mosquitodrome, where movies were shown three nights a week, rain or shine, and an occasional USO troupe or celebrity performed. It was here under the stars that we heard Noel Coward deliver his famous "Mad Dogs and Englishmen" and Paulette Goddard belt out a throaty "You'll Never Know."

My canteen was a one-room basha, a thatched-roof straw hut built on a concrete foundation. Inside, a bamboo-faced bar with stools spread across one wall, with card tables, folding chairs, and a few lounge chairs scattered about. A wooden bench accommodated a half-dozen men along another wall. Constantly in use was a windup Victrola playing Top Twenty tunes. Over in one corner a sweet soft-toned spinet piano, the reason for my assignment to Jorhat, beckoned me several times a day to beat out the swing tunes for clapping, singing, and dancing.

Tucked away among the jungle trees was the military housing: rough wooden barracks, army tents on concrete slabs, and a few bashas for upper-echelon officers. In their flimsy ground-hugging quarters the men battled jungle mold, mosquitoes, and an occasional deadly krait (snake), plus friendly frogs that dined on flying and crawling insects. Captain Stewart shared his warm house slippers with a little croaker whom he named Jessie.

Five miles from the post, over deeply rutted clay roads, we pampered females enjoyed the luxury of a comfortable tea planter's bungalow: a ten-room house on stilts, complete with broad verandas, overhead electric fans, two fireplaces, semi-modern baths, dressing rooms, a piano in the dining room, and twelve servants.

The term bungalow always amused us Americans for whom the word described a small, squatty, story-and-a-half dwelling with front porch and dormers. The Assamese plantation bungalow was a large square structure on heavy pilings with wide, shingled overhanging eaves and a wonderful veranda overlooking the tea garden. Underneath were flimsy storage rooms and a small pantry, with cookhouse out back. A tall hedge in the back hid mud huts where some of the servants lived. Two open stairways gave access to the main floor in front and back.

Luckily, wild and domestic animals, attracted by the cooking odors and enticing garbage below, could not climb upstairs, though plenty of roaches (up to four inches long), mosquitoes, lizards, green flies, and salamanders managed to crawl or fly upstairs, even into our beds and dresser drawers, where they munched on our fine cotton undies. Cheeky mynah birds kept us company on the veranda, helping to clear away the crumbs from our morning tea.

Our quarters included a large living room with fireplace, dining room with fireplace and an ancient upright piano in a corner, three large bedrooms with dressing rooms and baths, and two smaller bedrooms and a pantry off the dining room. Here Lou and I, Norris McClellan, club director, and three staff assistants lived comfortably. In June an English clubmobile worker joined us, so we moved our dining quarters downstairs to the vacant storage room.

Sparsely furnished at first, our bungalow soon became home, as our English neighbors and the British military hauled in dressers, comfortable chairs, a desk with a typewriter, and proper beds to replace the charpois. With a station wagon and an occasionally borrowed jeep or weapons carrier, plus a retinue of twelve servants, we enjoyed a luxury unheard of elsewhere for wartime field workers.

Majordomo of our household staff was a short lithe Christianized Hindu named Nanda, whose usually soft speech broke into harsh guttural invective whenever he addressed the sweeper or chastised recalcitrant lower servants. Because he had learned English in the local missionary school, he was made head bearer, household manager, and interpreter for the rest of the help whose total English vocabulary consisted of "Yes" and "No."

Nanda served the meals, brought up our chota hazri (coffee and toast in bed) and served mid-morning and afternoon tea to those of us not on duty. He also planned the meals, oversaw the cookhouse and garden activity, and supervised the housecleaning staff. On rush days at the post he helped serve coffee and doughnuts in the canteen.

For these services Nanda received the princely sum of 80 rupees a month (about $25) to cover all his family and living expenses—considered scandalously high by long-term British residents not yet accustomed to the higher wages brought in by a more affluent American military.

In addition to Nanda we enjoyed the luxury of two second-bearers who cleaned the bungalow and helped serve the meals sent up from the cookhouse below. Two paniwallahs trotted pails of hot water from the cookhouse to second-floor baths, and cold water from an unknown and probably unsavory source for our primitive toilets. Completing this retinue were a tall Hindu cook and his ten-year-old helper; three mahlis who cut and weeded the lawns and gardens; a dhobi who came from the village three times a week to do our laundry; and a weary, overworked, not-too-bright little sweeper, eternally underfoot as he squatted with his reed brush to rearrange the dust and dirt on the tile floors. Later in the year, when our clothes were wearing out, a durzi (tailor) brought his hand-operated Singer to replenish our wardrobes with shirts and shorts in exotic Indian fabrics.

In this whole staff there was no one to make our beds, put down our mosquito nets, order the bath water, or take care of our clothes. In India it was unthinkable that we should do these lowly tasks. After all, we were memsahibs. So Beeba came to do them for us.

Beeba and the Red Formal

She came to us one tinsel-bright morning in spring. As temporary burrah-memsahib (house manager), I was struggling with the household accounts and getting no-where. Twittering finches in the tea garden and human chatter in the cookhouse distracted me from the price of chicken in the market and the supplies-order from the base warehouse.

A flock of crows, circling above the big chinar tree in the far corner of the yard, screamed saucy protest as a thick four-foot snake, black as old fashioned licorice, slith-ered down the tree trunk into the knee-high jungle grass. Not an hour before, from that very tree, I had gathered the orchids now gracing my coiffure. In horror I watched the wake in the grass as the cobra undulated into the brush.

On the railing beside me two fat cheeky mynahs scolded for a while, then hopped to the tea table to peck poppy seeds from the leftover tea biscuits. A gregarious gecko made big eyes at me from the wall above my desk. The heavy odor of jasmine, spilling its white waxy blossoms under the porch overhang, enveloped me in a sensuous fog.

Over by the cookhouse two scrawny jungli-dogs licked their oozing sores, sniffed the air hungrily, and whined for handouts. I couldn't settle down to balancing the books.

A whisper of bare feet snapped me out of the hypno-tism of the tea garden. I turned to see Nanda standing beside me.

"Salaam, memsahib," he said softly, inclining his tur-baned head.

"Good morning, Nanda," I replied. "Did you get those rats out of the cookhouse?"

"Rats gone, memsahib. Cookhouse teek hai. I scare rats away."

Unfortunately, "scare" was probably all that had oc-curred, for I could not hope for extermination by a Hindu to whom all life is sacred.

"Cookhouse teek hai, memsahib," he continued. "New ayah here. You see her now?"

"Indeed I will," I said, welcoming any excuse to get away from those pesky books and happy to have my two-weeks search for a personal maid at last at an end. "Bring her up at once."

Almost before I finished speaking Nanda had slipped away. A moment later I heard the soft pat pat of two pairs of naked feet on the stairway outside. Then Beeba stood before me, a folded "chitty" in her hand.

Like millions of Indian women, she was about five feet tall, slender, and erect. She moved with the natural grace bequeathed her by countless generations who had carried their burdens on their heads. Glossy black hair, drawn to a prim knot at the nape of her neck, accentuated the plainness of her face. Parchment-thin, yellow-brown skin stretched over broad cheeks suggested Mongolian ancestry. But where did she get those blue eyes?

Beeba's manner was shy, her expression solemn, her bearing dignified. She wore a green-bordered white muslin sari wound round her wiry body and thrown over her head madonna-fashion. Her feet were bare and unadorned. On her left wrist three tiny glass bracelets tinkled when she moved. Beeba bore my scrutiny with true Oriental calm.

As I scanned the typewritten lines of the proffered chitty, I recognized at the bottom the angular signature of our British landlord, Mr. Carpenter.

"This servant, Beeba Sukuran," the recommendation read in part, "is clean, dependable and proud. Of Naga ancestry, she is reputedly descended from a chieftain. As a child she had some training in Christian principles from a transient missionary, though she has never renounced her own religion. She has been in my service only a few weeks and is as yet untrained. She appears, however, to be intelligent, willing and apparently honest."

This last-named quality was of prime importance, particularly in a personal maid with access to bureau drawers and unlocked jewel cases. I knew I could teach her to tend our rooms and care for our clothes, but I did not want the additional worry of police duty.

Nanda stayed throughout this first interview, for Beeba spoke very little English and my Assamese consisted largely of vague gestures and dubious facial contortions—far from an effective means of communication. With Nanda as interpreter we were able to make suitable arrangements.

Since Beeba was inexperienced, she was to receive a beginning salary of 25 rupees a month (about $8) plus 10 rupees for dearness allowance (board). Her duties included bringing up our chota hazri, dusting and straightening our bedrooms, making beds, letting down the mosquito nets at night, preparing our bath water, laundering the finer things we dared not trust to the stone-bashing method of a dhobi, and simple mending.

"You may show Beeba to our rooms, Nanda, and get her started on her duties," I said, to terminate the interview.

"Teek hai, memsahib," he replied, then silently led the new girl to our sleeping quarters.

During the next week I seldom caught a glimpse of Beeba except in the early morning when, bearing chota hazri on a small brass tray, she stood motionless and silent by my bed until her very presence awoke me. She did her chores when I was at the base, and was out of sight when I returned at four for tea and a change. If I needed anything, she was always within calling distance, but the one night I really needed to summon her, she had already gone home.

The following Saturday night was my night off and I was all aglow about the dance at the Officers Club, to which Major Davis, the post commanding officer, had invited me. A dashing fellow of the Hollywood type, handsome and unattached, he was also a handy man to know. Making a good impression on him was not only personally desirable but also professionally expedient. As CO he was a Houdini who could pull scarce items out of a hat. Maybe he could procure a badly needed ping-pong table for the base canteen.

At last I'd be able to get out of my drab uniform into something bright and sexy. I'd wear my red crepe formal and tuck a red hibiscus in my hair just for luck. The red formal, knotted up for months in a tight bedding roll, needed thorough ironing, but that was all. This was a job right down an ayah's alley.

Before going to work that morning I gave Beeba explicit instructions for preparing my dress. Since she had not yet mastered such complex English terms as "wash' and "iron," I pantomimed what she was to do. Pointing to the frock hanging on a hook in the dressing room, I pushed clenched fists up and down an imaginary washboard, shook my head, and said slowly, "Nay wash! Nay wash, Beeba." Then picking up the flat iron upended on the ironing board, I demonstrated the pressing technique and again spoke slowly, "Iron teek hai! Teek hai iron. Do you understand, Beeba? Malum?"

A smile of recognition crossed her usually serious face. She nodded, looked me squarely in the eye, pointed to the dress and then to the iron. Mimicking the motions I had just made, she said triumphantly, "Teek hai, memsahib. Teek hai. Fix dress."

That afternoon I did not return to the bungalow for tea. A new consignment of supplies had come in, so I stayed at the post to get them unpacked. It was the first big shipment of recreational equipment we had received since our arrival in Assam: hit tunes for the phonograph, library books, playing cards, and ping-pong balls. I wanted to get them ready to check out right away. By the time I got everything inventoried it was already eight o'clock. Major Davis was to call for me at 8:30. I made the five rough miles from field to bungalow by weapons carrier in a record fifteen minutes.

When I got to our quarters no servants were on hand to attend me. Beeba always went home after tea and the paniwallah disappeared as soon as the afternoon baths had been drawn. But the absence of a few servants could not dampen my spirits. On this hot night a cold sponge bath would be refreshing. Besides, my clothes would be laid out on the bed, freshly pressed, and my red formal would be shimmeringly smooth. Such were my thoughts as I ran up the steps of the bungalow.

My roommate Lou, sleek as a greyhound in her black draped jersey, was out on the porch waiting for her date. From the wicker couch she greeted me with her usual "Hi, chum! Better hurry up. Your true love doesn't like to be kept waiting, you know."

"Oh, I have plenty of time," I answered breezily. "Keith's always late. Anyway, Beeba has my dress all fixed."

Lou laughed dryly. "You're absolutely right, darling. Beeba has really fixed your dress."

Had I been decently attentive I would have caught the barb in Lou's remark, but I was in too much of a hurry to recognize any implication of disaster. Nothing could spoil my fun tonight. For a few minutes I busied myself in the bedroom, getting gold slippers, beaded purse, and satin slip out of the wardrobe. Then I switched on the dressing room light.

There hanging on a wire coat hanger was a red dress all right, but what a sad, shriveled, soppy mess it was now, about a size 6 and I was a tall, leggy size 12. A few drops of water still fell reluctantly from the sodden skirt onto the tile floor.

My first impulse was to sob. It was the only dance frock I had and it was too late to borrow another from anyone else. I wanted to bash that stupid Beeba's head against the very laundry stone she had used for my dress.

Laundry stone! So that was it! Suddenly the whole incident struck me as ludicrous. No wonder the girl had gotten mixed up. My demonstration of the washboard technique had been meaningless to her. I had forgotten that dhobis wash clothes by beating them against a stone. Beeba had tried to carry out my orders, but I wondered why she had never gotten around to using the iron.

That night I wore, for the tenth time, my other non-uniform dress—a short black crepe with pleated skirt and snug collared top. If Major Davis noticed the informality of my frock, he was gracious enough not to comment on it. Another great evening cemented my growing attachment to Keith. A ping-pong table was soon added to the club.

The next day, instead of braining Beeba, I called in Nanda, the head bearer. Restored to a spirit of benevolence by the success of the previous evening, I showed both servants how to wash our nylons and crepes in a tub. Within a few days Beeba became a first-rate laundress, American-style.

Assam Potpourri

On learning of my wartime services with the Red Cross in India, people invariably asked, "What did you do over there?"

At Jorhat, Assam we were three raw, fresh American club workers replacing three seasoned Red Cross girls, now transferred because of "officeritis" (spending too much time with officers and neglecting their duties to the GIs).

Our initial decision, to offset our predecessors' dating practice, was to forego all dates while we looked the situation over and got established. We needed to give our full time and attention to the job and the enlisted men. After ten days we began dating, casually to start. Our first dates were with enlisted men, to avoid the criticism of catering to "brass." On our day off we were free to date anyone, and that soon included officers.

At Jorhat we ran into our first big problem, a conflict between the military and Red Cross workers. Some GI squadrons had been favored over others, some ignored entirely. Vying for Red Cross attention, opposing factions pulled against each other in their demands for better recreational services. Our first job was to bring together these dissenting factions and to foster cooperation instead of competition.

We were to provide something for everybody. Coffee and doughnuts, card games, and darts were not enough diversion for GIs. Picnics, dances, sightseeing, concerts, music and art lessons, choral groups, and jaunts into the bush were needed to help stave off depression and boredom.

An early affair was a tea party for the "big" men on the post, both officers and GIs, to introduce ourselves and set forth our needs for the men and our projects. For the first time the opposing squadron leaders got together and ironed out many of their problems, with new working committees of officers and GIs from all units.

Ordinarily, as a lowly staff assistant my duties would have been serving food and drink to GIs, chatting with them, occasionally cleaning up the canteen, and playing the piano for singing and shows. Luckily I soon fell into the more stimulating job of APD (Assistant Program Director), though unluckily without the title and financial perks. But as an inveterate planner and party person, I had a ball from the first, as these letter excerpts reveal:

We are expanding the canteens already established and planning to open another. It means working longer hours than we are working now, but the men desperately need it. A cup of hot coffee and a doughnut, plus a smile from an American girl, mean more to these guys, who are flying under more strain than anyone in the States can imagine. Gosh, we really have a job to do and are thrilled to be able to do it. Sometimes I feel utterly inadequate to cope with problems of food supply, cleanliness, managing native workers, and transportation, but we do the best we can. Every tiny little thing is appreciated.

I'm in charge of the big canteen, which is already set up and working as a miniature club, but needs renovation. Running this thing is a big job, for the servants have to be driven all the time. The food (coffee, doughnuts, and cookies) must be brought from the house every day and sold at the canteens; library books and all sorts of games are to be given out; the place is to be kept neat and clean and in repair. The supplies need to be replenished all the time; and the men want to be entertained with interesting programs. I do it all myself with native help, plus volunteer help from the enlisted men.

Sometimes I wonder if I can do this huge job, but I guess I can. At least I'll give it my best shot.

In April, three new girls joined our staff. With this fresh breath of life we and our canteens were temporarily rejuvenated as we got back into the swing again. The rains abated; the skies cleared; the gardens blazed with color. Spring was here, at last, and it was time for a long overdue gala affair. We set about planning a party the men would remember long after the war was over.

On May 20, 1944 I wrote:

The party for the enlisted men last night was the most successful party ever given on this post. All the men had worked to get the place decorated, the games put into effect, the floorshow arranged, and everything ready. The dance hall was festive with flowers and fruits hanging down from a canopy of palms. Palm trees in pots decorated the sides of the room. In the back were tables and chairs for lounging and card-playing. A phonograph and loud-speaker system piped in dance music.

For dancing we had six Red Cross girls and seven Indian nurses who were cute and nice and who danced well. A group of men were self-appointed MPs to keep the dance from being a cut-in affair. The dancing was arranged by letting only as many men on the floor for each dance as there were girls. In the middle of the evening the men had a short floorshow of musical numbers with guitar, vocal solos, and parody songs.

Outside the mess hall was a hot-dog stand with Vienna sausages (the most common GI meat over here), specially made buns and onions, ketchup, and relish. The drink was a wonderful fresh lime punch. Dessert was devil's food cake and cookies.

Inside the storeroom, the men had piled up K-ration boxes for all sorts of penny-ante gambling games. One of the boys had made a roulette wheel, which was a colossal success. They also had a cute game of betting on a live mouse. Each person put his penny on a number that corresponded to a small box.

The mouse was let loose and whichever box he ran into was the winning one. This is an awfully funny game. Then there were pitch-penny games and quick sketching (in profile).

All the men had a grand time, with something for everyone to do. The party didn't drag for an instant and about 200 men enjoyed the fun.

By July the canteens were running smoothly, so I took on another job as house manager. I figured it would be good experience for later on.

This letter home describes my added duties:

We have an English woman employed as house-keeper who stays from 8:30 to 12 noon each day, but she has gone on leave and the house must be super-vised. So I'm doing it every morning, altering my rising hours. My duties include a daily inspection of the kitchen (water boiling, dishwashing, garbage collection, and cleaning), plus "driving" the servants and seeing that meals are served on time, keeping the house financial accounts, helping with the menus, overseeing the laundry, ordering supplies for home and canteens, giving orders to the tailor who works for us full time, etc., etc., etc.

It's a big job. I spent three hours Friday night or-ganizing the duties of all the servants, putting them down on paper and making a daily schedule for myself. This will cut down on my time in the can-teen a little, but it will give me something I've wanted and been entitled to ever since I've been here ...an extra night a week for dating.

It really is rather fun for a change. Guess I'm the domestic type after all. I don't mind running a house with plenty of servants. It's just that I don't like to do the dirty work. At present our biggest problems are the filthy kitchen and the garbage disposal, which hasn't been taken care of in weeks.

Within two weeks my new job seemed to be off and going well, as this letter attests:

Now the house is running better than ever. I have everything on a scheduled basis. The servants and I get along very well. They are happy and working

*well. All of which goes to show that if you are happy
and well adjusted and self-confident, you can do
almost anything.*

The long rainy season had left the men stir-crazy, so
when the roads became passable again we took the men
on a tour away from the post.

The Slit Trench

We arrived in Assam at the end of winter. The leaves on the trees had turned dark green before falling off to make way for the new leaves that would come out in February, a process of metamorphosis which in that part of India takes about two weeks. By the middle of March our tea garden was a riot of color.

One morning, as I sat on the front veranda, I visually feasted on the whole rainbow spectrum of bougainvillea, hibiscus, jasmine, poinciana, gold mohur, flame of the forest, and three varieties of wild orchids. In late March the heady fragrance of gardenias in the back yard brought memories of college dance corsages. In the fork of the big vine-covered tree out front a clear yellow lily-like parasite bloomed until in April the hybrid orchids began—lavender orchids to wear in our hair and sheaves of white orchids for house bouquets. In the summer red hibiscus and yellow jasmine graced our coiffures and brightened the canteen tables.

Spring also ushered in a plethora of insects, birds, reptiles, and animals. Our trees became the homes of mourning doves that cooed sorrowfully all day long. Dozens of pilfering crows stole trinkets right out of our rooms. Jaunty little brown birds boldly sneaked tidbits from the tea table on the porch. A tribe of monkeys did trapeze tricks in the trees for our enjoyment. Cattle egrets stalked the compound. At night we could hear jackals crying like human babies and occasionally a hungry leopard roaring in the distance.

Always the threat of snakes made walking in the yard inadvisable. Coral snakes lurked in the bush. Kreits occasionally turned up on the post. One morning I saw a five-foot black snake inch his way down a tree in the yard, then slither off into the knee-high jungle grass beyond. Just the day before I had picked orchids for my hair from that very tree. Two years later, after I returned to the States, I learned that the only black snake in India is the cobra.

In this bucolic scene only one change had been made since the beginning of the war. The grass around the bungalow had been mowed and a small slit trench had been dug there out of the clay, for use in case of an air raid. In such an eventuality we would receive ample warning, via the hospital siren, which was about 200 yards from the bungalow.

I used the slit trench just once, and this is how it happened. Some of the Red Cross girls had fallen into the habit of mid-morning tea, English style, on the veranda. Most of us worked in the afternoon and evening, so this early tea became our brunch and a time for entertaining. A British major, commanding officer of a truck-repair battalion stationed in Jorhat, had taken quite a fancy to our club director and used to call on us with one of his lieutenants nearly every morning at 10:30. The next two hours usually sped by in a pleasant exchange of gossip and not-too-sparkling repartee, while Nanda, the bearer, brought hot tea and English biscuits.

One morning soon after my arrival in Jorhat, I was busily engaged in shampooing my hair while Norris, the club director, and Major Berkeley chatted on the porch. Suddenly, the peal of the siren jerked me out of the bathroom. Scrambling for my blue army bathrobe, with half my hair done up and the other half streaming little rivulets down my neck, I grabbed a mirror, comb, bobby pins, gas mask, and helmet, and headed for the slit trench.

Norris and the Major continued calmly sipping their tea as if nothing had happened. As I bolted past them down the stairs, Major Berkeley called out, "Oh, I say, my deah, where are you going in that rig?"

"To the slit trench," I shouted, without slackening my speed. "You all better get a move on." But they made no attempt to protect themselves from the oncoming air raid.

"Stupid fools!" I said to myself. "If they want to sizzle, it's OK by me. But I'm going to get out of the way."

Just as I was about to enter the lizard-infested trench, I turned around and shouted one last admonition. "Come on, you all. This is no time for procrastination." Then I settled down on my haunches to wait.

From up on the porch I heard uproarious laughter. They were laughing with the Japs practically on our necks!

"What on earth is wrong with you two?" I called from my safety. "Have you lost your minds? Get down here quick before you get burned to a crisp."

Then Major Berkeley called out, in his insufferable clipped English, "But my deah, that wasn't the air raid alarm. That was the twelve-o'clock whistle."

Blast! Without a word, I crept out of the trench, back up the steps, and into my room to finish my coiffure.

Bechty and Jitter

Soon after my arrival at Jorhat Air Base, Private Bechtel, the post cynic appointed himself my chief heckler. Eighteen monotonous months in the jungle, he reasoned, qualified him for tormenting starry-eyed females fresh from the States.

Bechty knew how to get under my skin. The bald lie, the direct gripe, the innuendo, the feint—he was master of them all. Hardly a day passed that he did not grouse about the hard doughnuts, the bitterness of the coffee, the slow service, the cramped quarters of "the joint," the general inefficiency of the Red Cross, and the off-duty life of the Red Cross girls.

"Hey, Lib, was that you I seen last night in the CO's jeep?" I denied the charge vehemently and he cackled, "You're just like all the rest. Can't see anybody but a officer."

At first Bechty's remarks irritated me. Working fourteen hours a day, we had troubles enough without the GI gripe. But by the end of the month my ears were deafened to the jibes. Then Bechty changed his routine and made me laugh. Soon he wormed his way into my affection and became my favorite GI in Assam.

His new approach alternated between tearing down and building up. In the morning, as he leaned over the coffee bar he would say, "Hey, Lib. Whaja do with the egg beater you combed your hair with?" In the evening as I closed up the canteen, he would plead, "Will you do just one little thing for me, you know, for a lonely soldier? How about giving me a little souvenir to remember you by? That sweater you're wearing will do." Then grabbing my arm in feigned ardor, he would plant wet kisses from wrist to elbow before I could pull away.

Once, after the arm kissing routine, he looked at me with a twinkle in his eye and chanted in a childish lisp, "I wish I was a cake of soap, I wish I was a cake of soap, I'd go slippy and slidey all down your hidey, I wish I was a cake of soap."

Bechty told wild tales about himself. He claimed to be thrice married and twice divorced in his twenty-seven years. He spoke knowingly of numbers rackets, racing forms, and big-city gambling joints. He boasted of the tricks he pulled on the MPs while in the guardhouse. Twice a sergeant, he was now a private, the rank he liked best. He claimed to love no one, to believe in nothing, and to aspire to nothing except his discharge.

This was the Private Bechtel who tended Jitter with a mother's gentleness, fed her from his own mess kit, shared his bunk with her, and scratched her ears to soothe her tantrums.

The first time I saw Jitter she was just a pair of little bead eyes peeping furtively out of Private Bechtel's leather flight jacket. For all I could see of her she might have been a baby jackal, a puppy, or even a tiny human being.

"Take a squint at my new roommate," Bechty said as he mounted a stool at the coffee bar, his arm cupped against his bulging jacket. "Jitter, meet Libby. Libby, meet Jitter. But don't come too close 'til you get better acquainted."

A volley of guttural chatter escaped from flashing white teeth as I leaned over the counter for a closer look. Soft gray hair, shaggy overhanging eyebrows, an ugly pug nose, and thin lips framing buckteeth marked Jitter as one of the little rhesus monkeys so common all over India.

"Where on earth did you get her?"

"Bought her off a wog for a rupee. She was half starved and vicious as a snake when I got her. But she's tame as a kitten now."

Each day Bechty brought Jitter into the canteen and demanded an extra doughnut for his friend. Once, I dared gingerly to offer her a bite, only to hastily withdraw my outstretched fingers when she bared her teeth in a snarl. "She doesn't like women," Bechty warned, as he took the dainty morsel from me and stuffed it into her waiting maw.

A few weeks later, we organized a gala outing at a British tea plantation for Squadron B. Among the men who showed up for the excursion was Bechty, along with Jitter, who was chattering like a bobby soxer.

"Better keep Jitter away from me," I cautioned, as we climbed into the back of the open six-by-six. "After all, I don't want to show up at the bungalow tonight with a scratched face. No one would ever believe I got it defending myself against a female monkey."

It was a glorious day for a picnic, warm without being sticky. As we bumped along rough dirt roads, past water buffaloes knee-deep in mud, the men forgot for a while their military life and the insidious fear of flying The Hump.

About three o'clock we pulled into a hedge-bordered driveway, passed through a wrought iron gate held open by a turbaned durwan, then climbed down from the truck into an expanse of bent grass. On a knoll ahead sprawled a large one-story mansion. To our left was a swimming pond with two rowboats at its edge, and to our right three sod tennis courts.

Locally the estate was known as the MacDonald plantation. But for thirty happy GIs that day it was a country club straight out of their hometowns.

For three hours we pretended we were back home, swimming, sunbathing, playing games, and hitting tennis balls. Only the incessant chatter of jungle monkeys, in the trees beyond the pool, broke the illusion.

By six o'clock we all were ravenous. Mr. MacDonald's bearers had set out our chow on a long oak buffet table on the manicured lawn. Someone leaned on the truck horn five times. Minutes later eager GIs sprawled all over the lawn, consuming potato salad, Spam sandwiches, chocolate cake, and beer.

In the meantime we had forgotten all about Jitter. Bechty had tied her to a banana tree away from the fun and food while he took a dip in the pool. But Jitter hadn't forgotten about us. Tethered far away from the crowd, she had watched the merry-making all afternoon with frustration. When the feast began her fury reached a peak. Tugging at her chain, she let forth a volley of heartrending shrieks. Her master hurried over to comfort her.

It seemed a pity that she should watch while we gorged ourselves. I grabbed a Spam sandwich, hurried over to the banana tree, and thrust the food toward her outstretched paws. Jitter seized the sandwich, threw it on the ground, and sank her knife-sharp teeth into my wrist.

I got away as quickly as I could, but not quite fast enough. Eight tiny droplets of blood oozed from the wound, making a perfect circle on my wrist.

During the next few days I was so busy at the canteen I had no time to worry about the wound. When a new soldier to the post came into the canteen and facetiously inquired as to who had bitten me, I told him the whole story.

"You'd better watch out for that, Lib," he warned. "Monkeys carry rabies, you know."

I turned pale. What on earth had I been thinking all this time? The soldier was right, of course. I had heard of natives dying horrible deaths from hydrophobia. Already nearly a week had passed and I hadn't even bothered to see a doctor. Like a marathon runner I sprinted out of the canteen to the post dispensary.

A handsome young captain examined the scabs. "When did you get this wound?" he asked, all seriousness.

"Oh, about a week ago," I replied, trying to sound casual.

"You should have come to see me then."

"I know. I just got too busy, I guess."

"Looks as though the skin was broken."

"Yes, it bled a little at the time. But what do I do about it now?"

"Nothing now." The doctor's voice sounded ominous. "We haven't any rabies vaccine in this area anyway. The nearest vaccine is in Calcutta. Just keep track of the monkey. If it dies or goes mad, let me know immediately and we'll have you flown to Calcutta for treatment."

My hands got clammy and I became conscious of a rapid thumping under my blouse, not induced by the intense blue eyes of the flight surgeon. Hydrophobia! Ever since I could remember I had feared it. Hardly a childhood summer went by that we didn't have to keep our fox terriers tied up. Years ago a friend had suffered the horrible treatment—twenty-four days of painful shots. More recently I had cried over the newspaper picture of a little boy who didn't get the shots in time. Now it could happen to me. Bechty had to be found and Jitter tied up.

Without wasting another moment I sent a message to the barracks for Private Bechtel to report immediately to the Red Cross canteen. After a few minutes the bearer of my note returned with the information that Bechty was on flight over the Hump and would not be back until the following day. That night was the longest I ever spent.

The next evening Bechty ambled into the canteen alone. There was no bulge under his flight jacket. No bright eyes peeped out from under his arm. He looked especially dour as he ordered his coffee at the bar.

"I'm sure glad to see you, Bechty," I said, handing him a chipped cup and two doughnuts. "Where have you been? I've been hunting all over for you."

Bechty's eyes flashed. "Looking for me, Lib? Oh, no! Don't tell me you're gonna break down and gimme that date you promised last month."

I was in no mood for this worn out joke. "Listen, Bechty," I said. "I'm scared. Take a look at that." I showed him the scabs on my wrist. "That's where Jitter bit me. By the way, how is Jitter anyway? Why isn't she with you?"

Bechty took a long time to scrutinize my wrist before he spoke again. "Jitter? Oh, she's so so, just so so. As a matter of fact, she hasn't been up to par lately. That's why I left her at the barracks. Think she's got a cold or something." Bechty watched my reaction out of the corner of his eye.

"Stop it! This is serious. She might have rabies. If she starts to act strange, you've got to let me know pronto. Whatever you do, don't let her out of your sight."

Bechty promised to watch Jitter carefully and to leave her with someone responsible whenever he flew the Hump. The men kept me apprised of her escapades, swearing veracity on a stack of Bibles. She was reported to have bitten half the men in Barracks A-2, to have lain in a stupor for days, and finally to have died after going on a wild rampage.

Down deep I knew that Bechty would tell me if anything really bad happened to Jitter. But the whole thing smacked too much of "Wolf! Wolf!" to suit me.

One day soon thereafter, as Bechty was giving me his "what-are-you-doing-tonight, Babe?" routine, his face darkened with sudden recall. "Oh, say, Lib. I almost forgot to tell you. Jitter disappeared last night. I've looked everywhere for her and can't find a trace.

"Look here, Bechty old man, can't you do better than that? That Jitter story is old stuff now. Surely you're smart enough to think up a new line. If that taxes your brain too much, you can always fall back on the sweater routine."

"Now don't get in a huff, Lib. I'm not jokin' this time." His face was deadpan. I waited for the usual flicker of merriment in his eyes.

"Bechty," I said wearily, "you need a good long rest. Why don't you go back to the barracks and sleep it off? Your sense of humor is deteriorating fast in this climate."

Bechty scowled. "Hell, Lib. I'm telling you the truth. Ask any of the guys. They'll set you straight. Jitter disappeared last night and I don't know where the hell she is. You asked me to tell you if anything happened to her. Well, this is it!"

"OK, thanks," I said. "I'll run right down to Calcutta tomorrow and have my tummy punctured, just for protection. You can take over the canteen while I'm gone. Be sure to keep the tables cleaned off and the ashtrays emptied."

"It's your skin, not mine, Lib. Take it or leave it!" Bechty said, as he shuffled out of the canteen. I still didn't believe him, but the danger period had passed and I was no longer worried.

Weeks later, when another soldier brought a pet monkey into the canteen, I asked Bechty how Jitter was getting along.

"Hell, Lib. She ran away. I told you all about it at the time."

"I thought it was all a gag—just another one of your tricks. Didn't you ever find her after that?"

"Nope," he said. "I figured she must have gotten tired of domestic life and headed back to the jungle. She needed a proper boyfriend anyway."

"So it wasn't a case of 'wolf-wolf' after all," I said.

Bechty scowled for a moment, then his eyes twinkled. "'Wolf, wolf,' did you say? That gives me ideas."

He grabbed my hand, gave it a resounding smack, and launched into his old routine. With sorrowful eyes and bleeding heart, he began, "Tonight I've got to fly the Hump. I may not come back, you know, Lib. Won'cha give me just one little souvenir to remember you by? Any old thing will do. That sweater you're wearing will keep me warm."

The Little Monsoon

Rain started in April—flash cloudbursts at first in mid-afternoon, followed by steaming sunlight that quickly dried the mud roads to fine dust again. Then night rains lulled us to sleep. Hard, hot, penetrating rain awoke us in the morning and abruptly ceased about ten, in time for tea with our British neighbors. Eighteen inches of rain fell in nine days.

By mid-May the "little monsoon" had arrived with such force that we hoped never to experience the big monsoon of midsummer. We now knew firsthand the meaning of the dark green on our grade-school maps that marked Assam with one of the highest rainfalls in the world.

At first we welcomed the afternoon showers as a blessed relief from the enervating heat. But as the earth sopped up the water and began to give it off again in humid waves, the rain only added to our physical discomfort. The thermometer hovered around the 100-degree mark, often going to 120 in the sun. It felt as if we were in a steam bath all the time, with perspiration pouring in rivulets from our arms and legs.

No wind dried the sweat soaked into our seersucker uniforms. Whenever possible we changed clothes three times a day. But this did not prevent nasty blotches of heat rash on our necks and arms. Even the lacquer melted off our fingernails, so we gave up wearing it until the heat abated. Some of the men passed out cold from exposure to the sun and heat exhaustion.

The natives carried huge black umbrellas, not to keep dry in a downpour, but as protection from the searing sun. One of the funniest sights I saw in all India was an Indian in a rice paddy astride a water buffalo, clad only in a loincloth, under an open umbrella.

We managed to stay fairly comfortable at the bungalow. All the rooms and porches had overhead fans that ran 24 hours a day. The air moved easily through high-ceilinged spacious rooms. Tall trees shaded the yard and cooled the veranda. Bearers were always at hand to bring us ice water and cool drinks. Bungalow life was informal, so we were able to strip down at home to shorts and halters.

But, the heat in the canteens was well nigh unbearable. The increasing malaria and dengue fever menace brought a new Army ruling that everyone on the post had to wear thick slacks, heavy socks, high shoes, and long sleeved shirts after dark. Even this, plus sticky mosquito repellent, was not a guarantee against bites. One of the girls, who had observed all the precautions, was bitten through her slacks by a hardy mosquito that attacked her through the cane seat of her chair. Men and girls alike sweltered in silence for three months, but the natives sang merrily as they planted tiny shafts of rice in knee-deep mud.

The rains brought new life to the jungle and tea gardens. Almost overnight the bamboo thickets grew ten feet. Grass in the bungalow yard grew as high as wheat between cuttings. Even the two scrawny banana trees in front of the canteen leafed out and bore bunches of tiny tasteless four-inch fruit.

In the water holes, daily increasing in number and size, noisy frogs held community sings at dusk. Sometimes they sang louder than the tired men in my canteen who gathered 'round the piano to hum their favorite blues. The kill of deadly kraits on the runways escalated. Lizards climbed the canteen walls and up the bungalow drains into our bathtubs. Roaches, as big as small mice, made nests in our dresser drawers and feasted on silken undies and cashmere sweaters.

We rode the five miles from home to post four to six times a day in an open weapons carrier, piled high with jangling coffee cans, doughnut baskets, several bearers, and Red Cross girls. Each day the rain came down heavier, the mud got thicker and ruts got deeper. Each day we bounced harder against the rough board side-slats of army vehicles. Getting stuck in the mud was almost a daily occurrence.

As if the weather were not enough to dampen our spirits, we had the added worry of the Japanese menace, which for the first time since the war's beginning was something to be feared at Jorhat. The British had been driven back at Imphal and the Japs were daily pushing closer to the Burma-India border. Our airbase security was threatened, with no trained guards and only a few anti-aircraft guns. When the situation became grave, 400 trained men were shipped in from the nearby base at Misamar to strengthen security. A corps of our own men was put on guard duty. Everyone was required to carry a gas mask. Guns were issued to all the GIs. New gun emplacements sprang up like mushrooms and all roads within a five-mile radius of the post were constantly patrolled.

One day an officer came into our canteens with a startling command. "Get ready to leave in an hour," he said. "The Japs are near Gologhat. There's a jeep outside to take you to your quarters to pack a bag. Major Davis has a plane ready to take all you girls to Chabua. Hop to it."

"But I'm not going to leave," I said to myself, as I climbed in the jeep. "I'm staying here with Keith."

Back at the bungalow, while Lou and the other girls rushed to get ready, I stood to one side and smiled.

"Get a move on, Lib," Lou admonished. "Or are you trying to be the brave little consort who stands by her man?"

Just as everyone was packed up and ready to leave, the phone rang. It was Keith calling from the base. "Alert cancelled," he said. "False alarm." Then back to our canteens we went, only slightly relieved to have missed the excitement.

Right after that I was issued a Colt .45 for my own protection. I carried it with me everywhere and slept with it right under my bed where I could reach it easily. The men called me "Pistol Packin' Mama." Lou said she feared me more with the gun than she feared the Japs. But I was glad to have it aboard later when a drunk passenger in my jeep became unruly.

Everyone was jittery. And still it rained.

Paulette and the Cats

In 1944 the commanding officer at the air base in Jorhat, Assam, was Major James Keith Davis, a former civilian pilot from Montclair, New Jersey. Soon after my arrival there in January, we two became what is now called "an item." As the CO's "steady" I was the logical hostess for entertaining dignitaries and famous performers who came to entertain the troops.

In early April, Paulette Goddard stopped by overnight at our base on her extended tour of the CBI (China, Burma, India) theatre and I was her temporary companion.

In late March, Keith and I began making plans for her visit. Her manager came a few days early to get the lay of the land (literally) and to tell us something of Paulette's desires and habits so that we could accommodate her comfortably in a jungle outpost.

We had planned for her to stay at the Red Cross bungalow and have supper with us. But, alas, our plans "gang aft aglay." Her manager, after riding just two miles over the rutted dirt road in a weapons carrier, exclaimed, "Don't go any further. Miss Goddard cannot possibly be subjected to this road. You'll have to find accommodations for her on the post."

The upshot of the whole thing was that Keith and Major Morris moved out of their new but only partially furnished basha and turned it over to Paulette for her stay. So that she would have company, Keith asked me to come over and spend the night at the basha, which I did.

Keith and I sat down to plan the basha's decor. "We should do something about those drab plasterboard walls," I said. "Maybe paint over the dirty white and pretty up the windows with gay curtains for color and privacy."

"What color do you think they should be?" Keith asked.

"How does American Blue grab you for the walls?"

"Sounds great! And how about a touch of red somewhere to set them off, maybe in the curtains."

"Welcome to the decorator's world," I said. "That's the perfect color combo for the military. I think I can rustle up some stuff to brighten up your dreary abode. Let's see what we can find in the Jorhat bazaar."

It took some scurrying and scrounging to make the thatched hut comfortable for guests. I had a ball adding the final touches to those bare quarters.

From our British army friends we borrowed an ancient settee, two extra straight chairs, a chest of drawers, and several faded Chinese throw rugs. A local durzi stitched up gay Indian prints for the two small windows. Two volunteer GIs threw a fast coat of American Blue paint on the walls. A final touch of elegance was added when I brought over my own handcrafted brass tray for a coffee table.

Saturday afternoon Keith and I waited two hours at the air strip for La Goddard's special plane to arrive. Hordes of GIs and officers formed a long reception line behind us. The only thing lacking for a queen's welcome was the post band, which had not yet been organized.

Paulette stepped off the plane carrying a sheaf of hundreds of tiny lavender jungle orchids, given her as a parting gift from Chabua, her prior stop. She wore a fitted brown gabardine suit, her chest covered with the insignia of the units she had visited. Her feet were encased in mosquito boots, a sensible fashion for the CBI. She looked exactly as she does in the movies, like a wholesome American girl with a glint in her eye. Obviously she was enjoying the whole "ordeal."

For her nighttime performance she wore a short tight dress in bright yellow, printed with multi-colored circus figures and highlighted with dazzling sequins. On her head drooped two bunches of red iridescent grapes, one bunch over each ear—a most fetching headdress, I thought. She had concocted it herself from trimmings stolen from a hat. Her platform shoes, made of woven straw, were sheer fantasy, as was her long white ermine coat, casually thrown over her left shoulder.

Paulette was not a raving beauty. Her complexion, teeth, hair, and general features were just average. Her figure was a little on the droopy side. But she had a husky, sexy voice and a stack of personality that sent the men into stomping and whistling.

Her show was mostly a two-way conversation with GIs, plus a few current hit songs with the small combo that accompanied her. I would hardly call her a singer, but the GIs loved her and shouted for encores.

The officers had planned a post-performance party for her at the Area H officers' club. But Paulette, exhausted from her one-night stands, would have none of it.

"Won't you come for just a few minutes?" the CO asked. "We planned the party just for you. We'll let you off early."

"Nope," said the weary Paulette. "I'm going to bed right away. Goodnight, gentlemen. But thanks for the invitation."

A crowd of crestfallen officers watched as she and I climbed into a Jeep driven by an MP assigned to protect us from prowling beasts, jungle and human.

On the way back to our quarters the Jeep's headlights caught the shiny eyes of a tawny, furry midsize cat scampering across the road.

"What was that creature?" Paulette asked. "Looked like a wildcat I once saw in the Pennsylvania mountains."

"Might be a civet cat," I said. "It's too large for a domestic feline and too small for a leopard."

Back at the basha, Paulette washed her long wavy hair, put it up on pins, and went to bed.

A few hours later we were roused from sleep by a thud that sounded as if a huge animal had leaped against the back shutter of the basha. Paulette screamed. Then I heard a crackle of branches as the animal pad-padded into the bush.

"It's a leopard," Paulette shouted. "I saw him when he pushed the shutter open. Do you think he might come back? Can he get in the window?"

Our cries brought the MP from the "town" side of the basha where he had been taking forty winks in the long night of duty. He seemed to think it better to guard that side of the house against peeping toms than the jungle side against marauding jungle beasts. By the time he got around to investigate, the creature had fled. Only a damaged shutter indicated where it had been.

The next morning at breakfast Paulette said, "Oh, it's so thrilling! Now I can go back and tell about the leopard that tried to get in our house."

Paulette slept most of the time she was in Jorhat, so I had very little personal contact with her. But I liked and admired her. She was easy to please, sensible, and brave. She didn't panic over the leopard. And she had been closer than any of us club workers to real danger. In Burma she had performed at a post the day after it was taken from the Japs, the dead still lying in the streets and the enemy just a few miles away. From Jorhat now she had another hairy experience to relate at home.

Temples and Monkeys

For ten days we scoured the countryside for something of interest in the tea patches. Finally we turned up some ancient Hindu temples, the ruins of an old sports arena, and a beautiful lake with tree-shaded shores and an azure sky reflected in its mirror-smooth surface.

We hoped the rains were over, but in May you couldn't count on the weather. As we climbed into the covered six-by-six, a light warm drizzle dampened our spirits and kept our camera shutters closed. At least the rain settled the dust of the rutty roads as we jostled thirty miles to our destination.

Sitting with the GIs in the back of the truck, I endured with equanimity their disparaging remarks:

"What did they make this road out of anyway—washboards? With my weak belly there won't be a shred of me left by the time we get back to camp."

"Just like the Red Cross to take us on a tour of old relics. We thought we'd be treated to some hot nautch dancers. Ye gods, I wish I'd stayed in my tent."

"Say, Lib, what kind of grub did you bring along this time?"

"Oh, no, surely not that! Anything is better than sandwiches and potato salad. I thought we'd have fried chicken and apple pie."

"Come on, Jake, let's get out and thumb our way back to camp."

I could sympathize with the men about the long ride. Sitting on hard bleachers at a baseball game is theater seating compared to riding over rutted roads on rough wood benches. Our sore derrières and kinked muscles sent us for the rubbing liniment as soon as we got home.

Then I heard from up front in the cab, "Say, Lib, how about a song? Give us a pitch."

A resounding "Yes! Let's sing" from a half-dozen back-truck voices silenced the GI gripes. Starting with "I've Been

Workin' on the Railroad," then "For Me and my Gal," we soon had everyone in on the community chorus as we jogged along happily in tuneful reminiscence to our first stop.

About twenty miles out of Jorhat we sighted a group of ancient temples, three of them in a field on a slight rise above the road. Evidently these temples were no longer used, not even for sightseeing or pilgrimages, for there was no evidence of recent human activity. Entry to the compound was by a narrow footpath through waist-high grass. By the time we found a spot to unload the truck the rain had let up and all of us stiff and cranky sightseers were happy to stretch our legs.

The three small temples were similar to hundreds in that part of India. We saw nine of them that day, always in groups of three—the holy Hindu number. Only the larger temple at the lake, seen later, was currently a place of worship, with dozens of natives going in and out to pay their respects to multiple gods.

These Assamese temples, built of native terra cotta, were not as old as they appeared. Corrosion from the rains and heat had turned most of them into blackened relics. Built on rectangular stone bases, their exterior surfaces were covered with carved effigies of Hindu gods. The low sidewalls rose in a pointed dome surmounted by a three-pronged pitchfork.

Inside, the temples were virtually empty. Windowless, they presented a sinister, black, damp aspect to the visitor. A single candle lighted the interior of one temple. We peered into the dark corners with our flashlights and surprised toads, lizards, roaches, bats, and assorted creepy-crawlies. At the back of this vermin-infested interior was the tiny idol of a Hindu god. Flowers scattered by worshipers strewed the floor. Monkeys played in the temple yards, climbed to the pinnacles, and took over the inside for their private adventures.

Several hundred yards further on we viewed the ruins of an ancient sporting arena, used many years ago by the local maharajah for the entertainment of his guests. Nothing was left of the maharajah's palace or other buildings. Only this large stone structure, roofless and empty, remained.

We were able to reach a wide gallery above the walls that encircled the arena by using the massive exterior solid stone staircase. I imagined this gallery to have once been lavishly outfitted with comfortable couches and cushions. Now, hundreds of monkeys played there.

On the ground floor brown stones had been laid to form little enclosed compartments bordering a large open, central arena. Wild animals had been kept in the enclosures until they were released to do battle-to-death with other wild animals, for the pleasure of royal spectators.

Various contests had entertained the maharajah's guests, who especially liked the vicious battles between two felines—leopard and tiger; lion and tiger; leopard and panther. Occasionally boa constrictors were brought into the fray. Even elephants, rhinoceros, wild boars, and buffaloes did their part to please the spectators.

Farther along the road we could see the dome of another temple, covered with gold leaf, glistening in the distance. By the time we reached the little lake, the rain had ceased altogether, so we stayed there for the rest of the jaunt. Some of the men hired horses for a brisk canter, while the rest of us lolled on the fast-drying grass or walked around the lake.

After a picnic supper by the lake at dusk, with the inevitable potato salad, cheese sandwiches, lemonade, and chocolate cake, we climbed into the six-by-six and jounced back to Jorhat in the dark.

Dr. Kirby's Leper Colony

$\mathcal{O}$n early April, Lou and I went on a little trip into the boondocks to scout for gifts. Our destination was the leper colony where we could buy locally made carved animals, baskets, and embroidered linens for our GI friends to send home to their families. Years ago Dr. Kirby, a Baptist medical missionary, had established a small clinic and leper colony in a remote jungle compound about twenty miles from Jorhat. Mrs. Kirby helped her husband in the clinic and sold Indian handiwork to supplement their meager income and to give the local artisans an outlet for their wares.

The Kirby compound of some twenty acres, partially enclosed in a wire fence, bore no signpost or warning plaque that we were approaching a leper colony. An ordinary wire gate marked the compound entrance, where a turbaned durwan in dhoti and man's shirt opened the gate with his two fingerless hands. As we drove up to the entrance the durwan smiled, bowed in Indian fashion, and said cheerfully, "Salaam, memsahibs. Namaste."

En route to the Kirbys' residence we passed several clean mud huts where children played happily outside in grassless yards. When we saw some maimed residents going about their daily tasks, we were surprised at how deftly they performed them, as if the stumps at the end of their wrists were flexible appendages. Further on we passed two larger wooden buildings, which we later learned were the doctor's dispensary and laboratory. At the end of the drive stood a pleasant, well-kept bungalow like the ones for British employees on the tea plantations. Next to it a small car was parked, temporarily out of commission for lack of tires (unavailable in this war theatre).

"Hmm!" said Lou as we drove up to the house. "So the Kirbys have a car. I thought missionaries were dog poor and went about on foot or on horseback."

"Not necessarily," I said. "Certainly a car would be a necessity for a rural doctor. After all, there has to be some compensation for living in these parts. But how do you suppose the good doctor makes his rounds now that the car is on the blink?"

"Beats me," Lou said. "Missionaries depend on the love of God. Surely He will provide. In the meantime maybe they use a horse or ox-cart. Guess I just didn't expect them to live like other people."

"There you go again, Lou, believing everything you read. It's true that missionaries are poor. Otherwise, how would we be persuaded to give our donations and old clothes to them? But why should you think that a missionary is different from any other man of God? After all, don't most preachers at home have cars? Come down to earth, Lou. Times have changed since you went to Sunday school."

"You're absolutely right, Lib. I'll have to upgrade my religious thinking."

Mrs. Kirby, a big jovial woman, greeted us warmly, then ushered us through the comfortable living room onto the screened porch where we went through her stock of hand-embroidered organdy luncheon sets, delicate trousseau undies, baby dresses, fancy pillow tops, tooled leather wallets, wooden bowls, and jade jewelry.

As we picked out lovelies for our families and gifts for the men to send home, Mrs. Kirby told us about her life in Assam and about their two daughters raised there, now grown and gone.

"This has been our home for twenty eight years," she said, "and we plan to spend the rest of our lives here. The girls are on their own now, but Mary should be coming back this fall from the States to help us in the clinic, when she finishes her medical training."

Dr. Kirby had had some success in treating leprosy with a salve of his own concoction. He and his wife had lived very close to the lepers, yet neither had contracted the disease. The colony itself housed about 125 lepers and their families. The dispensary served many others not yet segregated into the compound.

Within the colony, the lepers led a normal family life. They had been taught the rudiments of cleanliness and disease prevention, as well as faith in God's help and healing. Beyond these simple principles they lived much like their compatriots on the outside. The Kirbys tried to make the families self-sufficient and provided enough land for every family to grow food. Some made a meager allowance helping around the dispensary and the farm. Contributions from American Baptists supplied funds for clinic maintenance. The Kirbys themselves contributed much from their own salary toward buying needed drugs and clothing for the children.

After our purchases had been stashed in the station wagon, Mrs. Kirby invited us for tea and cakes in the dining room. As she cleared the table of its clutter of account books and papers, she said, "Please excuse my messy house. I haven't been able to hire any servants lately. They're all working for you folks and the military at higher wages than I can pay." Mrs. Kirby also apologized for offering us only mildly cool drinking water. "My Frigidaire has broken down and the part needed to fix it is available only in Calcutta," she said. Then she went into the kitchen to bring out the tea goodies.

At the mention of an electric refrigerator, Lou looked over at me and said under her breath, "Such luxury! So that's where our hard-earned donations go!"

"I can't imagine living out here in these broiling boondocks without one," I countered. "Mrs. Kirby needs a fridge much more than anyone at home. I wonder how she stays so cheerful with so few conveniences."

The high point of our visit came a few minutes later as we sat down for tea. We bowed our heads in thanks as Mrs. Kirby led us in the simple prayer I had learned as a child:

> Thank you, God, for the world so sweet.
> Thank you for the food we eat.
> Thank you for the birds that sing.
> Thank you, God, for everything.

Lifting my eyes after the "Amen" I was surprised to see that another person had joined us at the table. A happy little native lad had crawled up into Mrs. Kirby's ample lap. Enfolding him in her arms, she said, "This is my son Shama. He is five years old and has been with us since he came into the world. He is my special helper in the kitchen. And I couldn't keep my garden weeded without him. Say hello to the ladies, Shama."

Shama beamed with pride. "I set table for you," he said, "and I help make cookies." Evident affection between foster mother and child showed in the warm hug and loving verbal exchange as Mrs. Kirby sent the boy to play elsewhere.

As we chatted over tea and sugar cookies, we learned that over the years the Kirbys had taken dozens of babies into their home and brought them up as their own, to keep them disease-free. Loving connection was maintained with the birth families who were grateful to parent healthy children. Mrs. Kirby home-schooled the little ones. Boys learned farm chores and carpentry; girls were taught household skills and embroidery. Each child stayed with them until able to work outside as a bearer, an ayah, or a helper on a nearby plantation.

We drove back to the base, laden with our purchases and aglow with Mrs. Kirby's "gift of the Spirit."

Terror in the Night

One night at the height of the "Jap scare" I happened to be alone in the bungalow. All the other girls were on duty. It was my night off and I had a date with the post CO, but he had been called suddenly for flight, so I was left alone in the big, empty house out in the boondocks. No servants were on hand, long ago gone to their huts. I could see no light in the other bungalows in the compound. The hospital was beyond earshot.

At first I had no fear of being alone. In just a little while some of the girls would be home. In the meantime I settled down at the desk on the veranda and wrote a long letter home.

As I clicked away on my trusty Underwood portable I suddenly felt the house grow big with emptiness and silence. What was that movement in the bedroom? Before I had a chance to scream, a cat scampered onto the porch and down the front steps. I breathed a sigh of relief. I switched on all the bedroom and living room lights. Then, just to be safe, I got out my Colt .45 and put it on the desk beside me.

Soon thereafter I heard a gentle, nameless sound quite close to me. A few minutes later I had the chilling sensation that I was being watched, as if sly eyes were peeping at me from behind a tree in the blackness of the tea garden. Momentarily I was frozen, afraid to turn around, even to lift my head. Then slowly reaching for my gun, I got up and wheeled around. Nothing was behind me. I cautiously walked around the porch, peered into the rooms, and then returned to my desk. Then I saw him. There on the wall, directly above where I had been writing, was a big bulgy-eyed lizard watching my every movement.

I was horror-stricken and relieved at the same time. I dared not move away, for fear that the gecko would strike at me with his darting, sticky tongue. His eyes never left me. Though the nine-inch lizard was much less harmful than a Japanese sniper, he was almost as repulsive to me.

Finally, I decided to stare him down. Easing gently into the desk chair, I went on with my typing, with one eye on the ogling reptile. An hour later, Lucia, returning from the canteen, found me still in the lizard's thrall.

"Oh, look at the perfectly wonderful gecko," she said as she came up on the porch. "He's quite the biggest one I ever saw. Wasn't it nice of him to keep you company 'til I got home?"

"Very nice," I replied dryly, my strength and good humor spent.

"What's eating you, Lib?" Lou said, sensing my mood. "Surely you aren't afraid of that harmless fellow. He just wants company. So what's the problem?"

"Oh, nothing! Nothing at all! Just cats and reptiles and potential Japs, that's all! Just try staying home alone sometime. It teaches you how the other half lives. Goodnight, Lou. Sleep well." And off I went to bed.

Sleep was slow a-comin' that night. When it did arrive, my exhausted body soaked it up like a sponge. For several hours I slept the sleep of the dead. But a peaceful night was not to be my lot.

About two o'clock in the morning I awoke in a state of terror. A heavy hand clutched my chest. Only half awake I reacted instinctively rather than reasonably. In order that the "thing" might not get away, I grabbed it with my left hand and tried to get out of bed to turn on the light, all the while keeping a death grip on the marauder's arm. I discovered to my horror that I couldn't move. I was caught in a vise.

Then understanding dawned on me. My right arm, on which I must have been lying, had gone to sleep and was resting heavily on my chest, When I grabbed it I could feel nothing. When I tried to get out of bed I was tied up in knots until the prickle of the awakening arm alerted my mind to what had happened. The next day Lou and I had a good laugh over "the arm of the intruder."

But the troubles of this night were not over yet. Just after I had gotten back to sleep, Lou called softly to me, "Lib, there's someone out on the porch. I heard him come up the steps. Listen! Sounds now as if he is heading for our room. Maybe he's a Jap spy. What on earth shall we do?"

"Don't scream," I whispered. "He might kill us. I've got my .45 right here," I said through chattering teeth, "and I'll use it on him if he comes in here."

The footsteps got closer. The person must have been tiptoeing, for his step was light and evidently hadn't awakened the other girls. I saw the dim shape of a uniformed man framed in the open French doors of our bedroom.

Reaching for my trusty .45 I shouted, "Stay right where you are! One step further and I'll shoot you through the stomach." I fumbled with the gun, trying to cock it.

"Oh, excuse me!" a man's voice said. "I'm looking for the British Troop Movement Headquarters."

"Oh, no you don't," I said. "Don't you dare move a muscle or I'll have you full of lead."

"Wait a minute, Lib," Lou said. "The man said something about the British Troop Movement Headquarters. Maybe the poor soul is lost. Maybe he isn't a Jap spy after all."

"Well, speak up then, man," I said. "What are you doing here this time of night?"

A shaky voice replied, "I've been sent to Jorhat on orders to report to the BTMH. My train got in late and I've just arrived from Massani. The truck driver let me out at the gate in the dark and I took this to be the place. Evidently I got off the track."

"Oh, for heaven's sake, man." I breathed a sigh of relief. "You scared us out of our wits. You took the wrong lane from the main road. The British troop headquarters is on the other side of the tea garden. You can go through the garden if you aren't afraid of snakes, or go back and take the other lane at the fork in the road."

"Thank you, miss. Guess I'll go back and try again. Sorry to have disturbed you." His voice sounded tired and frightened. We heard him tiptoe down the stairs.

"Poor fellow," Lou said as we settled back to snatch a few winks before morning. "I'll bet he was scared to death.

You sound so formidable when you get that gun in your hand."

"But it may one day save your life," I said. At least I liked to think it offered some protection.

"Goodnight, Lou," I said wearily.

"Goodnight, Lib."

Little Joe

Some years ago the media circulated a poignant photo of a wailing naked waif running in terror on a bombed Vietnam road. This called to mind the Burmese child I encountered in WW II—a little boy picked up by an American flyer along the Ledo Road and brought to the ATC air base at Jorhat, Assam. They called him Little Joe.

Even though I had yet to meet him, I knew about Little Joe through the men of Company C who used to talk about him at the Red Cross canteen. Between gulps of coffee, they would chortle over the latest obscenity Little Joe had flung at the mess sergeant or the slick way he had of filching the CO's cigars. Their remarks indicated the same lack of feeling for the boy that the men of Company A had for Private Bechtel's pet monkey. For a time the monkey had eased the boredom of the sultry summer days. I hoped I would find this new pet more appealing than Bechty's ill-humored Jitter.

The first time little Joe came into the base canteen, he got in without my noticing. As usual I was behind the counter washing coffee cups. At our busiest time the native bearer characteristically had failed to show up and I had to make twenty cups serve fifty thirsty men.

We got a lot of ragging from the GIs, particularly when we were rushed. That day the barrage came full and strong from counter-hounds and table-squatters pounding demands for service. Even the usual canteen din could not drown out the remarks I heard above the blare of the Victrola playing "Tangerine" and the two-finger rendering of chopsticks on the piano. The loudest ruckus came from the Company C crowd in the far corner of the canteen.

"Let's have a little service around here! How about a cup of coffee!"

"Put your finger in my cup, pretty lady, and I won't have to bother with sugar."

"Gad, these doughnuts are like bricks. Where d'ja bake 'em, in the post kiln?"

"Hey, Lib. Wha'cha doin' tonight? Keeping the CO happy?"

"Say, guys, look at the new dishwasher! Kinda cute, ain't she? But awfully light for a wog, don't you think?"

"Hey, babe. Gimme cup coffee!"

This last demand, though the words were familiar and never a cause for response, made me turn around. Uttered in a metallic, rasping voice, I knew they had not come from a soldier. Before I had a chance to figure out who had spoken, I heard the grating voice again.

"Hey, babe. Gimme cup coffee!"

Wiping my hands on my apron, I went over to the table in the corner. If there was a good mimic on the post, I wanted to draft him for a part in our next show.

"What goes on here," I said. "Is someone's voice changing or is one of you a ventriloquist?"

Before I had finished speaking I saw him, a midget GI with dark skin and slant eyes. He was flanked on both sides by husky six-footers. So this was Little Joe!

"Meet Little Joe," someone said. "He's our newest recruit."

"Hiya, babe. Wha'cha doin' tonight?" piped the boy, to the delight of his sponsors.

Immediately I disliked Little Joe. He seemed to represent the antithesis of everything attractive in a child. Chronologically he must have been eight or ten, but he was no taller than a preschooler. His head, disproportionately large for his emaciated body, reminded me of a circus dwarf. Bright black eyes bulged out of a thin face too old for his years. His vocabulary consisted solely of GI jargon, picked up quickly and used liberally without understanding. He parroted the obscene intonations taught him by the men. His filthy gestures disgusted me. In place of an amiable, innocent child I saw a hardened little man.

The GI shorts he wore were hitched up with a piece of string and hung below his knees. His brown chest, thin arms, and scratched feet were bare. When he spoke, he added a clucking sound taught him by his ribald masters. In his pocket he jingled the copper coins given him by the men, then pulled out two annas and threw them on the table. Parroting his cohorts, he shouted again, "Gimme cup coffee, babe."

I left the table immediately to keep from losing my temper. In place of pity I felt only extreme revulsion toward the too-precocious lad. As I returned to my dishwashing I heard the tinny voice piping, "Hot stuff, eh!" to the accompaniment of loud bass guffaws. Table 9 got no service that day.

About ten days later, during a slack period in the morning, Little Joe paid another visit to the canteen. Everyone noticed when he entered and he immediately became the center of attention. The men threw jibes at him. Gales of laughter attended his obscene replies. Egged on by so much attention, Little Joe became bolder, and his remarks became increasingly off-color.

Enraged by his disrespect and the verbal filth he was using in the canteen, I bided the appropriate time to deal with him. Hearing the clucking sound again, I dashed over to where he was sitting with three Company C men. Wearing my meanest scowl I spoke in a less than jovial voice, "From now on, Little Joe, if you want to come in here, you will act like a gentleman or get out and stay out."

Then addressing his friends, "I don't care how you guys talk in your day rooms and barracks, but in my canteen this kind of language just won't go. You can either be decent or get out for good. I've got enough to keep me busy serving the nice guys. Malum?"

A few snickers indicated that some of the men considered me a prig, but on the whole the talk quieted down. Little Joe's mentors admonished him in stage whispers and he made no more trouble that day.

Later I regretted my harshness with the boy. After all, he was only a child. Probably he didn't even know the meaning of the dirty expressions the men had taught him. He knew only that American slang and curses made him popular and brought in the dough. Down deep, the thing he probably craved the most was a little affection—a pat on the back, a piggyback ride, maybe even a hug. Why couldn't I overcome my revulsion? I vowed that the next time he came in, I'd act differently.

In the meantime I made inquiries about Little Joe and pieced together, from local chit-chat, the following story. The American pilot had found him standing stunned in the ashes of a hut where his parents and siblings had been murdered by Japs. Touched by the lad's plight, the airman had brought him back to camp where he personally saw to Little Joe's needs. But soon the pilot tired of his charge, and after being assigned to another base, left the boy at the mercy of fate.

The men of Company C finally "adopted" Little Joe, fitted him with clothes from their own meager wardrobes, requisitioned a mess kit and canteen for him, gave him a pittance to spend at the PX, and taught him a whole vocabulary of colorful expressions. In short, they made a miniature GI out of Little Joe.

He slept in the barracks with them on his own little charpoi, ate with them in the mess hall, and sat with them thrice weekly under the stars at the outdoor movie theater. He was the plaything of the whole squadron but the responsibility of no one. He offered the men relief from boredom. For a time, he fared well.

Several weeks later Little Joe came into the canteen again, this time alone. I had already resolved to be as understanding and gentle with him as possible. So when I saw him at the door I smiled and spoke to him as though he were an old friend.

"Hello, Little Joe," I said in a cheery voice. "How are you today? Are you looking for someone?"

"Nope," he replied. "Gimme cup coffee. Gimme doughnuts."

Since the men had failed to teach him manners I was about to teach him some right then, but thought better of it. Maybe the lad was really hungry. He looked even thinner than usual.

"Well, have a seat," I said, "and we'll see what we can find for you."

"OK, babe," he said as he climbed up on one of the high stools at the counter. I wished I had some fresh milk for him, but we hadn't seen any of that since our troop-ship pulled out of its Tasmanian stopover.

I diluted his coffee liberally with canned milk and sugar, put two doughnuts on a saucer, and carried the food to his table. He pounced on the doughnuts like a starved animal, hardly chewing them at all. I wondered when he had eaten last. Surely the men were looking after him.

"Gimme 'nother doughnut," he demanded, almost before I had gotten back to the counter. I took him four more doughnuts, which he dispatched with alacrity. Then he leaned back in his chair, rubbed his bare stomach, leered at me as I removed the dishes, and uttered an obscenity that would have stuck in the craw of a hardened top sergeant.

My reaction was immediate and instinctive. All my fine resolutions for kindness vanished in a flash. I went over to his table, took him by the arm, and escorted him out the door. "Don't you ever come in here again," I said, pushing him into the yard. "I won't have such language in this canteen. From now on you can get your snacks from your Company C buddies. But don't ever come back here."

He got the picture and never bothered us again.

After that I suffered a hurting conscience. The men no longer mentioned him and I wondered what had become of him. One day I asked the Company C officer how the boy was getting along.

"Not so good, I guess," he answered. "He got a little hard to handle and the fellows got tired of him. Guess they haven't been looking after him very well. Someone said the cook got mad at him and wouldn't let him in the mess hall. The fellows sneaked food out to him for a while, but I guess that stopped too. The last I heard he was scavenging the garbage pails. To tell the truth, I haven't thought about the kid for some time."

I was shocked by this news and very much ashamed of my own behavior to Little Joe. Something would have to be done about him. If Little Joe starved to death or got into serious trouble, we could consider ourselves indirectly responsible.

That night I took the matter up with the post CO, who promised to act immediately to find a home for the Burmese boy. Two days later Little Joe, thin and dirty, but still voluble, was sent to the home of a Baptist missionary nearby, where he was to be fed, clothed, and taught a trade.

I have often wondered about those first weeks of Little Joe's adjustment to the rigid principles of a Baptist missionary. I'd give a rupee to have been around when Little Joe let loose with some of his choicest GI remarks.

Beasts in the Jungle

Patriotism sometimes makes us blind to danger. Men in war rush into enemy gunfire and do their shaking after the battle is over. We Red Cross girls had our moments too, when serving the men took priority over safety.

One such occasion was a wild nighttime ride in 1944 during the monsoons in Assam. The road from the airbase to our bungalow was a series of mud holes, with ruts up to the hubcaps, and one great mud hole about two feet deep. Our Red Cross station wagon was always getting stuck, but usually we had men along who could push and tug to get us moving again. Even the weapons carrier with four-wheel drive got mired up twice and we had to send to the base for help. A British lorry or two got bogged down in the big mud hole nearly every day.

The road cut through the tea patches and rice paddies. On both sides stretched open country, with no sign of human habitation except a few mud huts. Once we girls started on our way we had to depend on our own wits and strength in case of emergency, unless we were lucky enough to flag down a passing truck. At night along our route, flashing animal eyes peered out from the roadside, while civet cats, jackals, and monkeys often crossed in front of our vehicle.

It was my night off and I was getting ready for my date who was to arrive about nine. At eight the telephone rang—Lucia calling from the strip canteen.

"Say, Lib," she said, "we're out of doughnuts already and a big load of troops is due through here in half an hour. We've just got to give them something to eat. Can you load up the rest of the doughnuts in the cookhouse and send them over right away?"

"But there's no one here to take them. Marion has a date coming at nine. Besides, she can't even drive. And I've never driven the station wagon."

"We can't let these guys down, Lib. We can't even keep them waiting, 'cause their stopover is only for an hour."

"But, Lou," I protested, "the doughnuts are for tomorrow morning. We've got to have food tomorrow for our own men too, you know."

"This is an emergency," Lou insisted. "Stop being an obstructionist. The cook can whip up some sandwiches by the time the canteens open tomorrow. In the meantime, we've got to have doughnuts, but quick."

"Well," I said, after a moment's hesitation, "I suppose I could bring them out. Doubtless the station wagon drives like any other car. Give me half an hour and I'll have your doughnuts on the spot."

Lou began to have second thoughts. "Gosh, Lib, maybe it isn't safe for you to come alone after all. The roads are so terrible, you might get stuck, or something might go wrong with the car. Just skip it. We'll give the boys coffee and a smile and forget about the doughnuts. Thanks anyway."

"I'll have the doughnuts there for you in thirty minutes. This is war, you know, Lou, and the least we can do is feed the men."

"Yes, but . . ." Lou began.

"No buts about it. See you soon."

I slammed down the receiver, jumped into slacks and a sweater, grabbed my Colt .45, and stumbled down the stairs and out to the cookhouse. In five minutes I had the station wagon loaded and was on my way.

The station wagon was a right-hand-drive job. Other than that it handled like any '38 Chevy and drove smoothly. I hoped the gas tank was full.

As I pulled out of our lane into the road, I felt like Florence Nightingale. "This is fun," I thought, "but gosh, it's awfully dark out here. Things look so different at night. Wow, that's really a deep rut. Come on Jezebel, get up on the high ground. Good! There we go again. OK, I'll give her the gas. A little mud isn't going to stop us this early in the trip. Yikes, what's that spotted beast that crossed the road? Couldn't be! We're too close to civilization, but he looked as big as a leopard. You just keep going, Jezebel. I don't care to have a heart-to-heart talk out here with one of those felines. Whoops, girl, what's the matter? Can't you make it? For heaven's sake, don't stop here. I'll be the rest of the night waiting for someone to come along. Oh, no! Not that! So you won't go any further. Then we'll just have to back-up and try again. That's it, just a little further. OK, now here we go. Good for you, Jezebel. Keep on going. Don't let me down."

At 8:45 I pulled up to the strip canteen. A line of hungry soldiers, midway in flight from Calcutta to China, stretched for a hundred yards outside the canteen. When they saw the doughnuts, a dozen eager lads lunged from the line to carry them into the canteen, pilfering a few for themselves on the way. The others cheered lustily, smacking their lips. The trip, as far as I was concerned, was eminently worthwhile. I could defy a herd of wild buffalos for a response like that.

I hung around the canteen for about half an hour talking with the fellows, and then got in the station wagon to go home. Lou came outside to see me off.

"Thanks a million, Lib," she said. "You saved the day. But you'd better have someone go back with you. I just don't like the idea of your going back alone. I'll get one of the fellows to ride you home and he can come back with Keith later on."

"And just what will he do while Keith is calling on me, pray? No thanks, Lou, I don't want any more situations. I'll be all right. Didn't have a bit of trouble coming out, and don't count on having any going back. So long. See you later."

I started up the motor.

Just outside the post gate, a soldier waved at me, thumbing a ride in the direction I was going. Maybe Lucia was right. A little masculine protection might come in handy. Besides, he would recognize the empty Red Cross station wagon and might accuse me of being snobbish if I didn't pick him up. We always filled the car with hitchhikers going to and from the post.

I stopped the car and the soldier climbed in. He had some difficulty in opening the door and fell heavily onto the seat beside me. A strong odor of booze struck me full in the face as he lurched too close to the driver's side. I was leery of the help this soldier could give in an emergency. In fact, I feared he might become the emergency itself. However, I dared not show him that I was frightened.

"Where ya headed for, soldier?" I inquired brightly.

"Jes' goin' to ma quarters...hic. ... Live at the hospital." At this point he dragged a half-pint bottle out of his hip pocket and uncorked it.

"Have a li'l drink, sister," he said, lunging toward me with the open bottle in his hand.

I moved over, hard against the door on my side.

"No, thank you," I said with as much dignity as I could muster.

"Oh, come on now, jes' a li'l tiny one, sister. I won't tell on you. I wouldn't tell on a Red Cross girl."

I stiffened. The odor of the soldier's breath was revolting. The situation called for tact, for obviously he was going to be difficult.

"Thanks a lot, soldier, but I'd rather not tonight. Never touch the stuff on duty."

"So yer on duty, are ya? I'll bet yer goin' home right now to have a date with some officer. Tha's the trouble with all you girls. Ya can't see anybody who ain't covered with brass." The soldier took a big swig from the bottle, and then returned it to his hip pocket.

"Say, sister. How 'bout a date some night?"

"Sorry, but I'm all dated up for the next three months."

"What'd I tell ya? A GI ain't got a chanct. Jus' 'tween you 'n me, I think the Red Cross stinks."

"Sorry about that, soldier, but we try to do our best for you guys. Suppose we change the subject to something more interesting." I stepped on the gas as we started to sink into a rut.

"So you want to change the su'jeck, do ya? Well, I don't." He edged over closer and put his arm around my shoulder. "Let's stop this old crate and pitch a little woo. How 'bout it, sister? Maybe I'll like the Red Cross better then."

"You're making it hard for me to drive," I said, pushing his limp body over into his seat. "And you will please keep your hands to yourself." Fingering the weapon in my pocket, I added, "I have a gun in my pocket and if you make another move, I'll put you out and you can hike to the hospital."

At that moment the car headlights shone on a khaki-clad figure in the road, with thumb pointing in the direction I was headed.

"Thank God for small favors," I said under my breath, as I brought the car to a halt.

"Hop in," I said happily. "I'm going all the way to the hospital compound."

As soon as he opened the door, the second hitchhiker realized the situation. Grabbing the shoulder of the slouched figure beside me, he said in a tone of command, "Into the back seat, soldier. The lady and I have something to say to each other." The soldier's voice sounded vaguely familiar, but I could not see his face.

"Hey! Wha'cha tryin' ta do? Get in the back yerself. I'm ridin' up front, see!"

"Oh, no you're not. You're going to climb right in the back and take a little nap right now." The soldier spoke with the voice of authority.

The drunk reluctantly climbed into the back, where within a few minutes he was snoring and snorting.

"Gee, I'm glad you happened along just now," I said to my new passenger.

"Has he been giving you trouble?"

"He certainly has. He was on the point of becoming unmanageable. I picked him up about a mile back. I didn't know he had been drinking until he was in the wagon. I didn't really want to use my .45 on him."

"Probably got hold of some bad Indian hooch."

I reached into the glove compartment for a pack of cigarettes. As I fumbled to get one out, I heard "Light?" and the click of a lighter from the seat beside me.

Are you stationed here in Jorhat?" I asked.

"Nope. I'm on my way over the Hump. Our plane needed some minor repair, so we're just here overnight. I have a buddy in the hospital and thought I'd drop over to see him."

"And did you really expect to walk the whole five miles?"

"I figured to flag down a ride sooner or later, even though I suspect there isn't much joy-riding over these ruts. How do you manage to get through at all?"

"Mostly by sheer will power, strong arms, and an occasional prayer directed upward. You'll probably have to get out and push before we get there."

As if to prove the veracity of my statement, Jezebel slowed down, spun her wheels, and finally settled down into a deep rut, refusing to budge.

"Let me take the wheel," the soldier said. "There's quite a trick to driving in mud—almost as bad as driving on ice. You have to rack the thing back and forth until the tires can get a little traction."

Alternately putting the car in low and reverse and feeding lots of gas, he finally got us out of the ditch. I told him all the turns to take and we finished the rest of the trip with only one incident of having to push. It turned into a merry ride, with soprano-baritone duets and lots of laughter.

At the lane into our bungalow compound, where the main road diverged, the singing soldier roused the sleeping one. "This is where you get out, buster," he said, helping the reeling man to his feet.

Turning to me, he said, "Think you can make it the rest of the way?"

"Yes, of course. The hospital is just up the other lane about a hundred yards. You can see the lights where the road branches."

"I'll find it all right. Goodnight, lovely lady. And thanks for the nicest ride I've had since I enlisted."

"And thanks to you," I said. "You were a life saver. Have a safe trip over the Hump. Stop by Jorhat again sometime."

The night held still one more scare. Parking the station wagon under the porch, I heard low voices upstairs and knew that the dates had arrived. As I got out of the station wagon, a blood-curdling roar came from the cookhouse area. Only in the zoo had I ever heard such a sound. Instinctively I ran up the stairway and into the arms of Marion's date, who had jumped to his feet at the roar.

"Get a flashlight quick," he screamed. "That was a big cat." Then he dashed down the steps in the direction of the cookhouse, his gun cocked.

No trace was found of the hungry animal. The next day, Nanda, the head bearer, told us that an old leopard, no longer able to kill his own food and therefore ousted from the pride, had been seen wandering in the tea patches nearby, evidently attracted by the savory smells from the cookhouse.

Several nights later we heard the roar again in the distance, but never had another close visit from a leopard while we lived in Assam. I'll never forget the hair-raising sensation caused by that roar.

The Naga Hills

At long last, a whole day off and the long-awaited trip to the Naga Hills, or rather the foothills of the Nagas. For weeks I had been planning a jaunt to the region of Beeba's birthplace. But clear weather and the availability of Army transportation for private use never seemed to coincide with off-duty time. Happily, my long wait was rewarded with a full day of sunshine and John's ability to commandeer a Jeep. (John was my newest love, now that Keith had been transferred.)

On May 4 we set out after lunch over the deeply rutted, miry roads through the jungle, grown lush from the early spring rains. John had made inquiries among the locals about what route to take in this unfamiliar countryside. I didn't worry a minute about his navigation. The whole trip was made without a wrong turn.

About twenty miles north of Jorhat we drove by a native village—a cluster of mud and thatch huts boasting two or three tiny dirty shops and a public well. Here the Nagas came once a week, walking for miles down out of the hills, to buy rice and sundry provisions. That day was market day in the little village, so we got to observe the natives as they chatted in front of the shops. After an hour or two of bargaining and laughing, they piled their purchases in strange cone-shaped baskets strapped to their shoulders and balanced by another strap across their foreheads. Then they slowly walked back, single file, the ten or fifteen miles to their hillside huts.

The Nagas are a strange looking people with a yellow glow over soft brown skin. Their faces are broad, chins and foreheads square, eyes wide set. Their black hair is long and straight. Mongolian ancestry shows in their light complexion and short, stocky bodies. They appeared healthy and happy, or at least stoical, in what we would consider dire poverty. Though in the past they were reputed to be headhunters, they showed no propensity for either belligerence or friendship, only a great curiosity as they poked at the Jeep's tires and seats, gingerly fingered John's gun holster, and laughed at their reflections in my hand mirror.

We had difficulty in distinguishing the Naga men from the women, except that the women were better covered below the waist. Over their shoulders these hill people had thrown thick hand-woven woolen shawls, reminiscent in color and design of American Indian blankets. Some of the men wore loincloths, some not. One old man walked alone in the road, unabashedly naked from his waist down, his gray pointed beard sticking out straight in front of him. When we drew closer, however, he pulled his shawl down over the exposed area and continued on his way.

Leaving the little village, we took the narrow trail deeper into the jungle. Dense foliage brushed against the jeep on both sides. As we drove along we heard in the distance a slow, weird thud-thud and a hollow scraping sound—frightening to our unaccustomed ears. I visualized all sorts of strange jungle animals attacking us in our open vehicle.

"Sounds like an elephant to me," John said. "Maybe if we drive a little faster we can catch up with him."

"I hope you're a good shot with the .45 just in case it's a wild elephant?"

"Oh, I think I can protect you, in one way or another," he said.

"OK, then step on the gas. I'm ready for more adventure."

John speeded up a bit. We could see no large footprints, but the freshly scraped area ahead indicated that something had been dragged along the trail. Shortly we heard the clanking of chains. The thud and scraping noise grew louder. Finally, at the curve just ahead we saw two elephants pulling huge timbers along the road. No driver or mahout was visible. We hastened to get a closer look, but the big beasts disappeared into a jungle path too narrow for us to negotiate in the jeep. Not dressed for jungle wandering, with snakes and insects and small varmints

lurking in the tall grass, we deemed it inadvisable to follow the elephants.

After about two more miles we came upon a crude saw-
mill where large timbers were stacked, waiting to be cut.
Another five miles up the hill the road came to an abrupt
end at a cliff overlooking a clear shallow stream. On the
other side of the water a footpath wound into the forest
beyond.

Parking the Jeep at the cliff, we got out the picnic provisions and explored the area for a spot to pitch our camp
for the rest of the afternoon. Directly across from the cliff
was a little peninsula of white sand, made by a bend in
the stream, a perfect spot for our picnic. We climbed down
the cliff, waded to the sandy beach and spread out the
feast of fried chicken, deviled eggs, tangerines, cake, cookies, and canned fruit juice, which had been prepared for
us by the bungalow cook. All around us, from the trees on
the banks, bird song and monkey chatter entertained us
in our peninsula hideaway.

Nothing is more beautiful than the jungle in spring.
The trees have new foliage and the trailing lianas make
an impenetrable green mass, dotted with flashes of red,
yellow, blue, and orange, as birds fly among the branches.
All the birds in Assam seemed to be congregated around
the stream that day: cocky long-tailed black and white
birds with smooth round heads, green parrots with crests,
red-winged blackbirds, big gray birds that looked brilliant
blue in flight, even two condors sitting on a dead limb like
philosophers contemplating the meaning of life. These big
black fellows, with thick white curved beaks and long white
tails, eyed us calmly as we ate. We wondered what carrion prey would constitute their supper.

We lolled on the little beach until just before sunset,
then reluctantly made our way back to the Jeep. As we
crested the hill, we beheld a band of curious Nagas clustered about the vehicle, pulling at it here and there, tapping
the hood, fingering the steering gear, and trying out the jump
seat. When they saw us approach, they made no move to
leave. So we decided to put on a little show for them.

John climbed in, started up the motor, and turned the vehicle around on a dime. The Nagas laughed out loud at the performance. Then they became entranced with John's green baseball hat, as he pulled the bill fore and aft. Next, John took out his gun and shot it in the air several times. Again they laughed and mumbled to each other.

I put on the last act. Taking out my vanity case, I did a complete make-up job for their benefit. The Nagas chortled at the sight. We gave them our two empty fruit juice cans— a gift that pleased them immensely and for which they would find a use. Finally, they continued their journey single-file down the steep incline, through the stream, and up the path on the other side.

As the sun dipped below the horizon, we left the jungle to the birds and beasts and its interesting human inhabitants.

Raj Justice

About the middle of August, with the arrival of three new Red Cross girls, we hired a second native girl to help Beeba.

Sherie, the new ayah, was everything Beeba was not— tall, slender, beautiful, and joyous. Had she matured in pre-war days she might have become a concubine in the household of a bachelor planter. Since she came of age in the '40s, when most of the planters were in military service, she had fallen into the "world's oldest profession." Somewhere along the line she had learned the duties of a lady's maid, so we hired her because she needed no training.

Beeba instantly disliked her.

On the ninth day of Sherie's sojourn with us, Kay, who was taking her turn as burrah-memsahib at the bungalow, reported the theft of 300 rupees (about $100) from the chest of drawers in our bedroom. After counting the monthly receipts, she had left the money on top of the chest while she went down to the cookhouse to check on supper. When she came back to the bedroom, the money was gone.

Up to that time we had never missed any cash at the bungalow, so we had grown lax about keeping it under lock and key. Little things like scissors, eyebrow pluckers, and fountain pens had disappeared, but money had never been touched. In fact, the servants made quite a ceremony of returning annas they occasionally found on the floor. Today's theft, therefore, made quite a stir, both upstairs and below in the servants' quarters.

The theft occurred at a time when all the servants were on duty, so any of them, except the cookhouse crew who never entered the bungalow, could have slipped into the bedroom unnoticed. We strongly suspected Sherie, since she was the newest member of the household staff and had been in the bedrooms after tea, ostensibly to let down the mosquito nets. With the help of Nanda we questioned her first. In brittle Assamese she sputtered her ignorance of the theft. Eyes flashing, hands waving, she put on a good show. We weren't convinced of her innocence, but we could not act on suspicion alone.

The next step was to cross-examine the other servants. At Kay's request Nanda had them all gather in the back hall where, lined up in the order of their rank in the household hierarchy, they submitted docilely to our interrogation. No one appeared to have seen or heard anything unusual that day.

As a matter of routine we questioned Beeba along with the other servants. Far more eloquent than her faltering denial was her look of shattered pride. I realized then that this public inquest had been unwise.

Having no clues to go on, we called on Mr. Carpenter for advice. Surely, we thought, in his thirty years upcountry he had encountered a similar situation. He had, and many times. He recommended that we try the local British method of recovering stolen sums. It seemed a harsh scheme to me, but we knew of no alternative action.

The next morning Kay again summoned the servants to the back hall. Translating Kay's orders into Assamese, Nanda announced that twenty-four hours would be allowed for the recovery of the money. If, by the end of that period, the loss had been returned to the burrah-memsahib, no questions would be asked. If, however, the money did not appear, ten rupees a month would be deducted from the wages of each servant until the entire deficit had been made up.

When I returned to the bungalow that afternoon for tea, my bath water was steaming in the tin tub, fluffy towels hung on the rack, and on my bed were clean nylons, a change of undies, a fresh uniform, and a scarlet hibiscus for my hair.

Beeba was standing in the doorway to the dressing room. I wondered why she stayed on, now that her day's duties were over. I asked if anything was wrong.

"Oh, memsahib," she burst forth, "I no take money. I Christian girl. Christian say wrong to steal. Please, memsahib, I no steal."

For the first time in my life I had no ready reply. Though never doubting her innocence, I lacked a vocabulary adequate to console a girl whose virtue, as she believed, had been put in jeopardy.

"I know you didn't take the money, Beeba," I stammered. "None of us suspected you. But we had to treat all the servants the same."

"Teek hai, memsahib..." she faltered. Then she slipped away.

I heard the gentle tinkle of glass bracelets as she crept down the outside stairway. Then the tinkle died away in the distance. That was the last we ever saw of Beeba.

After breakfast the next morning Kay found 300 rupees lying on the chest of drawers, just as she had left them two days before. No one knew who had put them there. But before nightfall the almond-eyed Sherie, ostracized by the other servants, returned to the village and her former trade.

Dashed Hopes

$\mathcal{M}$y last two months in Assam were bittersweet—fruitful from a work standpoint, but full of personal and staff problems.

Personnel problems, starting in May, had continued throughout the summer. On June 20 I wrote:

We now have three canteens under three separate program directors. We are supposed to help each other out on big events such as dances and picnics. Instead of a spirit of cooperation in these matters, there exists a spirit of competition. The three new girls who arrived most recently are darling girls, but very, very cliquey. When they plan something they turn out 100% for the event, but when I plan something they always have an excuse for not being there.

Yesterday I worked all day and invited six British nurses as guests for my musical program. It would have been a very successful evening if we had just had some more Red Cross girls there. I'm supposed to have help from other staff assistants, but they refuse to do anything that cuts into their dates. I'm the only one on the staff who works regularly at night.

Then to complicate matters, Lou and Nancy were taken to the hospital with dysentery, the club director got sick in the afternoon, and my most dependable canteen bearer, who had celebrated too much after pay-day, was home sick. Lou will be in the hospital four or five days. In the meantime I'm taking the responsibility for keeping her canteen open, plus making plans for special Easter music and decorations.

This past week has been the worst and hardest one yet. Our sanitary system at the canteen went on the blink and the dances planned for the post did not pan out. I was all set for the dances, had the men working and enthusiastic, only to discover that the

*five local women we were counting on had left town
and the other new recruits for dancing were not permitted to come. That leaves only five Red Cross girls
to run a party for two hundred men once a week.*

Despite these problems I had high hopes for promotion to APD (Assistant Program Director), in which capacity I had already served for the past six months. In July I
wrote:

*Here is a secret that boosted my morale last night
when it particularly needed boosting. Mr. Paxson,
my boss, had just returned from regional headquarters. He says that I have quite a reputation there and
that my promotion will go through immediately.
Moreover, he says that I can go right to the top, if I
wish: i.e. to club director (which means starting a
whole new club). But I really prefer programming
to being a club director, for the latter is largely ad-
ministrative and has an interminable amount of
bookwork and responsibility. It is nice to know that
they think favorably of me and are considering me
who was just a mere staff assistant.*

A later letter continued to boost my hopes:

*I have been recommended for a promotion, which,
if it goes through, will mean a salary increase of
$50 a month. I'll even be given two girls to assist
me. There is only one reason why the promotion may
not go through. If the new shipment has too many
APDs, I won't get a promotion. If it has a prepon-
derance of staff assistants, I will.*

The shipment came loaded with club directors and
APDs, so I stayed on as a staff assistant in rank and pay,
but with continuing duties in program planning.

By July we were all discouraged. I wrote:

*The situation here is hectic. Last Saturday every
one of us at different times during the day threatened to resign, or ask for a transfer, but after a little
while we all calmed down.*

We learned yesterday, much to our surprise, that our installation is the best in the CBI theater, that other installations are having much more trouble than we are, and that we have the best staff and best esprit de corps in the theater. In fact, one whole group of girls who just came over is being sent back home and the installation closed for some sort of charges made against them. I guess everyone is having problems. Certainly the army isn't having an easy time of it.

My workload escalated as I rushed to set up a new club before going on leave. Without the help of the military we could not have met the late-August opening deadline. My right-hand man was Captain John Stewart, who gave all his non-flying time to help me in planning and procurement. In August, 1944, I wrote:

John has been an invaluable help in the crisis. He fixed the Victrola spring so that now we have one machine that runs. Today and yesterday he worked on the piano, which has been terribly out of tune and in need of repair. He made artistic signs for the grand opening and painted the red crosses on the invitations. John is to act as art instructor temporarily. He carted me all over the countryside in a Jeep on club errands and has lent his interest and energy to everything we are doing. We are both wearing ourselves out, but we will recuperate on leave.

The stress of overwork was alleviated somewhat in early August by an evening off and a short interesting visit to a nearby base, as recorded in this letter home:

Saturday night John and I drove down to the Brahmaputra (big river) for the first time. You can't imagine anything more beautiful by moonlight. It was quite still, except for the haunting melancholy chant of a native nearby and the occasional passing of ox-carts. Even the banana tree leaves were not moving, for there was no breeze. Someday, if ever we can get transportation, we want to take one of the funny little junks down the river to find out what lies beyond the bend.

The other day I got to sit in on a fascinating event. Another US airbase was having a big celebration in honor of Chinese Air Force Day, with stage business, operas, and formal Chinese dinners. We were invited down, but could stay only for the morning events.

While we were in the major's basha, talking informally to several officers, orders came for a bombing mission.

The men casually got dressed while we sat there, then had dinner with us. I sat next to a Chinese major general, one of the biggest moguls in the Chinese Air Force. Afterwards we went with them to the airstrip, where we inspected their planes, and then watched them take off on their mission over Japanese territory.

It was really a thrilling experience to see the bombing mission go into action. One thing that particularly impressed me about the men at this particular base was the feeling of real comradeship between the officers and the men. There was no saluting or 'sir'-ing. Everyone seemed to be on a par, with no feeling of strain among the ranks.

By late August we were ready to open the new club. I wrote:

For the opening a big general is coming and bringing eight R.C. girls with him. Also, six or eight from other areas will be coming in for the day, so it will be a gala affair. The officers are invited in the afternoon for an informal "at home" just to view the building. We will have a small orchestra and two accordions. Decorations will be masses of water lilies (the only thing blooming now) and some sort of red flowers.

The affair at night is to be formal, with the girls dressed in their evening dresses. We have planned a short program, including the appearance of the general, plus a few variety numbers with an orchestra and two accordions in the small rooms. Ice cream, a real treat for the Gis, will round out the evening. Only GIs, local girls, and British planters and their wives are invited in the evening.

Several days later I wrote:

My program for the following week includes piano lessons, bridge lessons, art club (with John as instructor), swimming in the afternoon; birthday parties, Bingo, a show, classical music, chorus, game tournaments, and dancing lessons at night. It is a massive program to put over and I'll be 'as busy as a gas meter,' as Dad used to say.

As fate would have it, just as I get this program set up and the opening night taken care of, I'll be moving out of here. Such is life!

By September I was ready for a change. After eight months in the steamy jungles of Assam, three weeks in cool Kashmir would refresh me for the unwanted assignment to a city club on India's arid west coast, where Karachi's KGA Hall awaited this seasoned Red Cross club worker.

Paulette Goddard arrives at
Jorhat airbase, 1944. Shown
with Major Keith Davis, CO.

Major Davis receiving
Presidential citation for
Jorhat airbase, 1944.

Chatting with GIs at Base Canteen at Jorhat, 1944. Left to Right: Nancy Hemingway, Norris McClellan, (Club Director), Libby Appel.

Village market, Jorhat, 1944.

Lord Louis Mountbatten with Major
Keith Davis, CO at Jorhat, 1944.

Bechty and Jitter
Jorhat, Assam.

Part Four
North to Lotus Land

"My eyes will never be poor again,
having seen Kashmir.
I saw such beauty in people
and things."

Rumer Godden in
"Kingfishers Catch Fire," p. 2.

Stopover in Calcutta

The struggle was over in Assam. After weeks of planning, packing, and happy anticipation, Lou and I were actually on our way to Kashmir for leave.

Such a time as we had getting out of Jorhat! We pulled up to the runway before 7:00, the hour of dawn as far as we were concerned, to board a cargo plane, along with a British major and his budget-size lieutenant.

As Damon Runyon might have said, our luggage was "quite somewhat." Travel orders called for a total of 130 lbs. luggage each, since we were changing stations; otherwise our allotment would have been 65 lbs.

The baggage officer surveyed our pile of bags and boxes, winked at us, and said, "Guess we won't bother to weigh you girls in. I'm sure those trunks are full of feathers anyway." Dear man, we could have kissed him.

Another officer checked our orders and then came the wait. "You may as well settle down and be comfortable," he said. "There are five folks ahead of you and we haven't any idea what's coming through or when."

So we sat down for what we hoped would be at most an hour. Planes were coming in and taking off every few minutes. We felt confident that one headed for Calcutta was even now taxiing onto the runway just to accommodate us.

We waited seven hours.

Once aboard the plane to our regional Red Cross home base, I had time to write to my family:

> Seven months in the jungle, with dysentery and malaria for some and ear-fungus for me, and now this: two days in the city, then three whole weeks aboard a houseboat in the Himalayas. Please God, let nothing mar our plans!

> We're to stop first in Calcutta to pick up orders for a new assignment and to see our Red Cross supervisor. John and Marty are to join us there. Then the

four of us are slated to fly To Delhi. From there on, what happens is up to the little red gods, for transportation out of Delhi is uncertain. But we don't care. The uncertainty adds to the thrill.

Right now we're flying over rice paddies and tea gardens that make a mammoth green-and-brown checkerboard below us. Thatch-roofed shanties in distant compounds look picturesque and pretty—we cannot see the filth and crudeness from up here. There lies the long Brahmaputra weaving in and out among the squares, its wide sluggish waters baring sand bars, tiny islands, and narrow deltas. A barge is carrying rice south and small dinghies are moving with the current in the same direction. In the distance jagged crests of blue mountains are lost in cotton-batting clouds. Assam from the air is a beautiful land. Goodbye, Assam!

That reminds me, you probably wonder who John and Marty are. Well, they're the Hump-flying pilots from Jorhat who are going on leave with us. We've seen a lot of them in the past few months and have found them to be happy, charming, and resourceful companions. Subjected to the grueling strain of hazardous flying, extreme fatigue, beastly hot weather, and tropical disease, they are among the very few flyers who still maintain their sense of humor. They combine the zaniness of Fred MacMurray, the suavete of Ronald Colman, the practical masculinity of Gary Cooper, and the romantic appeal of Charles Boyer.

We finally got off about 2:00 PM in a C47 full of cargo. But who are we to quibble about bucket seats and no leg space this late in the day? We have to make Calcutta tonight.

We are four aboard this plane, carrying on conversation across a center row of empty packing boxes and huge water jars. Across the aisle are a portly British major and his lieutenant pal. They're going

*on leave too and have the holiday spirit. Already
we've made a date for a get-together at the B and A
Club tomorrow in Calcutta, when John and Marty
can join us.*

We got into Dum Dum airport at about 8:30, after gas-
sing up and changing pilots at Lamanerhat. We ate a late
supper in the airport, then headed into Calcutta on the
shuttle bus.

Calcutta at last! Home at last! What fun it was to be
back where we knew the streets, to go again to our favorite haunts, to see familiar faces!

Calcutta is like New York. We always ran into people
we knew: Red Cross girls back in town for reassignment,
supervisors who visited us upcountry, men we met on the
boat; officers and nurses from former posts, and a few
friends from the States passing to and from their work
stations. In Calcutta chance acquaintances soon blos-
somed into full-blown friendships, where people greeted
each other as long lost buddies.

Many of the girls looked battered and beaten. But on
most faces there was a look of hope and all were in the
holiday spirit. Despite the squalor and hardship of the
low-caste Indian people, I'll always remember Calcutta as
an oasis of gaiety for us in wartime.

We had hoped to stay at The Great Eastern, but it
was full, so we ended up at The Grand, with private bath
and bearer service. Lou and I shared quarters with a
British nurse who also had just finished a seven-months
tour of duty in Assam and was also on her way to Kashmir. After the luxury of hot baths, we settled down early
for a good night's sleep, in anticipation of the full day
coming up.

Sometime in the middle of the night I heard a soft
pacing outside our door. "It can't be John," I said to myself, "not this soon. He's not due until tomorrow at the
earliest." The pacing stopped just in front of the door, as
if the pacer were deliberating whether to knock. Then it
started again accompanied by a familiar voice humming

"Stardust." There was no doubt about it now. That was John, all right, but how had he gotten here so soon? I looked at my watch. 2:30. What did he mean by waking me up at that hour? Hmm! Tomorrow I'd give him a piece of my mind.

The humming had aroused my roommates too. Lou whispered, "Who on earth can that be?"

"Shh!" I cautioned. "I think it's our friend from Jorhat. But don't let him know we're awake. He'll go away if we just keep quiet."

"Wonder how he got here so quickly," Lou said. "And where do you suppose Marty can be?"

"Probably sacked out in his room, where all good boys should be at this hour."

"Hmm! Sounds like John might have opened his Seagrams," Lou said.

"'Fraid so," I mumbled.

The British nurse jumped up with a start, at a gentle knock on the door, then settled back into oblivion. Lou and I did not stir. In a few minutes we heard retreating footsteps going down the hall and the dying strains of "Stardust" hummed a quartertone off key.

The next time I awoke, daylight was streaming in the window and outdoor noises indicated that Calcutta was bustling with life. I lay quietly for a minute and filled my ears with the city sounds I had missed upcountry: the hollow honk of taxis, squawk of crows, jingle of gharry bells, buzz of human chatter, low tong-tong of rickshaw bells, cries of hawkers, and weird melody from a scratching gramophone.

Then I looked around the hotel room. The bed across from me was empty. Evidently the British nurse was doing the splashing I heard in the bathroom. Our uniforms were hanging on the backs of the straight chairs. Our suitcases cluttered the passageway. Under the door I saw a bit of white paper folded like a chitty. Curiosity got the better of my sloth and I finally got up to investigate. The note, which was addressed to me, read:

To the lovely lady in Room 217:

Half the night have I paced before your door, hoping to call you forth from the dark. Half the night have I sung love songs to lure you from your lair. And what has it got me this morning? Stardust and moonlight to soothe my splitting head?

Alas, no! Only nothingness and disillusion. So, lest you persist in your silence and keep me away all day, I offer herewith my deepest apologies for disturbing your sleep and beg of you to breakfast with me at nine.

Till then, my love, I must remain your rejected swain in Room 224.

PS. Marty, unworthy skunk, slept like a baby all night and wanted to go to breakfast at seven. I finally prevailed on him to grant Lou two more hours of beauty sleep. We'll see you in the main dining room at the appointed hour. You will be able to recognize me by the chic ice pack on my head.

During the night, between snatches of sleep, I had composed a sermon to deliver at breakfast. But John's contrite epistle and the brightness of the Calcutta morning sunshine swept the nighttime diatribe clean out of my memory. After a breakfast of bacon and eggs and Noel Coward repartee, we set out for a stroll to the native bazaar.

The Little Brown Birds

Calcutta was again our city of enchantment. As we four walked abreast down Chowringhee Road, passersby must have thought us either crazy or drunk. We laughed and danced and laughed again, exuberant with the freedom of our first leave. No work, no duties, no rules, no reproofs! All that freedom had gone to our heads and we felt dizzy with sheer happiness.

Not far from the hotel a street vendor stopped us. He looked like a Tibetan monk, with long white hair and white beard down to his chest. In one hand he carried an empty birdcage. On the other four little birds perched on his thumb and forefinger, pecking playfully at his withered hand—tiny brown birds with sleek black heads and yellow bills, later identified as Australian sparrows. As we approached to admire the birds, the vendor put two of them on my fingers, where they sat contentedly and allowed me to stroke their backs.

Of course I wanted the birds. Who could resist the allure of tame birds so prettily marked? But what would I do with them on leave? Already I had more baggage than I could possibly manage. The birdcage would be just one too many items to carry. But, oh, what adorable creatures they were!

The old man put a third bird on my hand.

"Ver' nice pets, memsahib," he said. Then, indicating one of the birds that was pecking gently at my finger, he went on, "See, memsahib. He likes you. You buy him. I sell him you cheap."

"How much?" John piped up, before I could protest.

"Fifteen rupees, sahib. Tame bird. He worth much more."

The price was preposterous. I knew it, John knew it, the vendor knew it, and he knew we knew it. The vendor was prepared to spend the morning bargaining, but we were anxious to be on our way.

"You know we won't pay you half that much," I said. "Besides, the bird should have a mate. We'd need two of them as well as the cage."

"Teek hai, memsahib. I make you cheap price. Fifteen rupees for two birds and cage."

"We'll give you twelve and call it a bargain," John said, taking out his wallet.

At the sight of the money the man's eyes glowed. "Teek hai, sahib, you take birds with you." Then, putting all four birds into the tiny cage, the old man handed them to me as John counted out a ten-rupee note and two singles. The ancient vendor salaamed his thanks as we continued on our way.

Halfway down Chowringhee Road we ran head on into a bunch of enlisted men. Nodding greetings, we were about to pass on when one of them said, "What have you got in that cage?" The voice startled me. It sounded familiar. I looked again into the blue eyes of a handsome GI who had helped me out in a tight spot early on in Assam.

"Why, hello!" I said warmly. "How nice to see you. Are you stationed here now?"

"Nope, just passing through on leave. Don't tell me you expect to adopt those birds."

"Oh, yes. In fact, I've just acquired them and they're to be company for us on leave."

"What are their names?"

"Oh, this is John," I said, pointing them out one by one, "and this one we call John, and the one in the corner is John, and the one nearest me is John. Aren't they adorable?"

"Amazing originality in your choice of names," the soldier said dryly.

"Well, I guess it does seem strange. But we can't tell them apart anyway and we don't know the Johns from the Jills, so it's just easier to call them all John."

"Do I detect partiality to that particular name? Seems I've heard rumors since I left Jorhat that a certain captain had replaced the CO in your affection."

"Could be," I admitted. "Oh goodness, my friends are already halfway down the street. Goodbye, and have a wonderful leave."

As I caught up to the other three, Marty said, a bit sarcastically, "Personal friend of yours?"

"No!" I said. "Just one of the fellows who used to haunt my canteen before you and John showed up."

"Well, at least you might have introduced us," John teased.

"Sorry, but I'm not even sure of his name."

When we returned to the hotel to change and rest before the evening festivities, I put the birdcage on the balcony railing of our second-floor room. "You'll be so much happier here," I told the four Johns, "than in our dark room. And there are still two hours of sunlight for you to enjoy. You can chirp at the people below and even sing a little song, if you have it in you." They seemed contented out there, so I left them there all evening.

What fun we had at the B and A Club, as we dined and danced and sang to celebrate the birthday of the British major Lou and I had met on the plane. John and Marty met him at tea that afternoon while we girls were putting on our glamour. I wore my purple embroidered sari; Lou was ravishing in a Chinese-red gold-embroidered Benares silk that set off her black bobbed hair.

After the party we rode through Victoria Park in an open gharry, with facing padded seats, each just wide enough for a close embrace. Garbo herself never spent a more glamorous evening than we two Red Cross club workers that night in Calcutta.

My first thought on returning to the hotel was to check on the birds. I beat everyone else up the broad stairway to our room, jammed the key in the lock, and ran to the balcony singing "John, John, John, John, I love you!" all the way.

The little brown birds were gone.

The bearers pleaded innocence. The street vendor, still at work, professed no knowledge of their whereabouts.

"These not your birds," he insisted. "I got lotsa birds and cages to sell. You want buy a nudder one?"

"Not on your life!" John spoke for us all.

We never found out who or what had stolen our treasures. Possibly a street urchin had climbed up from the outside to the railing, taking them to sell or to return to the old man, who would reward him with a few pice. But at least there was the consolation that we wouldn't have to care for them on our leave. At last, we were really free.

Into the Vale of Kashmir

Kashmir, Kashmir. Would we ever get there?
During a two-day layover in Delhi, John and Marty had combed all possibilities for travel to Rawalpindi, jumping off point for ascent into Kashmir. With military transport booked solid for the next ten days, they had to settle for a tiny Indian Airlines practice plane.

We arrived at the terminal a half-hour before our scheduled flight. Two hours went by and a dozen British and U.S. planes took off. What looked like a double-winged mosquito was warming up just off the runway. To my untutored eyes it appeared to be an early descendant of Orville Wright's craft, or at least a blood brother of Lindberg's little eggbeater.

"Good heavens!" Lou exclaimed, as the ancient four-seater taxied toward us. "Surely that can't be our plane. I'm surprised those antiquated flying machines are still in service."

"Don't forget this is India," Marty said. "Our castoffs are still useful to them."

"Maybe it isn't our plane," I said. "Maybe it's just a training plane."

A lanky khaki-clad Indian, with wings on his epaulettes, approached us.

"Are you the ones who have tickets to Rawalpindi?" he asked in a perfect British accent.

"Yes," said John.

"Good! This is your transport to Pindi," he said, pointing to the relic. "But we can take only three of you on this run."

"That plane holds four passengers," John said. "What's the matter?"

"I've got to check out a pilot on this run," said the Indian, "and that leaves only three seats for passengers."

"Hmm!" Lou said. "This is a fine kettle of fish. When does the next plane leave for Rawalpindi?"

"There's another flight in an hour or two that should get you to Pindi about eight tonight. I'm sure you could book passage on that one."

"Well, that's the luck of the draw," Marty said. "Some of us will just have to wait and it may as well be us, Lou. John, you and Lib take this flight. Lou and I can get some exercise while we wait. We'll see you tonight at Fleishman's in time for a cocktail or two."

"OK," John said. "We'll check out the facilities in Rawalpindi and make the arrangements for the drive up to Srinagar. So long. See you tonight."

"Pleasant journey!" said Lou, with a wry smile.

"Sarcasm will get you nowhere," I countered. "You'll be flying in one of these this afternoon. Pleasant journey to you!"

A few minutes later we were chugging along to take-off, then climbing to 1,000 feet for cruising. Once in the air we felt a little more confident, despite our uneasiness with the pilot-in-training. The senior pilot, however, assured us that there was no danger. The young man in front had had several hundred hours in the air, the flight was not a hazardous one, and he himself could take over the controls in case of emergency.

We settled back to enjoy the ride. John whiled away the time penciling a sketch of the handsome check pilot and I gazed upon the scene below.

The terrain between Delhi and Rawalpindi was quite different from the rolling hills and dense forests of Assam. From Delhi to Lahore the land was flat, alternately marshy and sandy. Irrigation canals crisscrossed the fields. Low bushes bordered winding streams. Inside some of the squares little mud huts huddled together like sheep in a pen.

Beyond our gas-stop at Lahore, the terrain changed from farmland to stratified, barren soil dotted with scraggly shrubs. The canals and streams were gone. Only a few native huts indicated human life. Then we crossed over barren foothills. Finally in the distance Rawalpindi, last outpost before the Himalayas, crept into our view. As the pilot jog-trotted the plane onto the narrow runway, we breathed a sigh of relief and thanked God for His protection.

A British truck driver offered to take us to the hotel, where we had made reservations weeks ago. Taking us for naïve tourists, he regaled us along the way with tales of the primitive life in this picturesque town.

"You'll feel right at home here," he said. "Fleishman's is right out of your own West, with gun slingers propping their feet on the porch railing and wild boars in the woods nearby."

"Great!" said John, ostentatiously taking out his .45. "Give me an hour and I'll get us some pork for supper."

As we drove up to Fleishman's we saw a rambling adobe structure resembling a hotel in the Mexican desert. While the exterior was anything but grand, inside it was another story. We were pleased by the well-appointed entry and really delighted with our sleeping quarters. We had ordered two double bedrooms at the usual Indian rate. What a surprise to be ushered into elegantly decorated two-room apartments. In the Spanish style sitting room a clean sofa and comfortable chair faced a marble-mantled fireplace. Overhead fans cooled each bedroom. Hot clear water spewed from the bathroom faucets. A pitcher of ice water and two glasses awaited us on a polished brass tray in each living room.

Before a late tea John and I toured the town in a conveyance new to us, a tonga. Reminding us of the pony carts of our childhood, this little two-wheeled vehicle is balanced to allow a little horse to pull it fully loaded all day long without becoming overly tired. The driver, with his whip, sits up front on a raised seat behind the pony's switching tail. Beside him is room for a small child or someone who can squeeze in for a front view of the passing scene. The other passengers sit behind the driver, facing backwards and often have to grip the side rails to keep from falling out when the pony climbs a hill.

In Rawalpindi we were treated to another new sight, which later in Karachi became old hat—camels being used as beasts of burden. Tame as horses though not as well mannered, some pulled heavy loads on long, low wagons. Others bore huge sheaves of straw hanging on each side of their single hump. A few provided transportation for their owners, who perched atop the hump on a throne-like wooden pad. All the camels were adorned with colorful necklaces, knee bracelets, and anklets. Loping slowly with an air of dignity, they reminded us of Victorian dowagers decked out in all their finery.

After our tea in Rawalpindi John made arrangements for a local taxi to take the four of us the next day to Srinagar, capital of Kashmir. The driver agreed to come for us at 7:00 am for the 200-mile trip up the mountain, which, if all went well, would take about ten hours. With the very real possibility of mechanical problems and landslides blocking the road, we would consider ourselves lucky if we arrived before midnight.

By 6:45 the next morning we were outside Fleishman's all packed and waiting. The cab driver showed up at 8:45, complaining that he had had difficulty in getting petrol (which probably was true). We loaded the baggage on top of his ancient English sedan and joined the steady stream of vehicles going up.

The long ascent from Rawalpindi to Srinagar took us over a narrow, winding macadam road, full of large holes and rocks. Often we had to drive perilously close to the edge of a precipice where landslides had taken out the main road. Our driver tried to maintain a steady speed of 20 to 25 miles an hour. We experienced the usual delays: a flat tire, lunch at a Dak bungalow (simple wooden shelter), customs inspection at the entrance to the state of Kashmir, plus a long stop so that our driver could offer consolation to a colleague whose taxi had broken an axle.

All the way from Rawalpindi to the outskirts of Srinagar, we marveled at the scenic splendor. As we rose above the green foothills, the trees gradually changed from hardwoods to hemlocks, northern pines, and strange conifers. No matter how high we went, there always seemed to be another mountain ahead. Finally, just at

sunset the terrain flattened out into a softly rolling mead-
owland. In the distance the lofty Himalayas poked their
snow-capped peaks into red-gold clouds. We had climbed
nearly 6,000 feet into the legendary vale of Kashmir. The
air was cool and invigorating as we entered the fertile valley.

"Let's get out and stretch our legs," Marty suggested.

It was an enchanting bucolic scene. Shepherds in
goatskin jackets were bringing their fat-tailed flocks from
mountain meadows back to compounds for the night. Both
shepherds and sheep looked content and healthy. Further along we saw the picturesque homes of well-to-do
landowners, two-story structures with brick below and
highly carved walnut upper stories, reminiscent of Swiss
chalets. Children played in the clean, well-kept compounds.

By the time we reached Srinagar darkness had fallen,
so we did not see the squalor until the next day when we
ventured into the city. Our driver took us directly to Nedoe's
Hotel, the taxi-terminal, and left us there to find our way
to the houseboats on Nagin Bagh (lake).

Hardly had we alighted from the taxi when hordes of
natives pressed upon us, poking business cards at us and
shouting their offers of every kind of service. Our mention
of Nagin Bagh brought a barrage of offers to take us there
and find "best accommodation."

"You go Nagin Bagh, sahibs? I take you there in my
shikara (taxi-boat). She ver' fine shikara. Only ten rupees
Nagin Bagh."

"See my fine taxi. She take you there twenty minutes.
Nagin Bagh just five mile. Cost you ver' cheap."

"You want houseboat, sahib? I got fine houseboat. I
take you there in my shikara. No extra charge."

"My taxi finest in Kashmir. Get you there quick."

"Razaka Badari! You look for Razaka Badari houseboat? I take you there."

Actually, we were looking for Razaka Badari's houseboats. We had been weeks in correspondence with him
about renting two of his boats. But thinking that this last

hawker was just another seeking our business, we paid no attention to his persistence at first. Then an envelope was poked at me and a soft voice said, "You look for Razaka Badari? I Badari's son. My name Ahmed. I come take you to houseboat. See, here is your letter."

I recognized my own handwriting on the envelope.

"It's all right," I said to the others. "This must be our man."

"Follow me," the Indian said as he gathered up our paraphernalia and put it in the end of a long gondola-like boat where three scantily clad natives waited with heart-shaped paddles to take us the rest of the way.

We stretched out on embroidered velvet pillows. Soothed by the gentle rhythm of the paddles dipping into the water, we glided into the night. Above us the sky was full of stars. On the shores around us we could see the flickering lights of houseboats moored along the lake's edge. Low voices mumbled in the recesses of obscure shapes moving by in the dark. Tiny glass bangles, hanging from the roof of our shikara, tinkled in the soft breeze.

Fifteen minutes later the boat drew up in front of a dimly lit houseboat, with a tiny shikara tied up to its porch. "This *Astrea,* memsahibs' houseboat, said Ahmed. "Sahibs' boat is *Lancashire.* She moored behind cook boat."

"We'll get the girls settled first," Marty said, "then investigate our quarters."

John and Marty, with Ahmed's help, unloaded our bags on the porch, then carried them into the living room.

"Oh, no!" I cried, as we walked into the *Astrea.* "I can't stand it. We're not in India. We're right back in a Georgetown flat." In the dim light of a single hanging low-watt bulb the interior of the houseboat looked cold and drab and terribly middle-class American.

Taking a quick glance around, John said, "Not exactly the Mayflower or even the Burlington. But I guess it will have to do for the next three weeks."

"Before you guys leave we'd better make plans for tomorrow," I suggested. "How about a tour of the town?"

"Count me out if it's a morning tour," Lou said. "I for one need a decent night's sleep."

"O.K. by us," John said. "We'll join you for a late breakfast on your deck, then take it from there."

"Sounds good. See you tomorrow. Sweet dreams!"

We had expected the *Astrea* to be gaudy, exotic, and mysterious, with bright Indian prints at the windows, floors covered with gay tiles or sisal carpeting, chairs of carved walnut, and little tables inlaid with mother-of-pearl. Instead we found an ugly floral three-piece overstuffed "suite," a Sears knee-hole desk against one wall, and three Maxfield Parrish prints hung at ceiling height.

The next day, however, when a bearer brought us a 75-watt bulb and a bouquet of marigolds and asters, the *Astrea* seemed almost cheerful. With our own little jitney tied up at our wee front porch and two stalwart companions nearby to squire us, we would be happy here for the duration of our leave.

I could hardly wait to try out the little shikara. "Let's go into town tomorrow," I said to John. "I want to see if this little skiff is as easy to paddle as my Old Town at home."

"Maybe we can even rig her up to sail, and take advantage of an occasional breeze to rest our arms," offered John, who had won day sailing races on Lake Erie.

Like hundreds of their kind moored on the many lakes of Srinagar, the *Astrea* and the *Lancashire* (pronounced Lancasher) where John and Marty bunked, were long, low, flat-bottomed, flat-topped wooden boats, entered from the water by two steps leading up to a tiny front porch. Beyond the porch, in a straight line, lay the living room, dining room with serving pantry, and three bedrooms with "baths." With no running water, we felt like pioneers as we bathed in the round metal tubs and made do without flush toilets. Around the outside of the boat a narrow board walkway allowed the bearers access to all rooms via the windows. This was especially handy for the sweeper, who carried off the "night soil" several times a day.

Razaka Badari, our landlord and cook, was of high caste. Tall, white bearded, dignified and usually gentle, he never learned to speak English. But he was vociferous in his own language as he berated the sweeper. Subhan, age seventeen, was translator for his father. Tall like his father, bright and observant, he became our guide for sightseeing and shopping, pretending to get reduced prices for us from the Srinagar merchants. Ahmed, head bearer, worked with his father to direct the other servants and to serve our meals. These three lived on the cook boat out back, with unseen wife-mother and younger siblings. From somewhere outside came a paniwallah, who brought steaming water for our baths, and a funny little sweeper, who tended the "toilets" as he mumbled to himself.

Our houseboats were moored on Nagin Bagh, a narrow lake about two miles long and surrounded by low mountains. The *Astrea* floated parallel to the shore in the shade of a huge chinar tree that spread a canopy over our deck in the slanting rays of the afternoon sun. Across the bagh the snow-capped Himalayas, their heads hidden in the clouds, formed a picture-book backdrop for an ancient Hindu temple, whose gold-leafed exterior reflected sunlight back to us.

The *Astrea's* broad, flat top was a wonderful spot for viewing the passing parade on the water below. Its pleasant sunny deck, reached by an open outside stairway from below, became our daytime lounge, with its wicker furniture, foam pads, and live potted plants. On nice days we had lunch and tea out there. With Coppertone-smeared bodies, Lou and I munched on tomato sandwiches and scones as we gathered Florida tans in the fall sunlight.

From this rooftop aerie we watched the water-peddlers with their enticing wares. First to arrive at our front steps were the flower boats. Smart young salesmen offered the rarest of blooms for memsahib's flower bowls, "the choicest selection in Kashmir" of marigolds, stock, cockscomb, and bachelor's buttons. "Just one rupee per bunch for you, memsahib." Each day we filled the house with fresh flowers.

Then came the other peddlers. The fur trader enticed us with leopard skins, red fox jackets, broadtail vests, and great white coats of soft, thick, luxuriant snow lynx and ermine. The shawl peddler unfolded white pashmina shawls and soft cashmere wraps. The cobbler came by with house slippers and thong sandals and plush fur-lined scuffs in red, green, and dark blue velvet.

The little boy with papier-mâché boxes lured me down from the deck to examine his wares. "Such delicate flowers on those tiny jewel boxes," I said. "I'll have to have at least four to take home. And how can I resist those plaques with Mogul princes on horseback shooting tigers and bears?" I didn't. I bought three on the spot.

When the confectioner's boat came by, Lou, as usual, took charge.

"Close your eyes, Lib," she said. "Here comes temptation. I'll engage the little boy in conversation for a while, then send him packing."

"But surely one little piece of sea foam won't hurt me. See how daintily he fishes it out with tongs. His fingers never touch the sweets."

"Don't you dare encourage him," Lou admonished. "You know we've been told to lay off native food."

"But my supply of Hershey bars is nearly gone. I don't have enough to last even a week. A few pieces of sea foam or fondant or even glazed nuts would tide me over until I can get to town."

Lou was adamant. "Not on your life! Not while I'm your roommate. I refuse to nurse you through dysentery. So shape up and be strong."

Then she threw a rupee to the little peddler below and shouted, "No sweets for memsahibs. Jaldi! Jaldi jao right now, before other memsahib weakens."

"You didn't have to be so ugly to the little boys," I said as the confectioner's shikara drifted away. "Jaldi jao is awfully strong and certainly not ladylike. What will they think of American memsahibs?"

"Probably not much. But I don't think they'll bother us again."

I loved the variety of transport we had in Kashmir, including our own, sturdy feet. When we were flush with time and money we occasionally made a trip by taxi-shikara. In the early days we loved going by tonga, which gave us time to enjoy the fresh air and the rural aspect of Srinagar. But by the last week, with funds running low, we had to rely on bicycles, our own shikara, and our legs.

Our trips into Srinagar took us along the winding, picturesque canals leading to downtown, six miles away. Willows and Lombardy poplars bordered the waterways. Carved walnut dwellings clung like fungus to the steep sides of the canal walls. All along the way, as though sprouting from the very wood of the dwellings, strings of flowering vines trailed down to greet the lilies and lotus that clogged the shallow waters. In the center of the bagh, concessionnairés had cleared a large open space around a wooden float for swimming and tying up boats.

One day John and I paddled through the winding canals to do some shopping on the Bund, but the shops were closed. The streets were hung with bright flags and pennants. Cheering bystanders, decked out in finery, shouted at the parade of the maharajah's fine cavalry horses,

"I wonder what's going on," I said to John.

"Probably a festival day for a Hindu god."

"But I don't see any children waving flags or fakirs squatting alongside."

Then we spotted an American car carrying the reigning prince, his wife, and his son waving to the silent bystanders. It was the maharajah's birthday.

September raced by as we sunned on our top-deck patio, sailed and paddled in our little shikaras, swam from the floating pier, played tennis at the Srinagar Club, and enjoyed cocktail hours with new British friends. At night we danced and played bridge at the club or took in the shows at the Srinagar nightclubs. But my favorite time was after dark when John and I lolled like royalty in a velvet-padded shikara, counted shooting stars, and listened to the rhythmic plash of heart-shaped paddles dipping into the lagoons.

The Leopard Cape

$\mathcal{I}$ loved to window shop along the Bund in downtown Srinagar. Bargaining was great fun with the Muslim and Hindu proprietors of Suffering Job, Honest John, and Profit David. The latter, prosperous purveyor of furniture, rugs, and special services to tourists (whom he despised) intrigued me. His English was fluent and expressive, his turn-of-mind philosophical, and his sense of humor almost Western in flavor. He soon accepted the fact that not all Americans were millionaires, and that not all females could be hoodwinked by a smooth sales pitch.

Most Kashmiri merchants were masters of the subtle swindle. Their favorite tactics were bait and switch, covering up the price tag, exaggeration, and sometimes outright lying, or professing not to have change for a 100-rupee note. They were shrewd observers of human nature and played upon human weaknesses and desires, especially on females, by flooding all with compliments. "Come into my shop, pretty memsahib," they would say to us; "Good day, rajah sahib," to the men. Only occasionally did they stoop to whine about their ten hungry children and sick wives at home.

One day as Lou and I were looking for silver bangles and small papier maché boxes, Ramzana, the fur dealer, nabbed us with a broad smile.

"Memsahibs," he shouted, "come in my shop. I have special sale. Everything half price. Only one snow leopard left. Come in, memsahibs, Try on coat. I make you good price."

"But we don't need fur coats," Lou said. "Our next stop is Karachi where we'd roast to death in fur. And we have no way of shipping them back home. We're just looking for small gifts for our friends"

A sucker for fur since age three, when I had rabbit-fur "doggies" on my bonnet, I couldn't resist a peep inside.

The walls and floors were covered with skins of tiger, leopard, black panther, antelope, bear, fox in red and

white, and other exotic beasts. On a table in the corner
mink and foxtails and snippets of sable, ermine, and mar-
tin awaited a buyer who would fashion them into hats,
belts, and collars for cashmere coats.

Ramzana followed my eyes to the lush snow leopard
coat casually slung over the back of a chair. His quick
hands had that elegant garment draped around my shoulders before I could protest. Standing back he eyed me like
a connoisseur.

"Memsahib, is perfect fit," he said. "Just made for you.
Only lady so tall, so elegant can wear it. You must have
it."

"Don't tempt me," I said, as I surveyed my "elegance"
in the ancient mirror. "You know perfectly well I'm not
going to buy it."

"I cut price in half for you. Two thousand rupees, to
clear out shop."

"You're a thief," I said. "You know I don't have that
kind of money. Two thousand rupees is over six hundred
dollars."

Actually, the asking price for this rare coat was a bargain. At home it would have brought double that amount.
Though I really didn't have that kind of money, I was
hooked. My eyes wandered to a back wall where several
leopard skins hung, one of which was over six feet long.
Tan and dark brown had always been my favorite color
combination for winter clothes. Maybe I could squeeze
out a hundred rupees for a leopard hat, if Ramzana would
make it up for me before I left.

Ramzana unhooked a large skin and caressed the soft
fur. "Feel how soft the fur, memsahib," he said, as he
draped the skin over my arm. "This is finest leopard. All
yours for 500 rupees, to clear out my shop."

The wily Indian could tell from my facial expression
how much I coveted the skin. "Just to think about it overnight," he said. "I put it back for you 'til tomorrow." He
smiled. He knew I'd be back.

At dinner that night John and I discussed the pros
and cons of the purchase. John made up my mind. "Go

ahead and get it, Lib," he said. "Think what it would cost you back home. Have it made into a cape. It will be stunning on you and you can wear it forever, beginning next Saturday night at the club. I'll even get out my dress twills and we'll have a fancy dinner before the dance."

"And all us Red Cross girls will be green with envy," Lou said.

"I'll be the proudest pilot in Kashmir," John concluded. "And if you run out of cash, I'll finance you for the rest of our leave."

The next day John and I walked away from Ramzana's shop with a heavy bundle of pure luxury—a hip length, satin lined leopard cape, a Russian style leopard hat, and enough leftover bits and pieces to trim a half-dozen suits and coats.

But that isn't the end of the story.

A decade later Ramzana and Profit David showed up again, but this time not in person. I chanced upon them in Rumer Godden's 1954 novel, *Kingfishers Catch Fire*. Both had had been her friends when she had lived alone on a mountain near Srinagar in September of 1944, the same time that I had been there. That novel brought the Kashmiri merchants back to life for me.

After I returned home I wore the leopard cape a few times, until it seemed too formal for my casual life on wildlife refuges. I gave it to my niece, Julia, then at Vassar. In 2002, when she read this chapter of my book, she wrote from California: "I loved reading this story of how you came by the leopard cape you gave me. It didn't fit well, so I had it remade in N.Y.C. while at Vassar. Alas, I had only one or two occasions where I could wear it. Wearing fur in California, especially from an endangered animal, is taboo. But I still have the cape. I think it would be fun to take a picture of you in it now."

Shalimar and Gulmarg

One afternoon John and Marty hired a taxi-shikara to take us to the famous Shalimar Gardens on a lake seven miles distant from Nagin. En route to the gardens our shikara had to plow through a thicket of huge dark green leaves that covered the lake's surface.

"What are those amazing leaves?" Lou asked. "They're as big as the elephant ears we have in Florida."

"They lotus, memsahib," our boatman said.

"But where are the big blossoms? I thought lotus were like our water lilies at home."

"Flowers gone now, memsahib. They bloom in summer."

Then I spied something peeping out from under the leaf cover.

"Look over there," I said, pointing to a lone, scraggly, off-white lily amid a cluster of seedpods. We paddled over to examine it.

"So that's what a lotus looks like," John said. "I could swear it's a plain old water lily."

"Pick some seeds," Marty said, "and we'll test out the Ulysses legend."

"You try it," Lou said. "I prefer to stay alert, in case you go into a coma."

"I'll stand with you, Lou," I said. Then to the men, "And don't you dare call us chicken."

John and Marty munched a few of the tasteless brown seeds, hoping to experience the sweet forgetfulness of the Greek myth. But alas, no lethargy or strange sensations overcame them.

Before we cleared the lotus thicket and moved into clear water, our shikara-wallah said, "Now I make you hats to keep sun away." Slashing through the water with a fearsome gurka knife, he brought up two huge fluted lotus leaves. Deftly he cut off the stems, which he used as pins to draw the rounded back edges of the leaf together. Then he placed the charming creations on our heads, the fluted leaf-fronts shading our eyes. We wore these fetching chapeaux the rest of the day, much to the amusement of other boat travelers on the bagh.

As we approached the Shalimar Gardens we sang "Pale Hands I Loved," anticipating exotic blossoms along winding lanes, at least as lovely as the azaleas and camellias of our own Magnolia Gardens in South Carolina.

What a letdown when we alighted at a series of stair-step pools rising to a tiny drab temple on top of a small hill. We climbed through long-dead weeds and knee-high grass to the temple, mirrored in the still, silent top basin. Had we arrived earlier in the day we might have found a caretaker to turn on the famed fountains for us. Now the pools were lifeless.

"Looks like the caretaker has gone on vacation," John said. "I keep forgetting that the tourist season is over."

"Not to mention the fact that this is wartime," I added.

The next day we headed for Gulmarg, a mountain resort high in the mountains. Our dwindling funds did not allow the luxury of a taxi for this long trip, so we traveled native style in a second-class bus, vintage 1920.

In mid-morning we boarded our transport in downtown Srinagar. Squeezing our way along the narrow center aisle of the ancient vehicle, we found space on a hard wooden bench, with almost no legroom. Soon barefoot men in dhotis and a few women in cheap white voile saris crowded six deep into the seats, double the bus's capacity. Standees clogged the center aisle, some clutching each other for support while others sat on big bundles. A few hardy souls climbed onto the exterior of the bus and held on for dear life.

"It's a good thing we got here early," John said. "I don't think you girls would cotton to joining the wogs outside."

"Oh, I don't know," I said, "I think I could manage to hang on. Compared to abandon-ship drill, it doesn't look too hard."

In addition to driver and conductor, our crew boasted a co-pilot, a funny little man with droopy eyes who rode in the doorstep and hopped out every few miles to add water to the radiator and crank the vehicle. In twenty-two miles we stopped once for gas, twice to load passengers, once for customs, and ten times to add water. The 27-mile ride took two hours.

We still had a five-mile climb up the mountain to Gulmarg. For this last leg of our journey we hired ponies to take us up the steep, slippery trail through a spectacular evergreen forest. We shivered in the late September chill and adjusted our breathing to the thin air of the high altitude (10,000 feet). The long trek up the mountain nearly did us in, for none of us was strong in the saddle, especially English type.

"What a relief!" Lou said as we plunked down on the hotel veranda where hot tea and biscuits awaited us. "This could almost convert me to tea drinking. Even coffee never tasted this good."

Revived, we walked around the cluster of shops, which, along with the hotel, make up the village of Gulmarg, now empty of customers in the off-season. Behind the old clapboard hotel the snow-capped Himalayas cast eerie shadows—a stylized painting in blue and white. Then the midday mountain drizzle grayed the scene.

"Time to saddle up old Betsey," John said, "if we want a canter before the rain hits full force. I for one would like to see what this old nag could do on that level path out front."

"D'accord!" I said as we mounted our steeds and took off around the hotel.

The sky became overcast. Then rain poured down in cold sheets. Our return ride down the mountain took an hour as we slithered and stumbled along the rock strewn muddy trail. We all joined Lou in shouting "Hallelujah!" when we saw the bus waiting at the terminal. We just had time to wolf down bowls of fresh strawberries before the bus pulled out.

Back at our houseboats we learned that no rain had fallen there but that in the mountains it is a daily occurrence.

Lou summed up the day for us all: "A wonderful experience," she said, still shivering in her cashmere sweater. "I wouldn't have missed it for anything in the world. But I don't want to do it again."

Sky Watchers

The maharajah's private airport looked frightening: no runway markers, no signal tower, no radio devices— just an open field knee-high in brown grass and weeds. Its only building was a large white hanger, with no one around except an old Indian caretaker who didn't speak English.

A few days before John and Marty had gone into town to make arrangements for our return trip down the mountain to Rawalpindi then on to Delhi. Rumor had it that the taxi drivers had already exhausted their petrol rations and no more would be available for another two weeks. All seats on the sole bus had been reserved weeks before. Already a backlog of 200 British personnel on leave awaited transport.

We began to get alarmed. John and Marty faced possible fines or court martial if they overstayed their leave. We were in no financial position to offer bribes. John had seen the British provost marshal, who at first assured us standing room on an open lorry. But this was cancelled because of landslides on the road down the mountain.

Only one possible means of exit was left, and luck alone would determine whether it would be offered to us. During our stay in Kashmir we had frequently seen planes flying over the bagh. We had met British generals and American colonels who had flown into Kashmir in private planes, but currently had no connections with any of them. We thought it worth a try to go out to the airport and thumb a ride. So we packed up our bags, spent thirty of our fast-dwindling rupees for a taxi, and drove to the airport.

Today the hangar was shut up tight and no one was around except an old Indian caretaker who didn't speak English. With no shelter from the sun, we squatted on a charpoi (string bed) leaning up against the wall and scanned the blazing blue sky for a flying speck.

"I'm going to stretch my legs," Lou said as she strolled over to the far end of the hangar to examine the wind-stripped roster of incoming planes.

"Would you believe it," she called. "Nineteen planes have dropped in here this month."

"That's encouraging," Marty said. "Let's hope today will see one more."

"In the meantime," I said, "let's play some bridge."

Sitting cross-legged on the parched grass, we played four rubbers with the two decks I had remembered to tuck into my overnight case. The game was a real challenge without table or chairs. A light wind from the north sent us scurrying halfway across the runway for the dummy.

As the afternoon wore on, and the sun got hotter, we got tired and cranky. To ease our aching legs, we walked the perimeter of the compound. Our shoes became dusty and our ankles scratched from prickly weeds.

Again we sat against the hangar wall, cursing our fate as the sun sank behind snow-capped peaks. With each gust of wind, we cocked our ears to hear the distant whir of a plane engine. But nothing flew into Srinagar that day. At dusk we telephoned for a tonga to take us back to town, got rooms at a third-rate hotel, and hoped for better luck next day.

The second day of our wait distinguished itself from the first only by the arrival of two American officers, now making six of us who watched the skies. Another day we waited, and another. By the fifth day we were getting panicky. Already we had overstayed our leaves. John and Marty mentally calculated the size of the deductions from their next paychecks. Among the four of us we had twenty rupees left. We could not spend another night in Kashmir.

About one o'clock on the fifth day we thought we heard a plane. Our first impulse was to rush out and scan the skies, but we had done that often, and been fooled. We nonchalantly kept our places on the charpoi. Soon we saw a large bird in the sky and welcomed the roar of twin engines. A few minutes later a Dakota (C-47) bearing the insignia of the Canadian Air Force glided up to the hangar. It was a fairly large plane, able to carry at least fifteen passengers.

"There'll be room for all of us," Lou said.

Three men got off the plane. The pilot got the warmest welcome of his life, I'm sure, as Lou and I threw our arms around him and kissed him on the cheek.

"What a relief! You're a Godsend. We've been stranded here for five days and we're dead broke. Now we can make it back to Delhi."

"Wait a minute," the pilot said. "I can't promise you a ride back. I came to pick up my group captain and his party. He's the one to make the decision."

"Hmm," Lou said. "Just what kind of fellow is this group captain?"

"He's youngish, but very much the boss of things," the pilot said.

"How many people does he have with him?" I inquired.

"Eight other officers and all their hunting equipment."

"Then couldn't you take the four of us? We don't weigh very much and we can sit on bags."

"As far as I'm concerned, I'd take you all. But I haven't a thing to say about it. You have to get permission from Captain Cameron."

"What time is he due here?"

"He told me to pick him up about 2:00. I guess they'll be along shortly."

We sat down again to wait.

At 2:30 two taxis and a private car drove up in front of the hangar. Two men, two girls, and a woman climbed out of the car. A half dozen uniformed men piled out of the taxis and began unloading quantities of suitcases, bedding rolls, golf clubs, tennis racquets, and fishing rods. The pilot went over to talk with the captain.

From the deference of the woman and the "Yes, suhs" of the airmen we judged that the tall, blond fellow covered with ribbons was the group captain. The women had come to see the men off, with handshakes and smiles and invitations to return, while the officers thanked them for "a jolly good time."

John suggested that Lou and I make ourselves a little more apparent to the captain. "Just mosey up to the group and ask which one is Captain Cameron. It'll flatter him for a stranger to know his name. Then put on your sweetest smile and ask him for a ride."

Neither Lou nor I looked alluring after our five-day sun bake, but we figured that Canadians liked their women healthy and that the captain might overlook our peeling noses.

We didn't have to tap Captain Cameron on the back to get his attention. Seeing us coming, he was more than eager to pass the time of day with us.

"Good afternoon," I said sweetly. "Which of you is Group Captain Cameron?"

"That's me," he said.

"Oh!" I appeared surprised. "I expected an older man. I always think of group captains and generals as gray haired. I didn't know they made them young too." The captain smiled broadly.

"I'm Libby Chitwood of the American Red Cross. This is Lucia Cortlandt. We're stranded for a ride to Delhi and wondered if you'd take us along."

"Well, now," said the Captain, ogling both of us from head to toe. "I think we might find a place for you. Where are your bags?"

"Over there," I said, pointing to the mound near the hangar. "We've some friends who also need a ride. The pilot says you're not heavily loaded."

Captain Cameron surveyed the four men standing by the hangar. Then he frowned and shook his head.

"I couldn't possibly take all of them," he said. "You must remember that there are only twelve seats in this plane."

"They'd be happy to sit on the floor," Lou put in.

The captain was adamant. Blowing out his cheeks in a funny self-conscious way, he blustered, "No! No, they can't come along. There's only room for you two."

"But can't you squeeze in just two more? The others can wait for another plane. Our two American friends have already overstayed their leave waiting to get out of here. They'll get a court martial if they don't report back to-day."

Captain Cameron colored deeply. He made the blowing sound again, saying with finality, "I will take you two girls. The rest will have to stay. Now, if you'll have the men load your bags, we'll be off right away. I must be in Delhi at six at the latest."

"Well," I said, not too pleasantly, "if that's the case, we can't accept your offer. We certainly aren't going to leave John and Marty when they've been so swell to us." With that, Lou and I walked forlornly back to the group at the hangar.

The Canadian officers began to board. Just as Captain Cameron was about to join them he turned around. He hesitated a moment, as though in conference with his conscience. Then, in a voice full of irritation he shouted, "Oh, come along then. Bring your two friends if you must."

We were already halfway in the plane before he finished speaking. The captain directed John and Marty to sit on bedding rolls in the back. He found a place for Lou beside a good-looking first lieutenant. Taking me up front, he helped me into a special seat reserved for himself, then sat in a smaller seat beside me.

For the first hour of the flight Captain Cameron engaged me in animated conversation. "Wasn't it lucky," he said, "that you're going to Delhi, because I'm going to be there for several days too! Will you go out to dinner with me? I would like to introduce you to my Division Commander." The net result of his entreaties was my polite, but emphatic, "No, I am already tied up for tonight. No, I can't break the date with my former CO."

His final entreaty to me was, "Would you at least write to me?"

That evening our sunburned, weary, and jubilant party of four dined at the Imperial Hotel. The next day Lou and I excitedly boarded a C-47, off to a new assignment on India's western shore: KGA Hall, the big city club in Karachi.

Rawalpindi: jumping off town
to Kashmir, Sept. 1944

Kashmir: Libby falling
off bike at left.

Kashmir: *Astrea*, houseboat on
the bog in front of chinar tree,
showing cookboat.

Kashmir: Ahmed and Subhan,
bearers on houseboat,
sons of Rasaka Bedari.

Kashmir: houses along
Dal Lake in Srinagar.

Rasaka Bedari
houseboat
owner cook.

Kashmir: Libby and
John Stewart.

Under the chinar tree.
Libby in Kashmiri sheep-
skin hat, lavender halter,
and yellow and brown
Indian print shorts.

Part Five

Unwanted Assignment in Karachi

"May God give you grace to risk something big
for something good, grace to remember that
the world now is too dangerous for anything
but truth and too small for anything but love."

William Sloan Coffin

Night Flight Across the Desert

Our leave over, Lou and I reported to Red Cross regional headquarters in Agra for reassignment. I had asked for the post of program director at Agra, Lucia for the big city club in Delhi. After seven months upcountry, we felt entitled to some of the benefits of city life for a change. Besides, it seemed a good idea to spend the next few months near the central travel arteries, so as not to lose complete contact with our Hump-flying friends coming through Delhi. The last place we wanted to be was in Karachi, a western coastal city almost 2000 miles from Jorhat. Assignment there would guarantee loss of contact with our friends in Assam.

Assured by the Red Cross regional supervisor that our requests were receiving favorable consideration, Lou and I spent the two-day wait making plans for our new assignments. Lou mapped out a whole month's program of activities for a large city club, while I mentally furnished the one-room apartment I expected to occupy in Agra.

On the evening of the second day our orders came out. We were both assigned to Karachi's KGA Hall. Scheduled for flight that very evening out of Agra, we would miss the planned moonlight taxi trip to see the Taj Mahal. But we did catch a glimpse of that "wonder of the world" from a tiny window of the C-46 that carried us to Karachi.

It was a beautiful night for flying—calm, clear, and cool at 3,000 feet. As we approached the Taj our pilot obligingly dropped altitude to 1,000 feet and twice circled the marble mausoleum. In the soft haze of dusk the Taj appeared much smaller than I had expected. From my bird's eye view I could distinguish only the outline of this greatest of India's temples.

As we passed beyond the mineretted shrine I was reminded of what an American soldier had told me one day in Assam, as we heatedly discussed the relative merits of Indian and American architecture. My learned companion maintained that the Empire State building far surpassed the Taj architecturally and practically. He could see little beauty in a jewel, which in the cutting had cost the lives of many thousands of Indian people. He could see little utility in a shrine, which stood empty and unused by worshippers century after century. He summed up his whole feeling about the shrine in this way: "The Taj Mahal is a diamond necklace on the wrinkled neck of a mean, ugly old dowager. The Empire State building is a rhinestone necklace on the soft bosom of a beautiful young girl."

We soon became chummy with the crew. Our pilot was a chunky, tough looking type, assisted by a tall, skinny copilot with pendulous lower lip, receding chin, and lifeless eyes. The third member of the crew was a short, rotund radio operator by the name of Jake, who took special pleasure in keeping us girls on pins and needles.

As the plane gained altitude, I noticed a few sparks coming from under the wings. We increased our speed and climbed into cruising range. The sparks burst into fast-flying streams of fire. Frankly, I was afraid. Lucia, always confident and more experienced in air travel than I, insisted there was no danger.

"After all," she assured me, "they're just exhaust flames going off in the air like fireworks. Don't worry about them. Sit back and relax." Her explanation, however, didn't relieve me, for I had seen gasoline loaded into those very wings that were now trailing sheets of fire.

About this time Jake came back to keep us company. Running competition with the noisy engines, we gave him our usual Red Cross routine: "What's your name? Where ya from? Wha'ja do before the war? How d'ya like India?"

To the second question he countered, "I'm from Texas, sister, and you ain't seen nothin' 'til you seen a Texas moonlight!"

We dropped banalities and got down to the business of fact finding. Jake was most obliging in his answers, almost too obliging. "Yes, the plane was a pretty good plane. It has made only one emergency landing since I have been its radio operator. ...I guess we're going about 300 mph, which is her regular cruising speed. ...The pilot and co-pilot are swell guys. We've been flying together for four months now. ...Yes, we have an automatic pilot, but the radio went on the blink a few miles back. ...No, I am not a mechanic and could not fix the plane in an emergency. ...No, that occasional sputter in the engines did not mean we were running out of gas. ...Yes, you are right. That exhaust flame does not bode well."

Leaving us this last tasty tidbit, Jake hooked on a crooked smile and withdrew to the cockpit. Lou passively chewed up the morsel and swallowed it. I rolled it about on my tongue. Just what would one do if the plane blew up? Would a parachute help in such an emergency? I walked back and fingered the small pile of 'chutes lying on the floor in the rear of the plane. But what good would a parachute do, I wondered, if you didn't even know how to put the thing on? Lucia sat silent and stoic in her bucket seat.

A few minutes later, Jake returned. Switching on the light as he came into the cabin, he walked to the rear of the plane, sniffed the air, and shook his head. Then he ambled over to a window, wrinkled up his nose, and shook his head again. Finally, he came over to where I was sitting opposite Lou and tapped me on the shoulder.

"Do y'all smell that gas?" he said. His expression was sinister. I leaned over toward the window and sniffed. I smelled nothing.

Pulling open a window ventilator, Jake beckoned me closer. "Get a whiff of that," he commanded, pushing my face into the air stream that blew in from the open vent. I sniffed again. This time I caught the odor of raw gas coming from the same general area as the exhaust sparks still streaming below the wings.

Pulling back from the window, I shouted to Jake in a weak voice, "I smell the gas now. What does it mean? Will it do any harm?"

"It won't do any good," he replied without a smile, as he walked back to the cockpit. Now I was positive that the inevitable explosion was almost upon us.

During this little by-play Lucia had gone to sleep. I was tempted to awaken her and apprise her of her fate, but my better judgment told me that she would not appreciate my concern if nothing really was the matter. I envied Lou her self-confidence and relied on it now more than the prattle of the radio operator.

We saw Jake once again before the flight ended. Just as our engines were kicking up a last huge backfire, he appeared in the cabin doorway and uttered this parting shot: "There are only four parachutes and there are five of us aboard."

But by this time we realized that Jake was what my father used to call a great "whacker," which in ordinary parlance means "fibber." Evidently he got his kicks by watching unattainable females quail under his dire pronouncements.

About 2:00 am I dozed off, finally convinced that the good Lord was responsible for us from now on. I don't know how long I had slept when I felt someone tugging at my coat sleeve. The interior lights were on. Beside me sat both the pilot and copilot. I gasped to see both these men in the cabin. I had visions of that stupid Jake gripping the controls up front and dashing us all to extinction in the desert, where the jackals and buzzards would soon make bare bones of us. Yet the engines still rumbled smoothly and the plane appeared to be on course.

"Good gracious!" I gasped. "You're surely not letting that radio operator pilot the plane!"

"Why, of course not!" was the nonchalant reply.

"Then who, for heaven's sake, is driving this plane?"

"George."

"George? George who? I didn't see anyone else when we boarded."

"Why, George, the automatic pilot," replied two voices in unison. I wilted with relief.

"You needn't worry about George," the pilot assured me. "He's the best driver in the world. Besides, it's a clear night, no headwinds, and the air is as smooth as glass over the desert."

An hour later we spotted the Karachi beacon light in the distance. We landed as softly as a feather falling on water, and I was as happy as any sailor long at sea to be on solid ground again.

Looking for a Bed

You and I were exhausted after the trip from Kashmir to our new assignments in Karachi. On our arrival before dawn the airbase was bustling with activity with Jeeps, six-by-sixes, and gasoline trucks. Nearby we saw a corps of medical technicians transferring wounded men on litters from two ambulances to a C-54. From all corners of the field we could hear the roar of planes warming up for take-off. The rhythmic flash of the beacon, the red glow of runway markers, the bright gleam of the terminal lights, and the moonlit sky conspired to transport us momentarily back to the busy desert airport south of Los Angeles.

As we rode the seven miles from the air base to Karachi in an open reconnaissance car, the California illusion vanished. The terminal lights faded, and the warm-up hum died away in the distance. Save for our American driver, we were alone in a strange dark land where jackals howled in the night. Our eyes soon adjusted to the dark, helped by the moonlight. We could make out the contours of the terrain. Miles of treeless flat countryside stretched before us, broken only by occasional groups of native huts.

When the landscape revealed vague rectangular shapes close to the road, we realized that we had reached the city. Karachi lay like a monolith, silent, sinister, and dark. Luckily a native driver awaited us at the airport to take us to our hotel. Moonlight cast eerie shadows as the city slept. A stray dog howled. A prowling cat scurried across the road. The hum of the taxi motor did not arouse the beggars sleeping on the sidewalks.

Our driver was not familiar with Karachi at night. In the unlighted city we rode the quiet streets for forty-five minutes until finally, by a process of elimination known only to him, the driver found our billet. The Killarney Hotel stood back from the street, its wide yard enclosed by a high cement wall with iron grillwork gates. Luckily one of the gates opened.

Our heels clicked against the tile floors as we entered the barn-like lobby. In the dim light of a single bulb over the check-in desk, we could distinguish several dark leather-covered sofas set against the plastered walls. The woodwork was varnished walnut. A sleeping Indian man in European attire slouched in a chair behind the desk, his head and arms on the counter. Near his head was a night bell. This we tapped briskly several times.

Like a jack-in-the-box the desk clerk jumped to his feet, saluted, and said, "Good evening, memsahibs. You want room?"

"That is the general idea," Lucia said dryly. "Or if you haven't a room, beds will do."

Noticing the insignias on our uniforms, the clerk said, "Red Cross burramemsahib, she no tell me you come."

"Then obviously she will be surprised to see us," Lou said. "In the meantime, we'd like a room with two beds and a bath."

"But memsahib, Red Cross room all filled up. We ver' crowded."

Two little patches of pink appeared on Lucia's unrouged cheeks and gradually diffused into a rosy glow covering her face and neck. There was no warmth in the brittle voice that addressed the man behind the desk.

"My dear man, do you have the gall to stand there and deny us the privilege of spending the rest of the night in bed? Now, just suppose you get out from there right now and show us to a room, but quick!"

"Ver' well, memsahib. I show you room." He darted from behind the counter and picked up our bags. "You share room with 'Merican officer memsahib. She stay in big room second floor."

A moment later Lou and I were trudging behind him up two flights of stairs and down a dimly lit corridor to Room 223. The clerk put down our bags in the hallway before the door, saluted again, then silently disappeared.

Since we had been given no key, we tried the doorknob. The door seemed to be bolted from the inside. I couldn't help thinking that waking a strange girl out of a sound sleep is nasty business and quickly decided to let Lou do the dirty work. After all she was an old hand at it from her months of getting me up in the mornings.

Lucia knocked gently, a firm but feminine knock. We heard a small sound inside, as if someone on a straw mattress had stirred.

Then a woman's voice whispered hoarsely, "Is that you again? For heaven's sake, go away. You know you cannot come in here. If you come back again, I'll scream and make it really embarrassing for you. Don't you dare knock at my door again!"

Lou and I exchanged glances. The whisper seemed to have come from an angry middle-aged female with an unmistakably American accent. We were bursting with curiosity to see the owner of that voice.

"Please don't be alarmed," Lucia said in her tone of voice reserved for children and servants. "We've come to share your room."

With an audible sigh, "Oh, I thought you were someone else. Who are you and what do you want?"

"We're two Red Cross girls who've just arrived in Karachi. The other Red Cross room is full, so the clerk sent us up here to share your room. We're awfully sorry to bother you, but we really do need to hit the sack." Lucia's voice was candy sweet.

"But these aren't Red Cross quarters. They're on the floor below. Why must you disturb me in the middle of the night?"

Lou's voice turned to vinegar. "As I told you, the Red Cross room is full. And you have two extra beds in your room. We did not come here deliberately to disturb you. But there's a war on, in case you hadn't noticed, and we're tired and dirty. So, if you'll please open that door, we'd like to come to bed."

"Well," came the irritated answer, "if that's the way it is, I guess I'll have to let you in."

We heard soft slippers slide across the tile floor, then the click of the light switch and the rasp of the dead bolt. As the door opened, we looked upon a petite middle-aged woman with her hair up in bobby pins and her face covered with cold cream. She inspected us critically for a moment, then smiled a broad welcome.

"Come on in, girls," she said. "It's really quite all right. Sorry to be such a boor, but an adolescent officer has been hounding me all evening and it made me edgy. When you knocked I thought he was outside my door again."

She pointed to a narrow passageway inside the room. "The bath is right over there. There's plenty of hot water. I just got clean towels today, so help yourselves and make yourselves at home. Have a good night's sleep. I'll try not to disturb you when I get up at seven."

Within ten minutes Lou and I were sleeping soundly under olive drab mosquito nets. The next day, two more beds were moved into Room 107 downstairs and we took up residence with three other Red Cross girls.

Tropical Fever

Soon after starting duty at KGA Hall in Karachi I was "awarded" an unexpected and unwanted rest. I awoke before dawn one morning in a sweat, with nausea, fever, and backbreaking pain.

"You look like death," my club director said, as I stumbled into the club a few hours later. "What on earth did you do yesterday?"

"Probably too much sun at Sandspit," I said, my whole body shaking.

"It's sick call for you," Mr. Merritt said. "The airbase bus is just about ready to leave. Get out front as quickly as you can."

I groaned as two GIs loaded me into the bus. Several military hitchhikers going to work kept me company en route. One even held my hand and later came to see me daily at the hospital during my long siege.

In the emergency room I was too miserable to appreciate the handsome Army doctor who took my temperature and questioned me about my recent diet and activity.

"Sorry, sweetheart," the captain said, "sunstroke isn't your problem. Your fever is 103. You've a classic case of dengue fever."

"What in heaven's name is dengue fever? Is it like malaria?"

"Nope. It's a tropical disease, but not as bad as malaria. It doesn't recur after the first bout, but it'll keep you out of action for a while. The locals call it back-break fever."

"Sounds horrendous. How do you suppose I caught it?"

"You didn't catch it, sweetheart. It caught you, in the proboscis of a daytime mosquito. Have you been out on the water recently? This mosquito particularly likes soft succulent female flesh."

As a matter of fact, I had been out on a fishing trip the day before. Phyllis Greenleaf, a Red Cross co-worker, and

I had been fishing and sunning at Sandspit with Bob Shamblen and Tom Lawrence, OSS men who introduced us to Karachi's ocean and restaurant pleasures.

It was mid-October, 1944. We were ten female patients in Ward C at the US Air Force base hospital at Malir, out in the desert near Karachi (now in Pakistan). We were a motley assortment of sick nurses, English volunteers, civilians attached to the military, several young Burmese wives of GIs, an occasional missionary forced out of China or Burma by advancing Japanese troops, and me from the Red Cross. Early on I wrote:

> *I'm in for ten more sleepless nights. Yesterday another Burmese girl delivered a squalling bundle of joy. The other two Burmese girls here, married to American GIs, also have babies. Their husbands have gone home to serve prison sentences for breaking Gen. Stilwell's CBI order about not marrying non-Caucasians. The babies are cute, but they howl all night long.*

Those first few days in the hospital were really rough. Unable to keep anything down, on the fourth day I was introduced to needle food. That first intravenous meal wasn't too painful. I sloughed it off as an adventure. The second was less comfortable, but old hat. Then Captain Corbin, more businesslike than the sick-call doctor, said, "If you don't start tomorrow on regular food, you're in for a long siege with the needle."

"Could we start with fresh limeade?" I said. "I think I might be able to keep that down. If the hospital mess sergeant can't provide it, the girls can bring it from the club."

That did the trick. Within a week my temperature declined, nausea disappeared, and I felt like hopping out of bed.

In the meantime my eyes began to look like those of a cat. Blood tests revealed full-fledged jaundice, which often follows dengue fever. To bring down my elevated icteric, a dose of salts and a tasteless breakfast greeted me each morning. Every four days "Rosie the Riveter" punctured my upper arm and drew out a huge vial of blood, to monitor the icteric.

My skin turned yellow. Catcalls greeted me in the ward. "Hi ya, Chink! Meow, meow! How's our little canary to-day?"

Since the military would not discharge me until I was able to return to work, my blood index had to go down to 4, from its high of 25. I determined to enjoy my incarceration.

We did everything for ourselves there in the nurses' ward: made our own beds (which I hadn't done since leaving home), fetched our bath water, and returned our meal trays to the kitchen.

Hospital food was not calculated to be gourmet, especially for those of us patients on a fat-free no-salt regimen. I trimmed down two dress sizes. Friends called me "Slim." Our schedule of 7:15 breakfast, 11:30 lunch, and 4:30 dinner left us ravenous by late evening. Luckily our visitors supplied goodies for snacks and parties, but no Hershey bars for this chocoholic.

Most of us ambulatory girls spent the daytime hours playing games with the men from other wards, chatting with new friends, and entertaining officers and GIs from former posts on their way back home. Visitors from Karachi and the airbase brought us food and flowers and small gifts from the PX.

Almost anything became an excuse for a late-night celebration. When five officers came out of quarantine, we set up cafeteria-style food tables marked Regular, Bland, Fat-free, and Liquid. One of the officers who had won a lot of money playing gin rummy footed the bill. I wrote home:

> *Incidentally, yesterday I beat this same officer two games and won $250, only we weren't playing for money, darn it!*

Lieutenant Don Newsbiggle, who had been in the bus with me to the hospital in October, was truly "Old

Faithful" throughout my Karachi tour. Each day he brought me a token of his affection—a single blossom, a nonfat snack, and postcards for my album, a bangle bracelet, or a colorful scarf. He asked nothing of me except the acceptance of the nice things he did for me. After my return to work, Don squired me to the city's tourist sites, took me swimming and boating, rode horseback with me, and introduced me to the Gymkhana Club, where we spent many fun evenings. He was my favorite companion until my special corporal came along.

After the initial novelty wore off, boredom set in. But we managed to find duties and fun to keep us upbeat. On November 13, 1944, I wrote:

> *All is quiet in our ward now. I am a little lonesome and forlorn. Last night six of our patients were sent home and we gave them a grand send-off. Some had been waiting a month for transportation, so it was a gala moment when they were finally alerted. All went home on medicals, to be treated at hospitals in the States.*

> *Most of all we miss Sidney, a cute little black-haired Southern nurse with a handsome husband five years her junior, who now lives in France. She had been nearly killed when she fell from a third-story window onto a tile court below. Because her eyes don't yet focus properly, I've been doing a lot of her letters. Today I must write to her husband and tell him how cute she looked when she left.*

As December wore on I got antsy with confinement and finally finagled a pass into town. It was wonderful to put on a dress again and gaze on something besides white hospital beds. The sight of the desert thrilled me. The camels and milling people seemed out of this world. I shopped on Elphinstone Street and had supper at the Red Cross club. The men hadn't forgotten me, and the bearers were most solicitous of my health.

I was ready emotionally, if not physically, to get back to work. Most of my favorites had left the hospital. Final days in Ward C, waiting for my blood index to go down to four, were dull, with no designated duties and no one needing my attention.

One day in late November I accosted Capt. Corbin as he made his rounds. "Please, kind sir," I pleaded, "let me out of this place. I feel great and I'm aching to get back to work. Lying around doing nothing just isn't my thing."

"Your icteric is still over ten,' he said. "I can't take the chance of discharging you just yet."

"But you know that I'm in fine shape except for that darned blood test. I don't even need a convalescent leave."

He pondered a moment, and then said, "Well, I guess that anyone who can dance as you did last night doesn't need a leave."

Two weeks later I happily returned to work, eschewed the offer to goof off another two weeks on sick leave, and immediately started preparations for our Christmas celebration at KGA Hall and the New Year's dance to follow.

Burma Girl

For the three weeks since my arrival at the hospital the private room had lain empty, neat, expectant. When the retching of a malaria patient kept us awake at night, we longed for the solitude of the private room. But there was little chance that any of us ambulants would ever know the peace behind that door.

We had just turned in after a long bull session when a new patient was admitted to Ward C. In the dim glow of the hall light we saw them bearing her stretcher into the private room. She moaned as though she carried within her an alarm set at regular intervals. As the night wore on we timed her cries, increasing in force and frequency. The air inside the ward was hot and heavy. Outside, jackals wailed in the windless night.

The moans became shrieks. Just before dawn we heard the sharp click of a man's heels beating half-time accompaniment to the dull thud of the nurse's rubber soles. Then, as the yellow light of dawn filtered through the screens, we heard a resounding thwack and the feeble cry of a newborn baby.

We wondered who had borne the squalling infant. It seemed somehow incongruous and almost indecent for a baby to be born in an overseas military hospital. When the ward boy brought in our breakfast trays we besieged him with questions: "Who's the gal in the private room? What's her name? How old is she? What's she like? Is the baby a boy or a girl?"

The ward boy was noncommittal, professing ignorance of the case. "How should I know?" he said. "She's probably the wife of a GI. I don't know her name. The baby is a boy. Ask the girl herself if you want more details. She seems to be doing O.K."

From the night nurse we garnered more information. The new mother's name was Maria Teresa Loboya Blankenship. A refugee from the Japanese invasion of Burma, she now lived with her mother and three sisters in Karachi where she had met and married an American sergeant. We could piece together the rest of the story ourselves.

Well acquainted with the CBI theater order forbidding marriage between military personnel and girls of less than three-quarters Caucasian ancestry, we surmised that the Burmese girl and her American lover had eloped. When it became evident that a baby was on the way, the sergeant had had to announce his marriage. The usual steps were taken by the military to punish the offender. Sergeant Blankenship had been immediately packed off to Leavenworth, minus three hard-earned stripes and fifty dollars of his pay. At the same time, the army had seen to it that his wife and baby had medical care. Hence, Teresa, as we always called her after that, now enjoyed the benefits of this American facility.

We were a gregarious bunch at the hospital, friendly and inquisitive. In a matter of minutes we usually weaseled out the history of new patients. The next morning I peeped in the doorway of Teresa's room and said, "Hello! Welcome to the best hospital in the whole CBI." In perfect English, devoid of foreign accent, Teresa thanked me for my greeting and smiled.

Lying there in bed she appeared slight in stature. I judged her to be about seventeen years old. Her complexion was fresh and smooth, more olive toned than yellow. She might have passed for an Hispanic-American except for the gentle slant of her brown eyes, glowing now with happiness and hope as she gazed upon the little bundle cradled in her arms. She held the baby up for me to see— a wrinkled moppet with a mass of fuzzy black hair. The love in her eyes lit up the whole room. After that I went in to chat with her every day.

By the time she left the hospital I had learned a lot about Teresa Blankenship. Born and raised in Burma, of mixed Asian and European ancestry, she spoke with anguish about the pillaging of her home by the Japanese four years before, of the torture death of her Portuguese-English father, and of the rest of the family's escape into

India. The Loboyas had lived well in Burma, in a large house with four native servants. She and her sisters had gone to a missionary school where they had studied English, which she spoke with more grammatical purity and rhetorical elegance than most of us Americans.

In their flight from Burma the Loboyas had managed to salvage enough of their possessions to buy transportation to Karachi where, with the help of friends, the four girls secured clerical jobs in British offices and with the U.S. Army. The girls, their mother, and two Indian servants lived comfortably in a Karachi apartment, with more security than they had known in many years.

Three of the girls had met and married American soldiers, but none had left to join her husband in the States. They had no intention of giving up their comfort and security for the unknown quantity of life in America. Apparently their husbands, now stationed on the other side of the globe, did not push them to change their minds. But Teresa, younger than the others and full of adventure, believed in love that could span the oceans, break down prison bars, and keep her lover constant until she could join him.

On Teresa's bedside table the photograph of a three-stripe sergeant caught my eye. It was an enlarged version of many such photos I had seen in the wallets of soldiers, which were cheaply printed, un-retouched, and mounted in a gray cardboard folder. The pose was full-faced and stiff, as though someone had just shouted "Atten-shun!"

A garrison cap sat too straight across the soldier's forehead above protruding ears. His shoulders were hunched up as though tied in the back with a leather thong. The lad appeared to be about nineteen. His glazed expression was that of innocence or ignorance, I couldn't tell which. Across the lower corner of the picture was scrawled the usual sentimental greeting: "To Teresa, with all my love, Tom."

"He's much handsomer than the picture," Teresa explained as I picked up the folder to take a closer look.

"He's tall and as lithe as a bamboo shoot, but that doesn't show here."

"Where's he from?" I asked, working on a hunch I hoped would prove untrue.

"A state called Texas," Teresa replied. "His father has a big ranch there and they raise cattle and cotton."

"How much do you really know about your husband? How long have you known him? Has he always lived in the Southwest?"

Teresa ignored the first two questions. "A long time," she finally answered. "I guess he was born there, and his parents too. My, it must be wonderful to live all your life in the same place!"

"That depends on the place and the people," I said. "I've seen lots of towns in that part of the country that I'm just as glad not to live in."

"But it must be a wonderful place," Teresa mused. "Tommy says it's just like parts of India—warm and sunny and with jasmine growing in the yard."

"Parts of it are lovely," I said, remembering waxy magnolias in Galveston front yards in May. "But life there is very different from life in India or Burma or anywhere here in the East. Do you plan to go to the States soon?"

"Oh, yes!" she said happily. "Tommy says I'm to come just as soon as he finds a place for us to stay when he gets out of Leavenworth. And that shouldn't take long because he has nearly finished serving his sentence. I'm hoping we can celebrate Christmas together."

"Perhaps you could live with his family for a while. That's what a lot of war brides do until they find a home of their own. Has Tommy's mother written to you?"

"No, not yet. You see, we married quickly and Tommy said we must keep it a secret. He said that American families do not encourage elopements, so for a long time we did not tell his family. They did not even know why he was sent home until a few weeks ago, when he wrote them all about us. He said his mother would write to me. I do hope she likes me. If she does, I might not mind living on that ranch."

I pursued no further questioning that day. Several days later Teresa showed me an envelope addressed to "The wife of Thomas Blankenship, US Air Force Hospital." Splotches of lipstick covered the page she held in her hand, "Just think how lucky I am," she said. "First I marry big Tommy and now I have a little Tommy to take home to him."

I wasn't as convinced as she of the prize she had drawn as a husband. I had a hunch that wasn't getting any weaker with the passage of time. "Did he say anything about your going to the States?"

"No, not in this letter. I guess he just forgot to mention it. But I'm sure he'll write me soon about coming, especially when he knows he has a son."

"Do you really want to go to the States? Would you want to leave your mother and sisters? It's a long way back from there, you know. You probably would never see them again." I wanted to prepare Teresa for what I felt was to be a great disappointment.

Teresa's face darkened for a moment, then brightened again. "Of course I'd hate to leave my mother. But I am young. And I want to be with my husband. Besides, my mother still has my sisters and I'm sure she wants me to live where I'll be happiest. I don't want to bring up my son in India, I want him to be an American." She spoke with spirit.

"That's the way a girl should feel about her husband and her family," I said without real conviction. "Good luck, Teresa. I hope you have good news before the week is over."

Teresa stayed in the hospital for a week after that, repaying the calls we had made to the private room. With no more letters from Tommy, her happy spirit dulled a bit each day. But she never gave up hope.

"It's just the fault of the mail," she would say. "Sometimes no letter for weeks, then a batch of six arrives. But soon I'll have an answer to my cable and when he hears he has a son, I know he'll send for me to come." Teresa kept on believing in Tommy's love, but my faith in the

Texas lad, never strong, dwindled away before the week was out.

The day before she left the hospital Teresa kept to her room, not appearing for her usual morning chat in the ward. I wondered why until the nurse told me that Teresa had finally received a letter from the States. I knew that letter brought bad news even before Teresa read it to me.

In mid-afternoon I tapped at the door of the private room. At first there was no answer. Teresa must be sleeping. Then I heard a low, stifled sob behind the closed door. I knocked again.

"It's me, Trese, Libby. Is there something wrong?" There was still no answer so I gently opened the door and saw her lying on the bed, her face flattened against the pillow. "For goodness sakes, Trese, what's the matter? You mustn't cry like that. It's not good for you and it'll spoil little Tommy's dinner."

Teresa pointed to a letter on the bedside table, the pages crumpled and wet.

"Is Tommy O.K.?" I said. "I hope nothing bad has happened to him?"

"It's not from Tommy," she replied in a toneless voice. "It's from Tommy's mother. She hates me. She hates the baby. And I know she will make Tommy hate me too." Theresa turned over on her back and gazed blankly at the ceiling. Except for the sparkle of recent tears, there was no life in her eyes.

"Perhaps you misunderstood her," I said, trying to convince myself as much as her. "I'm sure no one would want to separate you and Tommy."

"But she does hate me. You read the letter. See for yourself."

Scrawls of blue ink on lined paper told the sad story in pinched and uneven penmanship. It was a short letter, crudely stated, cruelly frank. Mrs. Blankenship didn't want "no yellow trash" in her family, "Now just you get them ideas of coming to the U.S. out of your head, because my son don't aim to have nothing to do with you."

I tried to conceal my resentment of the letter. Teresa watched my expression as I read it. When I had finished, she said, "Tell me, Libby, why does she hate me so? I love her Tommy so much?"

It was a hard question to answer. For a moment I couldn't come up with a response. Teresa was intelligent, tolerant and good. I knew she would never understand the prejudices of such a woman as her husband's mother. But I had to tell her something.

"Some American women," I began after a pause, "are very strange. They believe that their sons should marry only American girls, just as Hindu families insist that their sons take Hindu wives, usually of their parents' choice. That's the kind of woman Tommy's mother is. She wants him to marry an American girl, preferably from her own community. But even if she were different and wanted you to come, I don't believe you'd be happy living as she does."

"What do you mean? His family has a big ranch and a fine house. My Tommy told me so."

"Did he ever show you a picture of his big fine house?"

"No, but he told me all about it. He said it has fourteen rooms and tall white pillars in front, and he said that twenty Negroes work the ranch and take care of the cooking and housework."

"American soldiers talk big," I explained. "And apparently Tommy Blankenship is no different from many of his kind. I doubt he ever saw that house from the inside and I'll wager he never had a servant in his life. His mother's letter sounds more like that of the wife of a poor sharecropper than a well-to-do ranch owner." But Teresa wasn't to be convinced. After all, her Tommy had told her so.

I tried a different approach. "You have a nice apartment here in Karachi, don't you?"

"Yes, five rooms and bath. It's really very comfortable."

"And you like the luxury of servants, don't you, plus the comforts of city life?"

"Of course I do, I couldn't get along without them."

"In Texas you would probably be living way out in the country without any servants at all. You'd have to do the work of a sweeper, cook, ayah, and bearer, plus all the washing and ironing." I waited a moment for Teresa's reply.

"For Tommy I guess I wouldn't mind," she said simply.

"But what about Tommy's parents? Would you like to scrub floors for the woman who wrote you that letter?"

For a moment Teresa was silent. Then she got up and bent over the basket where her baby lay asleep. She looked at him for a long time, her face angelic with love. When she spoke her voice was flat and lifeless. "I don't think little Tommy would like the United States after all. He's got too much of the Orient in him. See how dark his skin is and how slanted his little eyes are. I guess we won't be going to Texas after all."

Her beautiful face was drained of light. But Teresa stood before me calm, resigned, and wise beyond her years.

The Jewel

They brought her into our ward about midnight, a wee wisp of a woman, wizened beyond her years. A convulsive cough and racking asthmatic gasps seemed to predict a short stay in bed 10 for Mrs. Mac. We doubted she would last the night, yet when Nurse Wiggins made her rounds at seven to dispense morning medications, there she lay in deep, exhausted sleep. Mrs. Mac was a survivor. Little did I realize then the impact she was to have on my life forty years later.

Over the next few days, as she rallied and her body grew stronger, Mrs. Mac filled in the grapevine scuttlebutt with facts about her life as a Scottish Presbyterian missionary-teacher, ousted after twenty-five years of devoted service in northern China.

Like so many other Europeans, longtime in the Far East, she had escaped with only the clothes on her back, plus personal items and a few trinkets now rattling around in the elderly cardboard suitcase under her bed. Each day a nurse hauled the near-empty suitcase onto the bed, where Mrs. Mac fondled her treasures, while listening quietly to the confidences of hurting, homesick, and burned-out young women.

One by one over the next few days many of the patients on our ward stopped by to chat with her. A sort of aura about her gentle, sweet face drew them like a magnet to her bedside counsel, as they unloaded woes and worries, doubts and fears. Even war-worn, self-sufficient types eventually succumbed to her attraction.

Some of the girls visited her every day. Nurse-patient Mary Russell, with an inoperable brain tumor, was greatly relieved of long-term pain after a few sessions with Mrs. Mac. Everyone seemed calmer after chatting with her.

Once or twice I saw her draw, from her battered bag, a small object for patients who had held her head during a choking spell or had come to her in tears. I didn't know the nature of the trinkets handed out or what had transpired in these sessions.

Mrs. Mac quickly learned all our names. Each morning she called out a greeting in her thick Scottish brogue. Usually it was "A fine mornin' to you, Mary" or "A glorious mornin' 'tis, don't your think?"

Ordinarily, a missionary-type person, or a stuffy, teaching-and-preaching "servant of God" would have turned me off, but something unusual, beyond mere curiosity, was pulling the patients into long whispered confabs with her. I was intrigued.

One day, as I was coming out of the latrine, she called out to me "Libby, do come and sit with me a wee bit. I want to get to know you better."

Ashamed that I had not been friendlier to her early on, I now was eager to learn the secret of her allure, not to mention satisfy my curiosity about the contents of her suitcase. I joined the "club" at her bedside.

Much as I tried to query Mrs. Mac about China, where I hoped for a last assignment, she avoided all but the shortest answers, deftly turning the talk back to me and what it was that made me tick. She had a slick way of pulling out confessions I had never stated to anyone else, yet without laying a guilt-trip on me. As I started to go back to my cubbyhole, she called, "Wait a minute, Libby. I have something for you."

Rummaging among the remaining trinkets in her suitcase, she came up with a dime-size piece of lavender cut glass. Handing it to me, as though bestowing a jewel of great price, she said, "Please keep this as a memento of our time together and of the greatest gift I can give you." Then, after a moment's hesitation, she spoke slowly, "Let go and let God."

The next day she was gone, winging her way back to Scotland, her tattered suitcase empty of baubles, but filled with clothing, candy, and special treats from the post exchange, presented by her grateful American friends. I never saw her again.

Forty years later, in preparation for a talk on India, I was surprised to find the piece of lavender glass, hidden beneath letters and photos, untouched during the many moves of my married life. I wondered how it had survived not only the wartime flight back home across North Africa and over the Atlantic, but haphazard storage in twenty-five residences.

Then I remembered what Mrs. Mac had told me on its presentation: "Let go and let God." Surely there must be something special about it, I thought. Maybe it really is a genuine stone. I took it to a jeweler for an appraisal.

"It's an amethyst," the jeweler said. "Not the highest grade, but well worth a good mounting."

The intervening years have opened my inner eyes to understand the greatest jewel that Mrs. Mac gave me that day in Karachi—a reminder for me to let go of worries, doubts, and fears, and to let God take control of my life.

The amethyst, set in a gold ring with a tiny diamond on each side, now belongs to my granddaughter Joy. I hope that it will come to symbolize for her the maxim that I heard on its presentation to me many years ago. That maxim became the one I adopted as my way of life: "Let go and let God!"

Not an Ordinary Guy

The last big party of the year was to be a gala affair on December 29, 1944. The AACs (Army Air Corps) had engaged the dining room of a local hotel. a local band, and a caterer for a dinner dance. All available American, English, and Anglo-Indian women in the area, plus a few Parsi girls, had been invited to entertain about two hundred GIs.

All aglow with anticipation for an evening of fun, I put on my glamorous new gown, a vivid paisley Indian print of bright blue and red satin. An hour before my GI escort was to arrive, a special messenger delivered a gorgeous gardenia. That was the icing on the cake.

I had just tucked the flower in my hair when a phone call changed my mood. The bearer knocked at my door, poked his nose in and said, "Memsahib, sahib want speak you on phone." It was John, my current best beau from Assam, calling from the Karachi airport. He had flown clear across India to see me.

"I'll be right out to see you," he said, "as soon as I get a cab."

"But I have to go to a GI dance. I hadn't expected you so soon."

"No problem. I'll check in at the hotel and cool my heels until you get back."

"Oh, John, I can hardly wait to see you. Maybe I can leave the dance at eleven. That will give me two hours with Cozy and his friends."

"No problem," John reiterated. "Look for me in the bar when you return."

So I went down to meet my GI date with a smile. I was honest about the whole thing and explained to him why I needed to leave early. He seemed to understand the situation and made no protest.

Cozy ordered drinks for us as I busily caught up on the latest gossip with a staff assistant from another club. I did not notice the tall slim soldier who approached our table until I heard a low, rich baritone asking Cozy for permission to dance with me.

I looked up into the clearest blue eyes I had ever seen and my heart skipped four beats. Things certainly are picking up, I thought. Cozy graciously gave his consent and before I knew it I was swept into the corporal's arms.

Literally that was true, for I had no sensation that my feet were touching the floor at all. I was carried along in a strange Viennese-type waltz, with smooth twists and turns, dips and glides, runs and hesitations, in the arms of this graceful but erratic dancer. At first, I had a hard time following, but after a while I got the hang of it and let myself relax in his embrace.

It was time to start the usual where's, what's, and why's. "Are you stationed here permanently," I began, "or on a flying visit from another base, or possibly another planet?"

"Permanently," he replied, "though it seems like outer space as I talk with an angel. Actually, I live out in the desert with the kraits and geckos and jackals."

"And what do you do out there with the creepy crawlies?"

"Sit in my tent in front of my radio and guide wayward planes away from the ocean. It's called direction finding."

"Sounds fascinating," I said, "How long have you been stationed here?"

"Regularly for the last four months, off and on before that."

By now we were out of the initial embrace and gliding at great speed in and out of the two-steppers on the crowded dance floor. At arm's length from each other, we could have looked into each other's eyes, but my partner appeared to be off in another world. His gaze went over and beyond my forehead, and then dipped down to the side as he watched his moving feet. I soon realized that I was the one on cloud nine, while he was merely trying to avoid a collision.

"I've never seen you in the club," I continued. "Don't you ever come around with the rest of the fellows?"

"Nope. I'm not much for Red Cross clubs. But I didn't know that you were there or I might have changed my mind."

I was beginning to get really interested in this strange guy. "By the way, what's your name?"

"Appel," he replied. "Just call me apple. It's easy to remember."

"But what's your first name? I can't go around calling you apple all the time. I hate calling men by their last names."

"I haven't any first name," he countered. "Just initials. J.C. is the moniker I'm stuck with."

"You're joking. Everybody has a first name. Certainly you didn't get by the draft board and all the army questionnaires with just two initials."

"That's exactly what I did," he persisted. "And I had a damned hard time convincing them that J.C. is the only given name I have."

"O.K. I'll take your word for it, but I suppose next you'll be telling me you don't even know how old you are."

"That's right, I don't."

By now the pace of the dance was making me breathless. His strong hand on my back, steering me through his complex routine, sent prickles up and down my spine.

"Now, listen here," I stammered. "A girl will swallow just so much guff, but I'm not completely stupid. Be honest now. How old are you anyway?"

"Twenty-five or twenty-six. Take your pick. The county courthouse burned and my records were lost. And even my mother isn't sure which year I came along."

"You're incorrigible. I can't even have an ordinary conversation with you."

"That's right," he said, "but then, I'm not an ordinary guy."

"That appears obvious, but we'll just drop that subject and proceed on another tack. What did you do before you entered the service? I suppose you were one of those idealistic fellows who volunteered."

"Right again. You seem to know all the answers. But I bet you can't guess the answer to your first question. What would you guess that I did in civilian life?"

"Oh, I don't know. You might have been an engineer or a lawyer. How about a used-car salesman?"

He chuckled. "Thanks for the compliment, Lib, but you're wrong this time."

"By the way," I interrupted. "How did you know my name?"

"Oh, I've known it for several months, ever since I heard you sing in the post show one night. I engraved your name on my heart."

"Well, that takes care of that," I replied diffidently, while smiling inside. "Now let's get back to my other question. What did you do in civilian life?"

"Guess again, just one more time. Don't you think I look like a wealthy capitalist? For all you know I might be a distant cousin of John D."

"Heaven forbid," I replied. "I'm no good at guessing games, but I still am curious about what you did. Come on now, out with it! This dance is about over and I'll be going back to the table just dying of curiosity."

"Couldn't let you suffer like that, could I? Well, I built elevators. The last job I had back in '42 was with Otis Elevator at the Ford River Rouge plant in Detroit."

"Now I know you're fibbing. Elevators come ready made from factories and then are hoisted down into elevator shafts. Ordinary people don't build them. You might be a carpenter or a plumber or maybe even an electrician, but not that. However, for the present we'll assume that I believe all your stories."

Suddenly I realized that the music had stopped and we were the only couple on the floor.

"For heaven's sake," I burbled. "We're all alone out here. Cozy has that anxious look in his eye and I haven't even danced with him. Wills't be so kind, fair prince, to take me back to my table?"

"Will do, lovely lady, but not with pleasure." We joined Cozy and the others at the cabaret table. J.C. thanked me with a bow and took his leave.

Cozy ordered more drinks, so we spent the next few minutes sipping and gabbing. We agreed it was a good crowd of about forty women, and most of them passably young and good-looking. We wondered where the men had scraped up so many European females. I'd have to get hold of their guest list for our next club dance, and the name of their caterer of these scrumptious non-military refreshments. We sat out a whole dance evaluating the party and downing rum punch.

Just as Cozy and I were about to dance for the first time, the soldier showed up again and asked for another dance. I referred him to Cozy, who denied his request. J.C. again bowed low and melded into the dancers on the floor.

Later I did dance with him again and that time this zany six-footer crooned in my ear, a la Bing Crosby, "Up a Lazy River" and "I'd Like to Get You on a Slow Boat to China." Then he startled me by quoting from Shakespeare's sonnets and talking of Plotinus and Euripides. It just didn't add up. He was only a high school graduate, yet he knew as much about Elizabethan literature and Greek civilization as I did, and I'd spent nine years in institutions of higher learning. I'd have to find out more about this character, but in the meantime it was getting late. John, who was back at the hotel, was probably pacing the floor.

At eleven, Cozy took me back to the Killarney where John, resplendent in his dress uniform, complete with silver wings and bars on epaulettes, whisked me off to the Gymkhana Club for the rest of the evening.

Four days later J.C. came into the Club. I was painting a poster to promote weekend events. The bulletin board was my pride and joy, particularly the poster I had done for carol singing the week before, with its bearded Scotsmen singing "Wassail, wassail, all over the town." Today I was making a plain black and white poster to announce the coming dinner dance. Deep into lettering, I heard a step behind me, but didn't bother to look up since we were used to soldiers watching us work.

Then I heard the deep voice.

"You've got your letters too uniform," he said. "That sign wouldn't catch my eye if I were coming into the club."

I turned to look at him. "So you don't like my poster?"

"Not particularly," J.C. answered. "You can do much better, I'm sure."

"Just what precisely do you find wrong?

"Too much sameness. Nothing to catch the eye. Neat and well executed, but no life."

J.C.'s comments raised my hackles. "I'll have you know that my bulletin board is the talk of the whole CBI. Why, I've had people from all over come just to look at my posters."

"That may be, but this is not the best you can do." J.C. reached into his shirt pocket, pulled out a pack of Camel's, took out a cigarette, tapped it against the back of his hand, and put it in his mouth.

"They're the best I can do right now," I replied testily. "After all, I have a few other duties besides poster making, or in fact, wasting time with critical GIs."

"I know," he said. "You dance and sing and play the piano and spend ten hours a day batting the breeze with lonely soldiers. But it doesn't take any longer to make a good poster than an ordinary one."

"OK, if you know so much about it, suppose you tell me specifically how to make it better. I've had enough of your negative comments." That, I thought, will hold him. He's just another of those conceited fellows who think they know it all.

"Well, for instance," he said, "you can improve the lettering. Make some of the vowels big and hollow with rounded corners, like doughnuts. Shade some of the letters and make some of them uneven, as a child would draw them. Get away from the sameness of squares and rectangles." He puffed on the cigarette.

"O.K." I said, "I'll buy that, but get on with it. I haven't all day."

"Vary the poster sizes as well as the shape. And whatever you do, don't cover the board with a lot of little signs.

Display only one or two at a time. The way you have it now, nothing stands out and hence nothing is read."

Hmm, I said to myself, this lad has ideas. I tore up the old poster and started a new one. J.C. stood around a while to oversee the new construction. To get better acquainted with this weird character, I invited him into the office for coffee.

We chatted for another half-hour about his love of hunting and fishing, his cabin on the Rifle River, and his postwar plans to own a rustic lakeside lodge in the Michigan woods. But just before he left, J.C. made a major faux pas. "By the way, Butch," he said, "how about a date some day soon?"

The hair on the back of my neck bristled. Walking away from him with a frown and a freezing voice, I said, "How dare you call me that! Don't you ever call me Butch again. If you do, you're forever off my list."

Obviously taken aback, he thought for a moment, then said softly. "How about Princess? Will that suit your majesty?"

Appeased and relieved, I replied, "I guess it'll do. At least it's better than Duchess." And from that day on I was his Princess.

After that we enjoyed many hours together, walking hand in hand down Elphinstone Street in Karachi. We didn't dance together again until twenty-five years later.

Courtship in Karachi

$\mathcal{I}$t was wonderful to be back on the job after my long hospital stint. I was ten pounds lighter and down to a size 10. My new GI heartthrob told me I reminded him of a Michigan deer, his favorite animal to track and take. In January 1945 I reveled in return to health, the glamour of Karachi, and the prospect of an upcoming amorous adventure. The following letter to my family tells a lot about J.C. and hints at what was to follow.

Today is my day off. I'm sitting on the spacious veranda drying my freshly shampooed hair in the sun. It is warm and spring-like now, after the intense cold of last week. The sky is its usual intense blue. Below me the dhobis are spreading laundry all over the ground. A camel cart glides by, ankle bells marking time. I hear the tinkly donkey bells and the clickity-click of the gharry-horses' hooves on the pavement. India is a fascinating place, and I haven't got enough of it yet. I love it.

The beauty of winter is that it is inevitably followed by spring. The beauty of spring is the reawakening of emotions that have been lying dormant. Two things always happen to me in the spring: I get a yen for "things," usually hats, and I fall in love. I've got "that old feeling" again.

I haven't had a date with him yet. That comes tomorrow for the first time. But I've seen him at one dance and four afternoons in the club, and we've talked a lot. I met him at a dance 2 ½ weeks ago. He hadn't come into the club before then. Now he comes to the club about three times a week. He's a corporal.

Thumb-nail portrait of J.C.: tall (6'1"), thin, straight, lanky, not good looking in the conventional sense, close cropped hair about color of mine, intense blue eyes that droop at the outer corners, thin face, crooked teeth, of Danish and English descent (Jens

Christian was his grandfather's name), well man-
nered, has a beautiful speaking and singing voice,
attractive to me (though not the dashing type), very
intelligent, entirely self-confident, practical in his
life style and thinking, idealistic yet cynical to a cer-
tain degree, honest, sincere, has fine principles,
smokes a pipe, is 26 years old, can quote Shakespeare
by the yard, and likes me.

Education: as yet an unknown quantity. Past em-
ployment: elevator builder ($125 a month), electri-
cal contractor, bird-dog trainer, authority on hunt-
ing and fishing, woodsman, writer, etc. Plans for
postwar are to go back to Michigan, lease or buy a
large tract of land not too far from a city but still
fairly remote, build a large lodge for a home, lease
hunting rights to Detroit business men, raise and
train setters, and write articles for Hunting and Fish-
ing magazine.

As he says, he's the type who likes to live in the
country and get dressed up to go to the city, rather
than to be someone who stays dressed up in the city
and goes to the country to "rough it." To say that he
is interesting and different is putting it mildly.

When I turned down a date for a big officers' dance, I
said to myself, "Can it be that I am settling down?" But I
still had to go to GI dances with other GIs, or someone
would catch on that I liked him.

From our first encounter, J.C. criticized more than
complimented me and my efforts. Later, when his approach
had changed, he explained that it was his only means of
getting my attention in the competition of dozens of handsome officers. In the meantime, he often succeeded in
getting me riled and thoroughly intrigued at the same time.

In another letter home I wrote:

J.C. continues to be most interesting. He says that
I'm an over-educated, somewhat spoiled child who
has spent so much time reading about life that I've
missed out on living it.

Having had to fend for himself since he was a little boy, he thinks he has learned a lot of things that I have missed. He's had to take responsibility for years and has known hardship. I guess in some ways he is right, but I wouldn't change my life.

Incidentally, J.C. says I'm not, by any means, the smartest woman he has ever known. My PhD doesn't impress him one whit. He's appalled at my ignorance on many subjects, particularly practical electricity, geography, politics, etc. He says he doesn't like women to be too smart, so I guess it's all right.

J.C. writes much better than I, knows Shakespeare and other poetry, and is a much clearer thinker. This makes me wonder about the value of formalized education. He thinks that the high school system should be adjusted to last six years instead of four, and that during that period a lad should be exposed to carpentry, mechanics, plumbing, electricity, etc. by actually engaging in the trades themselves. Then the boy will know if he has any aptitude for any of the hand skills. If not, he can go into a profession. J.C. thinks we need more good plumbers and electricians. A lot of lawyers, he says, would have made better plumbers, and vice versa.

By mid-March J.C.'s offhand manner with me had subsided and I was deeply and emotionally involved. I wanted my family to appreciate this guy who seemed bent on eliminating the competition.

I like him more and more all the time and the feeling is mutual. He has all the good qualities I like in a man and is so terribly manly and attractive with it, as well as intelligent.

Lately, he's gotten recognition from all over the theatre for his fine work, and inspectors of high rank from the states have given him special commendation. They have set his unit up separately now and he is in charge of it. I can't tell you the nature of his work, but he has saved a number of lives lately and hundreds of thousands of dollars worth of planes. It's good to be in the life-saving business in a war where the taking of lives seems to be the big thing. You would all like J.C. and approve of him 100%.

Chilled to the Bone

Winter caught us unawares in Karachi one Sunday in mid-January. It swept down on us as quickly as an Assamese hawk bullets down on an unsuspecting pullet scratching in a dried-up rice paddy.

Ever since we had landed in India, more than a year ago, the weather had been hot and humid. December in Calcutta had been as sultry as June in Miami as we sunned atop our flat-roofed veranda, longing for a punka wallah to fan the flies from our sticky bodies. In Assam the sun shone even brighter and the mosquitoes multiplied faster. By the end of the monsoon season in Assam we had become oriented to the most intense heat and drenching humidity in the world.

We certainly didn't envision winter in an arid desert where in autumn we had to take extra precautions against dry heat. Deedee, our faithful bearer, was always on hand to bring us cracked ice and tanda pani (drinking water). Scarcely a day passed that he did not draw ten baths for his five dusty, sweaty memsahibs.

On Christmas day 1944 we basked in the sunlight aboard the *Mary Ann* (bundar boat) in the Indian Ocean outside Karachi, sailing back at dusk in a warm breeze. Had we been more observant, we might have felt a freshness in the breeze that night. There had been an added tang in the wind, but it brought such a gentle relief to the heat that we welcomed the little chills playing tag on our spines. In the stern of the boat, however, Captain Tipperary wrapped his dhoti closer around his bare legs and pulled a light jacket over his shoulders.

The cold crept in on the heels of a sandstorm that blew up a thick sand-fog and a heavy fish odor from the sea. Nothing unusual about that. Sandstorms occurred about once a month. For two days and a night the storm raged, unpredictable in its direction, devilish in its aim. Sweeping up dust and manure from the street, it swirled filth around our heads and pummeled our bodies. The natives said the storm would last until the moon changed. But the natives were wrong. At dusk of the second day the wind ceased and the street filth settled. We cherished the temporary cooling.

That same night I woke up suddenly, not knowing what had troubled my sleep. At first I was aware only of the absence of the usual night noises. Once before, in the mid-Pacific, I had experienced a similar situation when our ship's engines had stopped. The cessation of the familiar sound had awakened me and fear had sent shivers down my spine.

I had grown used to the night noise of an Indian city: coolies chattering outside a nearby café, cats howling on the high walls, the clop-clop of ghari-horses' hooves, the scratching singsong of a gramophone, the low distant clang of camel bells, the occasional honk of a passing taxi, the tinkle of a sweeper's bracelets, a plaintive weird lullaby coming from the servants' quarters, the incessant hum of mosquitoes, plus dozens of other unidentified sounds cutting through the night. Sometimes I fancied one could even hear a soul escaping from an emaciated, fever-stricken body. Now, as though silenced by the Almighty himself, these sounds had ceased.

Right away I realized that the stillness alone had not awakened me. A thick fog had come through the open windows of our room. Reaching for my scuffs under the bed, my fingers touched the tile floor and a chill shook my body.

Throwing on my robe, I went to the windows and tried to close out the clammy chill, but it was as though I had encapsulated the cold within the limits of the room. Then I went to the closet, unrolled the army blankets, spread two on each bed, and climbed back under my mosquito net.

In the morning Deedee arrived as usual, dressed in the cast-off American suit willed him by a former employer, but something new had been added to his customary garb. Around his neck he wore a khaki-colored wool scarf that he did not remove, even as he went about his household tasks.

"Good morning, memsahib," he greeted me. "Cold, memsahib. Winter here."

Nodding agreement, I gathered closer around me the woolen bathrobe I had thrown over my cashmere sweater and slacks. I thought of Deedee's wife, thinly clad in a voile sari, her feet bare on clay floors, going about her household tasks. I thought of Deedee's four children at home in their mud hut, shivering in front of a tiny charcoal brasier.

As though anticipating my thought, Deedee said, "Memsahib, you got old clothes? Other memsahibs give me clothes. My wife like 'merican clothes."

Rummaging through my boxes I found some old dresses, a new pair of warm pajamas (my favorite turquoise balbriggans), and an old gray Tyrolean sweater. Then I took off the blue robe and added it to the bundle he was wrapping into a self-contained ball. It seemed a paltry offering for a family, but Deedee was pleased.

"Thank you, memsahib. You nice lady." Deedee bowed out of the room, carrying the bundle in his hands.

Though we had stored our winter coats in Agra, we had had foresight enough to bring warm pajamas, sweaters, and wool slacks to Karachi. The army had put a plentiful supply of woolen blankets at our disposal. Even several layers of virgin wool failed to keep us warm in the days and nights that followed. To boost our body heat we played ping-pong at the club and deck tennis with the few soldiers who came to town. Sedentary games and lounging were temporarily out. Throughout the day we drank uncountable cups of hot, black coffee until we twitched with over-stimulation. We still shivered, and blew on chapped hands, and gaped incredulously at the outside thermometer that registered in the high forties.

The cold reached its peak about the fifth day. Every available scrap of heavy clothing had been hauled out of footlockers, bedding rolls, and suitcases. My search had netted two pairs of cotton and wool snuggies with undershirts to match, another pair of flannel pajamas, a pair of thick gray flannel slacks, and four sweaters. Most of these

I put on, looking more like a stuffed toad than a thin American girl just recovering from a debilitating bout with dengue fever.

Nighttime wasn't much better. Like Keats's owl, with all my covers, I was a 'cold. The icy chill seemed to have crawled from the tile floor, up the legs of my charpoi, under the mosquito net, beneath the six protective layers of blankets, and into the marrow of my bones. Dozing off, I dreamed of great golden radiators, gloriously clanking and sputtering with hot steam.

The cold lasted another five days, closing out the sunlight behind a thick layer of clouds and bringing in the fog each night from the sea. Then, as suddenly as it had come, it disappeared. On the fourteenth day we awoke to a glaring sunlit room. Outside, the coolies chattered around the cafes, peddlers cried their wares, mothers sang weird lullabies to their black-haired babies, dhobis spread laundry on the ground to dry. The streets were alive again. Never before, or after, have I suffered so much from the cold.

Deedee, bringing in my coffee, put a tiny spray of bougainvillea on my tray.

"Memsahib," he said happily, "bougainvillea bloom again. Winter gone! Spring here!"

Pinning the scarlet sprig in my hair, I went out into the blue and golden day.

Sacred Crocodiles

One sunny day in February 1945, we took a truckload of men on a tour of three Karachi points of interest. The GIs didn't mind standing all day, crowded like cattle, in an open six-by-six truck. They loved sightseeing, not so much for the sights per se as to get away from the base and chow down on decent food. Lou and I sat up front with the driver.

Hardly had we left the post when I heard: "I've Been Workin' on the Railroad," "My Buddy," and "Home on the Range," rising from the crowded truck. Sad wartime songs and bouncy swing tunes were next. "Waltzing Matilda" indicated that some of the men had stopped over in Australia. I tuned my ears to the back, to spot tenors and baritones who might be horn-swoggled into our canteen shows or a barbershop quartet.

We stopped first at Clifton Beach, the favorite native bathing area and site of the yearly Hindu festival Maha Shivati. Clifton Beach lies on the Arabian Sea, three miles beyond downtown Karachi, looking west toward North Africa. We climbed out of the truck to stretch our legs on the beach, but had no desire to wade in the waters, where tiny shavings of mica would cling to the skin. We found no shells on the barren beach, but it was refreshing to breathe the salt air and listen to the surf.

From the beach the land rose gradually to a little knoll topped by a domed pavilion and bandstand. A long bridge and a series of steep steps led down from the pavilion to a bridge at the high tide line. Adjacent to the pavilion, promenades wound through beautifully landscaped gardens dotted with concrete benches and children's swings.

In March, Clifton Beach takes on a carnival air as great throngs of Hindus from miles around pour into Karachi to celebrate the festival of Maha Shivrati. Strolling food peddlers, acrobats, balloon men, men in white shirts, and women in saris and nose rings mingle with naked fakirs. Peddlers, with rows of exotic shells spread out on the beach, were happy to sell a penny's worth a day. Snake charmers, dancers, and jugglers entertain the crowds as they arrive in gharrys, camel wagons, ox-carts, bicycles, a few autos, and on foot. All night long the roads are clogged with pilgrims. Thousands of Indians dance, sing and perform strange rites, then bathe their sins away in the mica waters of the sea.

Today the beach was empty. A mahli, clipping the low shrubs in the gardens, was the only person in sight.

Our next stop did not invite long inspection. At the camel mortuary, an arid, odorous, enclosed field strewn with picked-clean camel carcasses, offered little of interest, but it did give us a chance to stretch our legs. No camels had died recently, but the "clean-up crew" was standing by. Hundreds of ugly black vultures with white heads and necks, waiting sedately in a straight line on the fence, looked like tuxedoed stags at a sorority party. They eyed the truck with a lean and hungry look.

"We'd better not get too close," the truck driver warned as we got out to exercise. "Those birds could mistake you guys for their next meal and really do a job on your heads." Hearing the whir of lifted wings and raucous screeches as the birds began to fly, we scurried back to the truck.

Fifteen miles farther on we spied several Indians on foot along the road, toting five-tiered aluminum lunch buckets, on their way back to their huts after work.

"Hold on to your hats, boys," our driver yelled to those in the back. "We're going to have a little fun with these wogs."

Gunning the engine, he manipulated the choke to cause a loud backfire, like a gun or firecracker. As we whizzed by, the frightened Indians jumped into the deep ditch bordering the road.

"What's so great about scaring innocent people?" Lou asked. "I fail to see the humor in this joke." I heartily agreed with her.

At our last stop, Nagar Peer, a Hindu shrine deep in the wilderness, we saw from the road a shoddy little weather-beaten wooden structure leaning against an overgrown hill—a far cry from the jeweled marble mausoleums in Agra and Calcutta. Beyond the shrine a small stagnant pool housed the crocodiles we had come to see.

Many Indians, especially those of lower caste, worshipped these crocodiles, one of which was supposed to have a red streak on his forehead called a tilak, a Hindu religious symbol. In times past mothers threw their dead babies to these beasts. Occasionally a live child became a meal for the reptiles.

As we alighted from the truck a white-bearded old man in a dirty dhoti approached. "You come feed crocodiles?" he asked. "I show you. You wait here. I fetch goat."

"Wait a minute," I said as the man started off. "How much?"

"Twenty rupee," was the reply as he skittered away.

Docile beasts, basking shut-eyed there in the sun, the crocodiles didn't move as we prodded them with sharp sticks and sloshed the water around them. But when the old man returned with an odorous gutted goat, the drowsy creatures suddenly came to life.

"You pay me now," he said before releasing the bounty.

"How much?" the driver asked, knowing full well the going price.

"Twenty rupee."

"You've got to be kidding," the driver said. "We're not your gullible tourists. I've been here a half-dozen times before and I know your tricks."

"But I buy goat special for you. Long way out to farm."

"So it probably cost you five rupees, if you didn't raise it yourself."

"Please, sahib, you rich. Me poor. I got six child my house."

"No doubt that's true. But twenty rupees is way out of line." The driver reached into his pocket and pulled out a roll of paper money.

"Eight rupees and two for a tip is double what any Indian would give you."

The driver held out a single note. "Here's a tener for you and your six kids. Take it or leave it before I change my mind."

Before the driver finished speaking, the money disappeared into the midriff fold of the native's dhoti. Then the old man cut the stinking carcass into bleeding sections for the eager GIs, who gleefully tossed them into the stagnant pool.

Immediately the sluggish waters churned to life as the goggle-eyed crocodiles slashed their tails, opened their toothy maws, and wrestled for the tasty morsels.

Brandishing bleeding pieces, the GIs shouted, "Get ready for your blood bath," as they pretended to push each other over the pool wall.

"You're next," one GI said to me as I watched from a distance. "You'd make a toothsome morsel for that big eyed monster lounging in the back behind his harem."

"And he'd make a dozen pairs of shoes for me and my friends, if only you were strong enough to catch him," I countered.

When the feed was over the satisfied reptiles settled back into their lethargy, eyed us philosophically, then dropped off to sleep in the sun.

Jenna and the Nautch Dancers

In wartime, thanks to the military, we Red Cross girls had a chance to see more of India than ordinary tourists.

One night in March 1945, after our club closed, an MP from the Malir airbase came into Karachi to "show us the town," at least the part that we would never have dared visit alone. Four of us piled into his jeep and headed off toward Napier Road for a tour of the red-light district.

By day Napier Road is like any other quiet residential-business street in the native quarter, with rows of balcony apartments above tiny merchant stalls on the ground floor, many of which do not open until nighttime. That night it had all the color, noise, and gaiety of a traveling carnival, with throngs of Indians clogging the winding alleys. All the little shops seemed to be doing a good business, particularly the sweet shops and betel nut stands. Peddlers sold bright paper streamers tied to sticks. Beggars cried for alms.

Every building was aglow. Lamps lighted open doorways, inviting any and all to mount the stairways as the balconies beamed soft red beckoning glows from within.

Behind grillwork railings Indian girls in silk saris and gaudy baubles draped themselves enticingly on sofas or hung over the balconies to accost passersby. In the stairwells women stood in alluring poses and called to men in the street. Some of the girls were lovely, young, delicately featured and unpainted. Some of the "ladies" were old and ugly, heavily rouged, and dirty.

"We'll go up and see Jenna," the MP officer said. "She's a legend in these parts. I'll ask her to show you her tattoo."

We had heard much about Jenna from the soldiers. A longtime friend and informant for the MP's, she had been in Karachi for years, plying the trade she had learned in her native Syria. Already wrinkled and worn in her forties, she was still No. 1 in her profession. We were anxious to talk with a woman like this, just to see what made her tick.

Seeing us below, she shouted to the MP to bring us up. We climbed the dark narrow, vermin-infested stair-way to her home.

Jenna beamed with pleasure that four ladies had deigned to honor her humble abode. She had the simplic-ity of a child, a sort of innate innocence. We saw nothing here of the hardened cynical prostitute we had expected. It was obvious why, even after twenty-five years, she still had "regulars."

A thick coating of make-up accentuated the lines of Jenna's face. Straight, black, bobbed hair set off her white skin. Her ugly pink shift-style dress came just below her knees. Yet she had charm. Her eyes were bright, her man-ner gracious, and her welcome effusive.

"I am so happy you come see me, ladies," she said. "You make me ver' happy you come here. Please to have a chair and I bring you some tea."

"Oh, no thank you," I said hastily. "We cannot stay for tea, but we'd love to sit down for a minute and visit with you." Jenna remained standing throughout the whole visit, as much from deference as from the lack of seating for all of us.

"Oh, sir," she said to the MP, "these ladies so pretty, so fresh, so young and their hair so soft and curly. Ameri-can girls so beautiful!" She touched Lou's curls reverently.

"You so good to come here," Jenna went on. "I thank you ver' much." We felt that her appreciation was about as sincere as any we had had since leaving home.

Presently the MP, getting up to leave, asked Jenna to show us her mark. For a moment she was bashful. Then she lifted her skirt above her bare knees. There on her thigh was tattooed the legendary blue butterfly, her most prized possession.

None of us felt judgmental of her way of life, only com-passion for its necessity in a city that offered few options for an uneducated, poor female to earn her keep. Without a dowry, she could never have wed. We wondered what enticements had been offered her as a child for her to come to India. Possibly the enticement had been the promise to become a dancer or a child bride.

Across the street from Jenna's place we went upstairs again into a large windowless, brightly-lit room, redolent of burning incense and hookah-pipe smoke. Along the walls several Indian men in loose white cotton shirts and jodhpurs reclined on long purple velvet cushions. Four young Indian girls, in heavily embroidered bodices above bare midriffs, swished their full, brightly colored cotton skirts and stamped their feet to the beat of castanets and a native drum. As we were shown to cushions along the wall, the dancers withdrew to an inner room.

Arranging ourselves comfortably on the cushions, we waited for the dancers to return. The MP talked with the Indian in charge, slipped him a two-rupee note, and said, "Send out Rutna and Rama and their friends. And tell them to give us a good show, the real McCoy, and not some pasteurized version because of the girls."

Then the Indian gave each of us a little flower, which we were to place against our cheeks when the dancers came in. Each of us also was to have a rupee ready for later in the dance ritual. The drum began to beat again and the dancing girls returned.

This time six tall, beautiful young Indian girls filed in from the adjoining room, their heads, necks, arms, and noses adorned with jewels and silver trinkets. Tiny-belled bracelets on their wrists and ankles tinkled as they moved. Below a wide expanse of navel-revealing light brown flesh, red, blue, yellow, and orange "broomstick" skirts flared out to form swirling circles, as their bare feet tapped faster and faster. The graceful dance consisted largely of studied movements of arms, wrists, hands, and fingers, plus occasional glides to right and left and the frequent roll of hips.

Midway in the dance we pressed the flowers to our cheeks, as we had been instructed, as if to release their perfume. Then the girls plucked the flowers from our hands, giving us in their place little bits of perfumed cotton on a stick. Next we pressed the rupees against our cheeks and the dancers, after many tantalizing assays, finally plucked the rupees from our clutch.

We wondered if this was the dance customarily performed for the patrons of the place, for it seemed so decorous, or had it been cleaned up for the American memsahibs? The MP assured us that what we had seen was the real McCoy. Their dance was not an invitation to debauchery, for the nautch dancers are forbidden to arouse the passions of those who come to see them. They are not prostitutes, but are revered, much as are the geisha girls in Japan.

When we returned to the jeep from the stuffy scented room, a little boy of about ten approached the MP. "Anybody come tonight?" the MP asked the boy.

The lad looked up and down the street, then said, "No, sahib. No 'merican soldiers."

"Are you sure?" the officer asked. "My men told me that old Gus had seen a GI here." Then the MP put a bright, new rupee into the lad's hand.

The boy again looked all around, and then motioned the officer into the shadow of the building. When the MP returned to the jeep he drove us down a side alley at a rapid clip.

"Who's the little boy?" we asked. "And where are we going now?"

"He's one of our informants," our driver said. "He says he saw a corporal going in the direction of old Tammy's. We'll take a look down there and see if we can find him."

Luckily for the soldier, we didn't find him and the post brig had one less drunk to contend with.

Captain Tip and the Mary Ann

On a tiny barren island called Sandspit, jutting out into the Indian Ocean near Karachi, J.C. and I found our favorite trysting place. There, basking on the hot sand with only an occasional scrubby bush for cover, we spent many happy afternoons planning our future in a cool northern climate.

On a spring day in 1945 we invited Lou and her current beau, Sam, to join us for a whole day on the beach. On rented English bicycles we four set out at 10:00 in the morning for West Wharf, peddling the six miles against a strong ocean breeze. Our route took us past the warehouse section of Karachi, where progress was temporarily slowed by hundreds of camel carts loaded with cotton bales, huge timbers, and piles of straw. We finally reached the wharves where tankers and freighters had put in.

The only access to Sandspit was by bundar boat (called machwas by the natives). A large dinghy with high mast and a single colorful sail, it seated four to six people comfortably on padded couch seats. The captain-owner manned the tiller. He had a crew of four little boys, whose duties were to bring about the unwieldy sail at the captain's command and sit on the outrigger in high winds to keep the boat from tipping over.

J.C. and Sam had already hired our boat, so we did not have to endure the usual lengthy haggle over the cost of a day's sail. Captain Tipperary with the *Mary Ann* was waiting for us when we arrived.

On hearing the captain's name I had visions of a retired British captain with whiskers and a briny accent. The name, however, was truly "a snare and a delusion." Captain Tipperary was neither British, nor ex-military. His accent was British, but not of the salty variety. A tall clean-shaven Indian wearing a dhoti, white shirt, and droopy turban, he bowed and said, "Salaam, sahibs, salaam, memsahibs. *Mary Ann* all ready for you. Nice day for fishing. *Mary Ann* best boat in Karachi."

It was a good day for sailing. We had enough wind to carry us at a fast clip across the water, with real thrills as we rounded the buoys. Out in the bay the breeze died down enough for us to try our hand with the bamboo fishing poles supplied by our captain. We spent the next few hours pulling in croakers and blowfish. Hauling in our catch of forty-two critters reminded me of the fun I had many years earlier in Virginia, with an old black man who used "swimps" for bait. In India we used live prawns.

Lou and I had a great time with the blowfish. Lifted out of the water, they swelled up with air like tight balloons covered with sharp spikes. Thrown into the water again, they deflated to usual size and scuttled off into the bay. After an hour's fishing, Captain Tip dropped us off at Sandspit for the rest of the day, promising to return for us before six.

Sandspit was populated by hundreds of tiny sand crabs that scuttled into their holes as we walked along. Except for a half-dozen little shacks near where the dinghies docked, the white sand stretched nearly deserted for miles. Beyond the beach the sand humped into rounded dunes, many covered with milkweed and low sand shrubs. Along the beach an occasional net drying in the sun and an empty sailboat moored nearby indicated the presence of human life. The only sounds were the restless howl of the wind and the relentless surge of the surf. In the distance blue mountains reached up into the soft haze. It was said that from there on a clear day one could see the distant hills of Baluchistan, a strange land next to Afghanistan.

About three o'clock in the afternoon the wind increased to a squall. We battled stinging sand the rest of the day. It blew into our eyes, hair and even our teeth. It ground into the pores of our skin and tickled our noses into coughs. We ate sand in our sandwiches.

When the sun was low in the west we hiked back to the strand where Captain Tip had agreed to pick us up. As we rounded the little rise between ocean and bay, we looked for the *Mary Ann's* tall mast, but saw only rumpled water and blue sky. By seven the *Mary Ann* was still nowhere in sight.

"Damn these Indians, anyway," Sam said. "You never can depend on them."

Any other day a dozen boats would have been moored off the strand at this hour. Today there was none. The wind whipped up white caps in the bay. We waited and shivered and cursed the captain who had not kept his word.

At about 7:30 a little boy appeared out of the twilight. "Sahibs," he said. "You Cap'n Tip's boat?"

"Yes, we are," J.C. answered. "Where in the devil is the scoundrel? He was to meet us here at six and already he's over an hour late."

The little boy appeared to understand very little English. He spoke again hesitantly, as though reciting a speech he had memorized but now had mostly forgotten. "Sahib, Cap'n Tip break mast. He go get fixed. He say return soon. You wait for him." The boy smiled in triumph at the speech he had made.

"It's a lie," Sam said. "You haven't seen Captain Tipperary any more than you've seen the man in the moon."

The lad, comprehending little of Sam's outburst, grinned and stood still. Then he tried again. "Sahib, Cap'n Tip tell fishermen he be back. They tell me. I tell you. Gimme cigarette. Please!"

"You're much too young to smoke cigarettes," J.C. said. "Besides, I don't believe you."

The lad did not move. His face did not change. "Cigarette, sahib! Cigarette, memsahib! Please," he chanted, hoping for a messenger's tip, as he dug his toes into the sand.

J.C pulled out a half-pack of Camels, threw it at the boy, shouting, "Here's your set of coffin nails. Now scram." The little boy pounced on the pack and scampered away.

Night was coming on and the air was chilly. The wind had subsided to a gentle breeze, but there was a sting in it that raised goose bumps on our sandy sun-parched bodies. We drew our clothes on over our swim suits and waited.

Sam and J.C. made a tent of the army blanket we had earlier spread on the beach, to shield us from the salt spray blowing in from the oceanside.

We scanned the bay for a sail until we could no longer see. Then we waited while the stars came out, betting on the time and mode of our eventual rescue. A few sandwiches were left from our picnic lunch. They really hit the spot now. After a round of old songs, we told ghost stories. "Twas a dark and stormy night..."

Finally we heard an Indian song floating over the bay. The singing came closer. We heard a man's voice calling, "Sahibs, memsahibs, Captain Tipperary coming." Then a bedraggled, panting Indian came onto the beach, his turban askew.

"I ver' sorry, sahibs, you have long wait, but *Mary Ann* she break big mast in wind storm. It cost ver' much have her fixed."

"She seems to be in fine condition now."

"This not *Mary Ann*," the captain said. "I leave her there to get new mast. This *Eagle's Nest*. I borrow her to bring you back. I always keep my word, sahib. I never let you down."

Our tip to Captain Tipperary that night should have gone a long way to pay the repair costs of the *Mary Ann*.

Sailing back under the stars, we thanked the quirk of fate that had delayed our Indian skipper. Without it we would have missed one of the most beautiful, romantic sights in all India—Karachi Bay lighted only by the constellations and the Milky Way.

A Dismal Day in April

It was a hot dusty day in Karachi when the girls brought the sad news to me at our quarters in the Killarney Hotel. Always a late sleeper, I was still in my PJs, taking the bobby pins out of my hair at our makeshift dressing table, when my three roommates, ready for work in their drab gray uniforms, filed into the room. Their faces, usually smiling, were downcast and their shoulders drooped.

"We've sad news for you, Lib." Rachel's voice broke as she continued: "President Roosevelt died last night."

Meg (from California) piped up. "We know how much you thought of him." Then three pairs of strong loving arms held me and we all burst into tears.

On Saturday morning, April 15, I wrote my family:

> We've just returned from an official army memorial service for President Roosevelt. Sir Hugh Dow, Governor of Sind, was the principal speaker. Others who addressed the group were the commanding brigadier general of this section and this section chaplain. The orchestra played "God Bless America," "Faith of our Fathers," and "The Star Spangled Banner." It was a very impressive service, with representatives from the British military, civilians, and representatives from all the consulates, as well as our own armed forces and business people of the city.
>
> As a part of the general mourning, all dances in the theatre have been suspended for thirty days, as well as all noisy gatherings.
>
> The death of the President was a tremendous shock to all of us here, as I know it was to all of you at home. At first we feared that everything would go wrong immediately. I had a hollow feeling inside. But, as J.C. said, "He was ably supported by able men who will continue his work."

*I know how you must feel, Dad, because you felt
that he was absolutely irreplaceable, as indeed he is
as an individual. But maybe a group of men can
carry on.*

My mind backtracked to a memorable handshake in
1932—my sole encounter with Franklin D, culminating
my first and last political involvement.

A chip off the old block, I admired my Southern dad's
Democratic (and democratic) commitment. Sometimes he
split the local ticket, but always joked that "when you are
in that voting booth, with only you and God, you have to
vote the Democratic ticket."

A seventeen-year-old sophomore at West Virginia University, I had joined the small, unorganized group of Young
Democrats working for the election of Franklin Roosevelt.
We had no funds except the small sums eked out of our
personal allowances and a few quarters and dimes culled
from glass donation jars at checkout counters. After a first
disastrous publicity stunt, of offering free sandwiches and
coffee at a downtown rally, we ran out of money. Only
homeless, non-voters took advantage of our bounty.

Our second and last gesture was to create a bronze
plaque inscribed with hopeful words for winning, to be
presented to our candidate at the Monongalia County rally
in early May. To present this Victory Plaque from the WVU
Young Democrats Club, the garrulous Libby Chitwood,
never known to be out of words for any occasion, was
chosen.

When the great day came, there I was, sitting on the
same platform just two seats away from the man who was
to become one of the most respected and vilified men in
history. When I presented the plaque, with a few hesitant
words of hope now long forgotten, Franklin Delano
Roosevelt firmly grasped my shaking hand and said a few
appropriate words of thanks. He then launched into a
mellifluous flow that may have secured the state of West
Virginia for the next four presidential elections.

Memsahib's Bridal Slippers

One sultry spring afternoon in 1945 Lou and I moseyed through Karachi's Bori Bazaar looking for shoes
the color of the square-cut emerald on the third finger of
my left hand.

The question of a wedding dress turned up one day as
J.C. and I were window-shopping on Karachi's crowded
Elphinstone Street. I wanted a glamorous draped, white,
silk jersey, similar to the American gowns then in style for
afternoon wear—a dress to remember. But J.C. had other
ideas.

"It's not the kind of dress for you," he said, eyeing me
critically from neck to knee. "You need something soft
and full, to cover up those flat surfaces, and something
plain and simple over those extra bulges."

Like Iago, J.C. was "nothing if not critical." Thank heavens, though, he lacked the duplicity of the Shakespearean
villain. And his judgment was nearly always sound.

"The trouble with most women," he continued, "is that
they've got to be in style if it kills them. Take a gander at
that female across the street." He pointed to a bowlegged
Anglo-Indian girl in an above-the-knee western frock. "Why
in the devil doesn't she cover up those scrawny legs? Now,
if I were designing a dress, I'd..."

"O.K," I interrupted, "you design my wedding dress
and I'll promise to wear it."

Much to my surprise he took me at my word. In a little
draper's shop J.C. picked out a crisp white cotton pique
with green polka dots. I protested weakly in favor of a
fragile China silk, but J.C. stuck to his guns, practical to
the point of exasperation.

"I'll be darned if I'll design a dress to be worn once," he
said, "and then moth balled."

"But brides are supposed to wear all white," I reminded
him.

"So what! This stuff will bring out the green in your
eyes. Besides, who's designing this dress anyway? You're

only going to wear it. I'll be looking at it for the next ten years."

A few minutes later, as we sipped lime sodas in an out of bounds café, J.C. fished in his pocket, pulled out a blue envelope and sketched a frock with a peasant-style blouse, drawstring neck, and flared skirt. Three days later a pert little Indian durzi, sitting cross-legged on the ground before a portable Singer, studied the sketch, eyeballed my figure, then snipped and stitched until the sketch became a reality.

Now I needed green shoes to complete the costume.

Bori Bazaar, about the size of several city blocks, was a fascinating maze of cobblestone streets littered with garbage, surface sewage, and animal waste. For Lou and me the walking became a game of dodging stinking puddles, human spittle, and what rural Southerners call "cow pies." To city Indians these droppings from sacred cattle were pure gold: fertilizer for their tiny garden plots, fuel for their braziers, and warm insulation for their huts.

Each alley, just wide enough for a bullock cart, was squeezed between junky, two-story, wooden structures with overhanging balconies. Colorful cotton saris, strips of white turban gauze, and bright tie-dyed scarves dried on the fretwork railings. Behind each balcony a mysterious honeycomb of windowless rooms housed a hive of human drones and an occasional "queen," who plied her trade at night under the red lamp beside the stairway leading up.

Under the balconies, gloomy little shops were niched into the face of the buildings, one after the other as far as the eye could see, like berry boxes stacked closely together on their sides. Each shop specialized in a single commodity: rice, goat's milk and cheese, earthenware, brass pots, sweets, hardware, fruit, cloth, jewelry, saris, or shoes.

Outside the stalls, squatting merchants passed the time of day with each other, pondered the imponderables, and spat betel juice into the street. A buyer haggled for an hour over the price of a cupful of rice, not just to lower the price, but from sheer habit and for entertainment. Bargaining was a way of life for the Indian. Only the hurried tourist paid the first or even fourth asking price.

As we passed by, the shopkeepers, competing for our attention, shouted their friendly "Good morning, memsahibs," gaily oblivious of the time of day. But today we had no time to chat.

Because of the confusing sameness of stalls flanking identical alleys we often got lost in the honeycomb of the marketplace. Swarms of half-naked children, their torsos bound in ragged cheesecloth dhotis, jostled against us in their play. Green flies struck our faces in their flight from open drain to fruit stall. Lethargic cows and mangy dogs clogged the passageways.

The heavy odor of fresh-slaughtered goats, decaying in the afternoon sun, sickened me. Everywhere, we felt the outstretched hand and heard the nasal singsong of the child beggar, parroting American soldier-tutors. "No mamma, no poppa, no per diem. Bakshish, memsahibs, bakshish."

After a while my nostrils became desensitized to the stench, and instead, picked up the pungent odor of wood burning on unseen hearths. More noticeable now than the incessant chant of the alms-seekers was the gentle tinkle of street-sweepers' anklets and the low tong-tong of oxen bells. In place of focusing on peeling plaster and grimy walls, I learned to pick out the rich purples and gold of silk saris in the cloth merchant's stall. My eyes feasted on the contours of long-horned bullocks, shaggy fat-tailed sheep, lithe human bodies, square stalls, bicycle wheels, and smoke spirals from charcoal brasiers heating afternoon tea. Then the bazaar became a magnificent symphony, a contrapuntal interweaving of color, sound, shape, and smell. I loved the bazaar.

Several weeks earlier, during an afternoon off, I had noticed a pair of green suede sandals, displayed in an old Hanford's Balsam of Myrrh case in the shop of one Jehu Lalchand. At the time, the incongruity of the display case struck me more than the shoes had. Now, I remembered the shoes. They would be perfect for a bridal outfit. Hoping I could squeeze my big feet into them, Lou and I went again to search for the horse liniment box.

On the way we stopped at the brass merchant's stall, where I chanced to see the perfect gift for my father: a four-tiered round aluminum container with a cover on top and a carrying handle. I had first seen them swinging from the hands of native clerks on their way home from the shipping offices near the wharves.

"Oh, Lou," I exclaimed. "There they are! They're perfect for picnics. Mom and Dad will love them. Dad likes hot chicken legs and snaps for picnics and Mom always takes along her homemade hot cinnamon applesauce. What a wonderful way to carry them and keep them warm!"

"How much for the lunch buckets?" I asked the shopkeeper.

"Fifty rupees, memsahib, but I make you special price. Forty rupees to such a lovely memsahib."

"Flattery will get you nowhere. Here are three ten-rupee notes. I haven't all day to haggle."

At last we stumbled onto the shop with "Jehu Lalchand" printed in big letters above the stall. There were green suede sandals inside the glass-domed case, a trifle dusty, but just as elegant as I had remembered them. It was obvious that these little slippers, made for a petite Indian maiden, would never accommodate my size eights.

As I hesitated before the shop, a little boy came out of the cavern behind. I paid little attention to him other than to note that he was about nine or ten and anxious to make a sale. I looked around for the merchant-owner to serve me.

"Good morning, memsahibs," the boy said cheerily. "Nice day, memsahibs. You want shoes, memsahibs? I got nice shoes." He waved vaguely at the row of footwear behind him. "Come in my shop. I show you."

We went up the rickety wooden steps into the stall. Along the back wall hung rows of European and Indian shoes of every size, shape, and color: stiff black leather oxfords, shop-worn canvas sneakers, thick heavy "mosquito" boots, flat-soled native sandals with toe-spreading thongs, high heeled pumps in a dozen colors, plus a few gold and silver dancing slippers. Surely in this motley array I could find a pair to fit me, at least in open toes.

Hurriedly scanning the shelves, I automatically discarded all models that were not green. Then, against a jog in the back wall, I spotted a pair of green suede sandals, identical in design, but several sizes larger than the ones in the showcase out front.

The Indian boy watched me mentally reject all his handsome offerings until my eyes rested on the far wall. With the agility of a mongoose he snatched the green shoes from the shelf and held them up for me to try on.

"These, memsahib?" he babbled. "You like these green shoes? They just your size. Ver' cheap. You try on."

Before I could say anything, the boy had pulled up a low stool for me and was fooling with the ties of my black oxfords. In an instant he had replaced my sturdy American-made "regulations" with delicate, emerald-green handmade sandals. Losing myself for an instant in a haze of feminine daydreams, I let the Indian lad fasten the straps across my arches. The green shoes were a perfect fit. Three more weeks and I would be a bride, in emeralds and pique and green suede shoes!

An ugly sight jolted me back to reality. Looking down at the beautiful shoes I noticed the hands that had put them on my feet. At the sight of the open bloody sores covering the tops and palms of the small brown hands, I jerked my feet away. The boy's face, arms, and legs oozed yellow pus through several layers of dirt. I wanted to run away to my hotel and bathe my feet, hands, and whole body in a strong disinfectant.

I blurted out thoughtlessly, "Goodness, boy! You're covered with sores. What on earth's the matter with you?"

The boy looked at his hands. He smiled. Then, straightening up to his full, undersized height, he stammered with evident pride, "Me, memsahib? Me? I got, I got … gon–no–rhee–ah!"

A moment later I was out in the street, clutching a pair of green shoes for which I had paid twice the asking price. Ten rupees seemed a paltry tip for a little boy with the makings of a successful businessman and a disease that would last, in India, his whole short life.

Purviz

$\mathcal{N}$one of the Red Cross clubs at home and overseas could have managed without the local volunteers who gave so graciously of their time to help us entertain American GIs. English, Indian, and Anglo-Indian women in India were of invaluable assistance in club activities, dances, and off-post tours. They even pitched in to help us with pickup and cooking chores, as well as minor maintenance. Some even invited us and the GIs to their homes, where they treated us like friendly neighbors.

Mrs. McKensey's living room in Karachi became a private dating place for J.C. and me. Sheila, her English daughter, often invited our soldiers for jaunts in her Morris Minor. Kitty Drummond, an Anglo-Indian, became a GI favorite at dances and knew all the latest steps, and my best Indian friend, Purviz Pavri, helped entertain the men at KGA Hall.

In November 2000, an unexpected e-mail from Karachi, now in Pakistan, took me back fifty-five years to when I first knew Purviz. My letter of January 20, 1945, tells of a visit with her family.

> *Yesterday I had tea at the home of Purviz Pavri, a little Parsi girl I met recently at the club and have seen a lot of since.*

> *As you may already know, the Parsis are a small group of high caste Indians who control most of the commerce and big business in India. They are probably the richest and best educated of any caste and surely the most modern. A Semitic race, they first lived in Persia (hence the name Parsi), but were ousted for their Zoroastrian beliefs and sought refuge in India. Now they number about 300,000 of India's 450,000,000 (1945) population. Shrewd business people, they are known as "Indian Jews." Many of them have the hooked nose and large eyes of their Semitic origin. The Parsis pride themselves on caring for their own poor and have no beggars.*

*Each Parsi contributes generously to the mainte-
nance of homes and asylums for the poor and af-
flicted.*

*Purviz has the equivalent of a high school educa-
tion in our country, yet she is better informed than
many American college graduates. She speaks perfect English without accent, plays Bach and
Beethoven on piano, sings English and Italian op-
eratic arias, and converses intelligently on almost
any topic.*

*In WW II she is an Indian WAC, working as a
code-sender for the British Signal Corps. I met her
at our Red Cross club where she is registered as one
of our local hostesses. Last week she invited me to
her home to meet her family. I was delighted and
privileged to accept.*

*Purviz, single and in her early twenties, lives with
her mother and father in old Karachi, just behind
the YMCA in a modest flat on the second story of an
adobe structure. The tiny treeless clay front yard is
swept clean and imprinted with a traditional paisley Indian chalk design. Upstairs we entered an airy
living room furnished with table, upright piano and
several comfortable chairs neatly covered in tan
denim. Beyond the living room was the family bedroom and beyond that a large dining room where
we had tea.*

*Purviz's mother greeted me at the door in a gold
bordered, blue silk sari, elegantly draped over her
tiny figure. She is small and quite thin, with straight,
jet-black hair drawn to a simple knot at the back of
her neck. Her bright, interested black eyes smiled a
warm welcome as I came in. Though she spoke only
a little English, with the help of her daughter-trans-
lator we managed to understand and appreciate each
other.*

*Mrs. Pavri showed me her heirloom sari collec-
tion, which Purviz will inherit some day, though at*

the present, her daughter prefers American-style "trendy" dresses when not in uniform.

From an ancient silver-strapped walnut trunk, Mrs. Pavri drew out dozens of flat rectangular packets, encasing carefully-folded saris of gold and silver bordered Benares silks, delicate lawns in pastel prints, and vivid blue and red rayon satins in all-over paisley designs. Then she drew out a silky, open-weave, black garment with woven flowers in bright pink, turquoise, gold, soft blue, and silver. This she insisted I accept.

From her collection of blouses and bodices, Mrs. Pavri then selected two as gifts for me: an embroidered bodice-front in knock-your-eyes-out red, blue, gold, and black, and a stunning trim-set in bright orange embroidery. The all-over design, in buttonhole stitch with tiny inset mica mirrors, was the handiwork of the wife of the Pavris' milkman. This art is unique to Rajputana (now Rajasthan), where the raw mica is prevalent in Sind coastal waters.

At about four-thirty, Purviz's father came home from his work in the shipping business. He was small, but more corpulent than his wife. He wore a white duck European suit and a straw hat. Though he spoke only broken English, he too managed to make me feel very much at home.

At five o'clock Mrs. Pavri served tea with delicious sugar cookies and a fancy fruit bread, plus cake—enough for an ample supper. Then I went back to the club for my evening program and Purviz came along to help me.

Except for the differences in skin color, native tongue, and everyday attire, these dear people could have been my cousins in southwest Virginia. Purviz indeed did become like a sister to me.

In the '70s Purviz, brought up in the Zoroastrian faith, became a dedicated Christian. The sharing of our faith brought us even closer together and we have kept in touch, by mail, all these years.

Fakirs at the Fair.
Karachi, 1945.

Hindu festival of
Maha Shiva,
Karachi, 1945.

Deedee, our bearer
at Killarney Hotel.
Karachi, 1945.

Libby at Sandspit.
Karachi, 1945.

Left to Right: Phyllis Greenleaf,
Meg Walker, Libby Appel, Club
Director, British volunteer.
Karachi, 1945.

Kitty Pundole, Parsi
volunteer. Bungalow,
right, is similar to the
one we had in Assan.
Karachi, 1945.

Don Newsbiggle
and friends.
Karachi, 1945.

Libby outside Red
Cross Club in
Karachi, 1945.

Not an ordinary guy
in Mt. Abu, 1945.

Jim Peden, J.C.'s
best buddy, 1945.

Part Six
We Visit the Prince

"Friendship, mysterious cement of the Soul.
Sweetener of life, and Solder of Society."

(On Christmas card received from
His Highness Taley Mohammed Khan,
Nawab of Palanpur, 1945)

We Wangle an Invitation

Even now, after fifty-eight years, I am aghast at our audacity in concocting the letter and how quickly it had brought a response.

Grapevine gossip hinted at elegant visits to Zorowar Palace in Palanpur, Rajputana—for American officers, Red Cross workers, and a few civilians attached to the military. No GIs had presumed to aspire to the sought-after invitations, but J.C. and I were both ready for leave and had plans for where to go and what to do. Getting an invitation would take some finagling, but J.C. was an old hand at that.

My memory is short on the initial contact with Mr. Khan, secretary to the nawab of Palanpur (not the "Maharajah," as stated in the letter). In fact, I'm not even sure that an invitation had been issued, but J.C. needed something "official" to show his CO, detailing plans for a week's stay at the palace, before leave papers could be cut.

One day we sat down in my club and pieced together a few facts, purportedly from Mr. Khan, and added our own creative data about hunting and dress. The letter, on official Red Cross stationery (herewith attached), went off to both Mr. Khan and Colonel Munson, CO of J.C.'s airforce unit. For a week we sweated it out, fearful that J.C.'s furlough papers would not come through before our scheduled departure. When they finally arrived, just in the nick of time, the inevitable snafu occurred, this time occasioned by our high-strung Swiss canteen manager.

When I returned to the club after our usual Sunday afternoon sightseeing tour for the men, which was also the day before we were to leave, Mrs. Schweir rushed to me, babbling terrifying news.

With great alarm and concern Mrs. Schweir said, "A friend of yours is in the hospital at the point of death and is asking to see you immediately. You must grab a taxi and speed to his bedside at once, before he ... , before he ... ." Mrs. Schweir loved the dramatic and told the story in hurried phrases, with gestures and facial contortions worthy of the immortal Sarah B. With flair she continued, "Your friend is in the amputation ward, so be prepared for a shock when you see him. He says he's from your hometown and knows you well." As I listened to her, and her words sank in, my whole body reacted and weakened as I visualized one of my intimate friends breathing his last.

Past experience should have taught me to divide all that Mrs. S. said by four, but that evening I took every word as gospel. Finally I got up enough courage to ask the man's name. "Hodges," she said. "The nurse said his name was William Hodges."

Hodges, Hodges. I turned the name over in my mind. It didn't click. Hodges, Hodges—Bud Hodges, that was it! He was a boy who had been in my grade-school class. I hadn't seen him since. I'd hardly call him a close friend, but the least I could do was to go out to the hospital and investigate.

A native taxi-driver took me the fifteen miles across the desert to the base hospital. The nurse was expecting me and led me directly to a bed in the middle of the ward.

There lay the boy I had known in grade school, with his leg strapped in a Rube Goldberg contraption, that lifted his leg to the ceiling and one arm to the bed rail. Both limbs were heavily bandaged. He groaned frequently and breathed heavily. My heart did a pole vault up into my throat.

I took his unbandaged hand in mine and said as cheery a "Hello, Bud!" as I could muster. He groaned a feeble "Hi!" and smiled.

"Good gosh, Bud," I said, "You're all banged up. I guess you really had it upcountry."

"Upcountry?" he replied, between moans. "I haven't been out of Karachi."

"But didn't you get banged up in battle? Or did you go down with a plane?"

"Good God, no!" he said. "I'm not even in the army."

"Then how did you get in such a mess this far from home?"

"I came over here," he said, "on a little business trip for the government and was staying with a friend here in Karachi. You know how these Karachi houses are, with their unprotected upstairs porches." I nodded. "Well, I walked in my sleep last night and stepped right off the damned thing. No one believes me when I tell them that. They all think I had been out on a binge and fell on my face." But I believed him, because since childhood I have been a sleepwalker.

"What is the extent of your injuries?"

"A broken leg and fractured wrist that hurts like the devil."

"I guess you'll survive," I told Bud as I was about to leave. "But for heaven's sake, stick to first-floor bedrooms from now on."

Early the next morning we began the journey that was to change the course of the rest of our lives.

Departure at Last

On the pre-dawn stillness on Monday, J.C. and his buddy Jim Peden, picked me up at five o'clock in a gharry and we clop-clopped off to the station. Seated like Indian travelers on our sturdy luggage, we waited for two and a half hours for the train to pull in.

The station was crowded with lower-caste Indians and a smattering of British soldiers. We could hardly pick our way through the masses squatting on the quais and stretched out on the floor of the waiting room. We wondered how all these people could board a single train. But they did, huddled like sheep in third-class compartments. We Americans settled down in first class and thanked our government for providing wages that afforded such luxury. At our first stop an English lieutenant joined us in our compartment.

Rolling along at top speed (about thirty miles per hour), we surveyed the landscape outside our compartment window. The scenery was familiar to all of us, who had been stationed in Karachi for the last six months. Miles of flat yellow desert stretched out to join a cloudless sky, broken only by scattered clumps of sagebrush and an occasional camel caravan in the distance. We wasted no time observing the unchanging vista, but directed our attention to the more important business of procuring food.

We had not eaten since last night's supper and it was long past midmorning. Jim was the first to broach the subject of food as he rummaged in his B-4 bag, hoping to find in some remote corner of that overstuffed, shapeless mass the wherewithal for brunch.

"I don't know about you characters," he began in his Damon Runyon style, "but I'm gonna eat. The time has come to break out that hardtack we borrowed from the warehouse. If I do not mistake the rumblings in my lower regions, it is high time we have a little sustenance."

"It just could be that in this particular case you are right," J.C. answered, continuing the Runyonesque rambling. "If my eyes do not deceive me, the hands of my trusty Elgin would indicate that the time has arrived when the inner man must be satisfied. What are you waiting for, man? Bring out the grub, but quick."

In his corner by the window across from J.C. and me, the English lieutenant watched us as he silently puffed on his briar pipe.

Jim hauled out a package of K-ration, crackers, and a tin of cheese, to which I added a can of salted peanuts, saved from last month's PX ration. J.C. produced a minute can of grapefruit juice, the sole bit of potable liquid that the search thus far had netted.

"We've got to have something more to drink," I said. "That little can of battery acid will barely wet our palates."

"It seems to me," Jim said, "that somewhere in this bulky B-4 I have just the thing to staunch our thirst. If you'll cease your worry for the duration of a minute, Lib, I might be able to find the perfect thirst quencher."

It was two minutes, however, before his face lit up and he uttered a happy "Ahh!" as he dragged out a pint of Seagram's VO. Uncorking the bottle and noting the look of horror on my face, he said, "You can have the grapefruit juice, Lib, while we fellows drink the nectar of the gods. But be advised, my dear girl, you will never taste a better drink than whiskey at ten o'clock in the morning. Relax, woman, you're on leave."

Jim took a healthy swig straight from the bottle, passed it to J.C., then continued with his sermon: "Furthermore, with this stuff very much in the minus quantity, no one is going to force it on you. But if you will cease with the teetotaling inhibitions, we might let you have a taste, just to prove the truth of my contention." The Englishman sat silently in his corner.

After helping himself liberally to the breakfast drink, J.C. handed over the bottle to the English officer, saying in his most cordial tone, "Oh, I say, old fellow, do have a swig of this Seagram's. It's really very good stuff, you know."

"Thank you very much," the Englishman said, "but I don't believe I will. I had a regular breakfast before I boarded the train. I'm not thirsty, really I'm not."

"Oh, come now," J.C. persisted. "Be a good sport and join the fun. We'll be together a long time today, so we may as well get acquainted. Besides, it's fairly good liquor."

"No, thanks," the officer said. "I really shouldn't deprive you of it. ... Perhaps, though, just a drop or two, to see what American whiskey tastes like ..."

"Drink all you like," J.C. said. "We've got another bottle for future use."

The Englishman poured a little into the top of his thermos, drank it down in one gulp, and smacked his lips appreciatively.

"Oh, I say, that is good. I didn't know you Americans made such stuff. We think we have the corner on good whiskey, you know."

After that the Englishman loosened up and became an agreeable traveling companion. When the Seagram's was all gone, he took from his pocket a little silver flask and passed it all around. It was full of a clear liquid.

"It's only gin," he said. "We can't get good whiskey out here, you know. I'm almost ashamed to offer you this, but please help yourselves anyway."

"Why don't you save the gin for breakfast tomorrow," I suggested. And that is just what he did.

By afternoon we were all in the holiday mood and had almost forgotten the tribulations of the day before. The men settled down to comfortable conversation on the relative merits of English and American armed forces, while I set about writing a long letter to my family.

Bugs and a Bomb

At Hyderabad, Sind, we bade god-speed to our English friend as he boarded an outgoing train to Simla. Then we settled down for a four-hour layover in a dusty desert town quite unlike the large capital city by the same name southeast of Bombay. While the southern city boasted paved streets, mineretted palaces, jewel bedecked elephant palanquins, and a Nizam said to be the richest man in the world, the Hyderabad of our stopover had nothing of interest or even convenience. On that March day the place was hotter than Hades, dusty, windless, and devoid of shade.

We inquired about the best hotel, hoping to spend the waiting hours in the bar. There was no hotel, much less one with a bar. We asked the way to a restaurant and were directed to a small spare structure, where we dared order only fried eggs and black coffee.

At 4:30 a train from the north pulled into the station and carried us southward into the vast rural territory of Rajputana. All military personnel were checked in and out of the train. British enlisted men (known as BORs—British other recruits) were assigned to special railroad duty. The sergeant examining our tickets was dumbfounded to find two American corporals traveling first class.

"How can you afford to travel first class?" he inquired as he punched J.C.'s ticket.

"Oh, we save our money, then make a big splash," J.C. replied.

"Even so," the sergeant said, "we don't make enough to travel that way. It's the officers, anyway, that get all the good places. We always go second or third, that is, whenever we get a bit of leave." We had a hard time convincing him that American soldiers could travel any way they wished.

Beyond Hyderabad the train stopped about every half hour to pick up local passengers and mail. At Marwar Junction we saw a group of exotic looking women huddled together on the quai—a bright spot in an otherwise drab landscape. Above full skirts of bright red, orange, green, and yellow, edged with silver and gold braid, they wore tight muslin blouses, with tie-dyed scarves thrown over their heads. Their arms were adorned from shoulder to elbow with bands of silver bracelets; their bare ankles were encased in silver circlets. Each wore a lock of her black straight hair drawn down tightly over her forehead between her eyes, over the bridge of the nose, and affixed to a ring in the left nostril. Trundling babies on their hips and carrying large sacks, they chattered happily as they awaited their train.

After we had a good night's sleep on the benches and in the overhead bunks, an Indian army nurse, pint-sized compared to us tall Americans, joined us in our compartment. Very dark skinned, she wore her hair in a single long pigtail down her back. At an earlier stop the British dispatcher had asked us if we minded having a roommate. The nurse had a first-class ticket and ours was the only first-class compartment aboard. She had been riding for hours with friends in second-class. We, of course, said we'd be happy to have her join us, but we really didn't treat her nicely.

She was a pathetic looking girl in her flat black shoes, black cotton stockings, and drab khaki uniform. She entered the compartment with a look of misgiving, as though she felt unsafe so close to two stalwart American men. Even the presence of another woman did not reassure her. Instead of taking the logical empty seat on the bench where Jim was quietly reading a book, she perched on the end of the other seat with J.C. and me, slung her legs over the arm, and sat stiffly with her back to us for the rest of the journey. We tried to talk to her, suggesting that she take the roomier bench, offering her some of our dwindling chocolate ration, but all to no avail. We could not penetrate her silence, nor break down her wall of shyness.

The situation struck us as funny. Our seat was a little crowded, with its three occupants, while Jim was now stretched out full length across the way. We jibed him about his lack of appeal, suggesting that perhaps he needed the aid of good bath soap or a scented dentifrice. Jim is not in the least formidable looking. If anything he has a kindly, warm face. Yet, before long we had him just about convinced that he could run a close second to Bela Lugosi.

When it appeared that the nurse had resolved to spend the rest of the trip without movement or murmur, we lapsed into a silly mood, pouncing on chance incidents to make a joke. Two of them probably fortified any strange notions the girl might have had about American soldier-sahibs.

At one of the stations the conductor came around to make a routine check of our tickets. J.C. had already gotten up to let the man into the compartment, so I asked him to get my ticket out of the pocket of my uniform coat, which was hanging from the upper bunk. J.C. rummaged in vain for a moment. Then I said, "What's the matter? Can't you find it?"

"Nope," he said with a twinkle in his eye. "There's nothing in here but a bunch of beat up old hundred-rupee notes!" Our seatmate turned around with a start, her eyes wide with wonder. Here was real proof, she must have thought, of the rumor that all Americans are rajah-sahibs.

A little later we stopped at another station where two kinds of pests bothered us: myriad flies and peddlers, one group swarming inside the compartment and the other pushing their wares at us through open windows, then poking us in the ribs as we alighted on the platform to stretch our legs. Thoroughly annoyed, we sought to get rid of both flies and peddlers.

"Why don't you get out the bomb," I said, "and get rid of some of these insects. And while you're at it, reach in my bag for a hand grenade to scatter the crowds outside."

Jim reached in his B-4 bag for the aerosol bug bomb, which he poised gingerly between his hands with mock care. The little nurse turned around with a start, her eyes full of fear, just in time to see Jim unscrew the cap. As he sprayed the compartment with the evil-smelling gas, I'm sure the girl must have said whatever prayers a Hindu says just before she dies.

Two hours later, when we finally got off the train at Palanpur station, the nurse surely must have breathed a sigh of relief to be rid of such troubling travel-mates.

The Nawab's Safari Tent

As our train pushed south out of the desert region of Rajputana, bits of dull green began to dot the landscape as the sandy soil darkened to reddish clay. In the distance the flame-red blossoms of an occasional gold mohur tree brightened the drab vista where a few sheep and cattle grazed.

On our arrival at Palanpur station, the usual crowd of native spectators was on hand to watch the train go by. But these people were different from those I had seen in Calcutta and Karachi. No porters grabbed our bags, no beggars tugged our sleeves, no little boys shouted "Shoeshine, Joe?" or "Gimme cigarette!" The station itself was different, too. The low, red brick building had been newly painted inside and was swept clean. The quai and the walkway around the station house were trash-free. We did not have to pick our way around the usual mounds of manure.

As we got off the train a dapper Indian man, dressed in a European suit, approached us. "How do you do!" he said in perfect, if stilted English. "Welcome to Palanpur. I am Mr. Khan, private secretary to His Highness. He asked me to extend his cordial greetings and to show you to your quarters." Then he led us to a late model Buick and whistled for help with our luggage.

Two Indian men, bare-chested and dhoti-clad, stashed our luggage in an ancient truck. Before we had time to get out our tips they were gone. We climbed into the car with Mr. Khan and headed out into the countryside. Along the way, Mr. Khan filled us in on that morning's hunt when two black panthers had been sighted.

At the massive gates of a walled compound I caught a glimpse of the palace, a white turreted structure at the end of a drive. As we approached the palace, Mr. Khan pointed to a large colorful tent on our left with a scalloped roofline and a crested flag atop its center pole.

"That's where you men will be temporarily housed," he said. "Later, if a vacancy occurs, you can move into the guesthouse. Memsahib will stay in the guesthouse. Two American officers are already there."

The driver dropped all of us off at the guesthouse, a two-story white structure adjacent to a pretty little garden with bubbling fountain. We walked up a short flight of steps onto a porch, then into the large reception room where a welcoming English tea awaited us.

While we refreshed our thirsty gullets and silenced the growling of our tummies, Mr. Khan outlined plans for the next day's entertainment. Then he gave us a run-down on the other guests who had already arrived, but were nowhere to be seen at the moment. An American colonel and his young army sidekick were presently looking over the grounds. At the palace the nawab and begum were hosting the Maharajah of Porbander, for whom today's hunt had been specially arranged. Expected later were another Red Cross girl from Delhi and an American correspondent for a large midwestern newspaper.

After tea we retired to our various quarters to unpack and freshen up before dinner at eight in the guesthouse dining room. At first J.C. and Jim did not cotton to living in a tent. It smacked too much of earlier army digs. But when they walked into the nawab's elegant safari tent, Jim said "Wow!" J.C. added, "It's straight out of the Arabian nights. Bring on the belly dancers!"

The brightly colored tent, large enough for a circus, proved to be more than adequate for the men's needs. The nawab had used it in his sporting days when big game had been plentiful all over India. Actually, there were two tents, one a little larger, and placed over the other, providing a narrow corridor around the inner room for ventilation and access by the bearers. Canvas partitions divided the inner tent into three large rooms, each with its own bath facility. The inner walls were hung with bright red and yellow Indian prints and embroidered tapestries. Overstuffed chairs and a sofa sat on thick Persian rugs. Instead of string-and-straw charpois, imported innerspring mattresses provided comfort at night. A well-appointed desk, a stocked refrigerator, and a game table completed the tent's amenities. Hand-pulled punkas (overhead fans manned by little boys) cooled the air.

An hour later, as I leisurely dressed for dinner I heard, through the draped doorway of my room, heavy steps in the reception hall and snatches of dialogue. The first tantalizing tidbits were in unfamiliar voices. Then J.C.'s deep bass and Jim's baritone voice chimed in. I listened entranced.

"Two panthers. Think of it! And the Maharajah didn't score a hit."

"I could see pretty well from the tree stand."

"The nawab deliberately shot foul."

"The bombs sounded like big firecrackers."

"I wonder if any beaters were clawed."

By the time I joined the others in the living room the men were already on their second drinks. J.C. introduced me to short, plump Colonel Gilmore, who was in his fifties, and on leave from Calcutta with his tall, thin, twenty-four-year-old adjunct officer, whom we called Captain Charlie. The colonel at first was standoffish with the GIs, but loosened up later after he saw how much the nawab appeared to respect them.

A middle-aged Red Cross club director joined us the next day and took the colonel off our hands. Captain Charlie was "one of the boys" and hobnobbed with us.

As we gathered for drinks before dinner, we made short shift of small talk, for all were eager to hear the details of the hunt. Much to our chagrin we learned that we had missed the hunt by just four hours because of the long wait in Marwar Junction. This shoot was unusual in that two black panthers (melanistic phase of the leopard) had been sighted and shot at, yet neither was killed nor wounded. J.C. and Jim were disappointed to have missed the shoot, for big game hunting had been the main drawing card for this vacation. They were happy later, however, to bag plenty of lesser game in the two shoots specially arranged for them.

Dinner that first night was leisurely and delicious, prepared by the palace cook and brought to the guesthouse by liveried bearers. We dined on white damask with English bone china and Waterford crystal. Fresh garden flowers centered the table. Fresh vegetables, which had been cut into flower forms, and tiny orchids garnished each plate. At all guesthouse meals, except for breakfast, gold-edged menus cards, embellished with the royal crest leaned against our water goblets. This was the typewritten menu for our first dinner:

DINER

Consomme Froid en Tasse

Filets de Pomfret
Belle-Meuniere

Selle D'Agneau St. Menehould
Legumes

Coupe D'Oranges

D/20-3-45.

DEJEUNER

Poulet et Langue en Aspic
Dalade

Curry de Mouton au Riz
Plats a l' Indienne

Creme Renverse

21st. March 1945

Exhausted after our long trip, we all turned in early to be prepared for the next five exhilarating days of high adventure and fine food.

The next day we caught our first glimpse of our royal host when he came to the guesthouse in the morning to welcome us. J.C. and Jim had come over from their tent for breakfast and an early game of gin rummy. The nawab found us sitting on the floor in our bare feet.

"Good morning," he said with a smile. "Welcome to Zorowar Palace. I just came by to see that you are comfortable."

"Good morning, Your Highness," we responded as we jumped up to shake hands.

I was about to excuse myself to put on my boots, when His Highness said, "Oh, no! Please don't put on your boots for me. If you do I'll be obliged to leave," whereupon our royal host joined us on the floor and took off his shoes.

Ramad, the bearer, bringing our mid-morning tea, was shocked to see us in deshabille in the presence of his august master. Muttering to himself in his native tongue, he seemed to say: "These Americans! Sitting on the floor when the room is full of chairs! They must be crazy."

"Is Ramad serving you well?" His Highness inquired after the bearer had slipped away. We assured him that Ramad had been more than satisfactory, probably the best bearer we had encountered in India. His martinis were superb and his Tom Collinses worthy of the Waldorf bar.

"And has he kept your flower bowls replenished every day?" was the next question, addressed to me.

For a moment I was silent, not knowing what to say, for in this one respect Ramad had been remiss.

The nawab sensed my unvoiced answer. Immediately he summoned back the bearer. The tone of his voice, rather than his words, conveyed his displeasure. To the quivering Ramad he said, "You are to bring fresh flowers from the gardens at once for the bowl's in the memsahib's room. And do not let a day go by without refilling them."

Then the nawab put on his shoes, got up to leave, and said, "If you need anything, just tell the bearer or Major

Singh, my aide de camp. Her Highness and I expect you for dinner at the palace this evening. You'll meet the maharajah of Porbander then. My chauffeur will pick you up at 7:30."

"In the meantime," he added, "please feel free to enjoy tennis and billiards at my private club. My son will be happy to show you around."

We took up his offer that very afternoon, playing billiards for an hour before we dressed for dinner.

His Highness, Taley Mohammed Khan, looked every inch the modern prince. A little taller and heavier than the average Indian, he was stately in bearing. He held himself a little stiffly because of an old back injury, the result of a polo accident in his youth. His olive complexion was smooth shaven, his hair nearly white, and his dark eyes kindly and gracious. At age sixty-two he appeared to be in the full flower of health and strength.

At dinner that evening we met the charming young begum. Until recently the wives of Muslim potentates had never appeared in public, secluded night and day in their private quarters with servants and children. The first two wives of our host still lived in purdah and were never seen outside. His third wife, a beautiful Australian mother of his five-year-old son, was his traveling companion, partner in service to the people, and hostess extraordinaire. She presided at our table that second night of out stay in Palanpur.

For the occasion we Americans put on our best bib and tucker, which for Jim and J.C. were starched suntans and polished civilian shoes. The officers donned their "pinks." I wore my new formal sari of purple Swiss organdy embroidered with tiny flowers. However, in the rush of leaving Karachi, Jim had forgotten to pack his dress shoes. None of us realized this until we were busily chatting in the palace drawing room. I looked across the room and seemed to see nothing but Jim's big, worn out, army clunkers.

Two sedans called for the five of us and drove us the two hundred yards to the palace, where we gathered in one of the smaller drawing rooms. It was a charming room, with off-white walls, Empire furniture in soft luscious turquoise satin, and family pictures along the walls. Though the nawab's Muslim religion forbade smoking and drinking, he offered us liquor and Turkish cigarettes.

Here we met the Maharajah of Porbander, who acknowledged the men with handshakes and me with a deep bow. The tall, thin maharajah stood regally erect in jodhpurs under a long, black, silk tunic, closed from neck to hem with a single row of solid gold buttons. The nawab wore a formal white linen suit, double breasted, and buttoned all the way up to his neck with rubies and diamonds.

A few minutes before dinner the begum entered the drawing room. All of us were startled by her grace and beauty. Her peaches-and-cream complexion and shiny black hair, pulled straight back to a low knot on her neck, perfectly set off her white lace sari. Emeralds and diamonds cascaded around her neck, enveloped her wrists, and dangled from her ears. A single massive emerald pin on her shoulder kept her sari in place.

The nawab and begum both possessed the happy faculty of putting their guests at ease. Before we sat down our host made a special effort to talk with J.C. and Jim, since, according to protocol, they would not be close to him at the dinner table. Their wide-ranging conversation covered the panther hunt of the preceding day, the Bombay port explosion of the preceding year (where J.C. had been involved in clearing away the debris), the religions of India, astrology and fortune telling, and the works of Somerset Maugham.

Dinner was in a small informal dining room, with sixteen guests at a round table. The maharajah and the colonel sat at the begum's right and left;, while the captain and I flanked the nawab. The nawabzada (heir apparent), a family cousin, Major Singh, J.C. and Jim, plus five male local guests rounded out the circle. Trophy skins of tiger, leopard, snow leopard, and various antelopes, plus rhino horns lined the walls—a fitting setting for a post-hunt dinner.

After a dinner of lamb curry, rice, exotic vegetables, and boiled custard, the Indian men partook of their after-dinner betel nut, which is chewed like plug tobacco. At the instigation of the young nawazada, Jim and J.C. decided to try it out, much to their discomfort. At one time J.C. almost had to excuse himself from the table to avoid a mishap. Finally the two GIs just swallowed the stuff with a grimace, and vowed never again to be tempted by the Indian recreational "drug."

After dinner the men shot billiards in the game room, where the walls were covered with animal skins, big game trophies, and photographs of the nawab on safari. The begum and I watched the men play and commented on the nawab's skill with the cue. At ten the begum bade us goodnight and the royal cars drove us back to the guesthouse.

The next day a memorable meal was prepared by the nawabzada (heir apparent) as a special honor for me. Like many Indian princes he had learned to cook and prided himself on his culinary skill. He had spent the whole morning in the palace kitchen preparing a hot curry for my two companions and me.

At lunchtime a liveried servant appeared at the guesthouse door bearing a small silver bowl on a large silver tray. Bowing low, he silently passed the precious dish to me, then to my companions. Then he stepped aside to watch us sample his master's gift.

It was a curry to end all curries. "It's hotter than a whore's behind," Jim indecorously stated later.

My turn came first to taste it. Spooning a half-cup of rice on my plate, I gingerly poked a small forkful of the savory saffron curry, well encased in rice, into my mouth. I winced, coughed, sputtered, and swallowed quickly, then grabbed the water goblet by my plate. Tears filled my eyes and my breath came in spurts.

Jim and J.C., their palates accustomed to hot Texas chili, fared better. They actually ate all the rest of the curry, blinking from time to time and consuming lots of water.

"Not bad," Jim said.

"Best curry I ever ate," said J.C., who had never before tasted the Indian dish.

"Please give the nawabzada our heartfelt thanks," I said as the bearer removed the silver bowl. "And be sure to tell him how much we enjoyed his delicious curry."

We all guzzled ice water the rest of the day.

A-Hunting We did Go

Though we had missed out on the black panther shoot, we later enjoyed two hunts specially arranged for us Americans.

The Palanpur shoot was a whole different ballgame from the American or European versions of tracking and killing the quarry. Literally no hunting was involved, for the game was already located before any gunfire occurred.

For a princely shoot, you do not rough it. You wear decent clothes and ride in a car to a tree stand, or until you see the quarry, then fire at close range. There is no long tramp through the woods and brush for game, which may or may not be there. Game was plentiful in Palanpur, at least for the royal family and guests. The gunner did not even have to retrieve the bloody animal. Native men, following in another vehicle, rushed out to slit the slain animal's throat and carry it back to be stripped of hide and horns.

The set-up for our hunt was quite different from the maharajah's panther shoot. We set out one afternoon in two American cars, the lead Buick driven by the twenty-eight year old nawabzada, with the colonel beside him up front and the captain, the other Red Cross girl, and me in the back. Behind us, a Ford station wagon carried the nawab's aide-de-camp, Major Singh, along with J.C., Jim, and two turbaned assistants.

We started off down a dirt road but soon were traveling cross-country in an amazing fashion, through sand bars, over plowed fields, down deep ditches, and into thick cactus hedges, at about fifty miles per hour with the radiator spouting boiling water all the while. It was the most thrilling ride of my lifetime. That old sedan mowed down cactus hedges like a tank plowing through stone walls. If the Buick makers could have seen the test that one was put through, they would have upped their prices and cornered the Land Rover market.

Our hunt, arranged on the spur of the moment, was simpler than the one for the maharajah. That earlier shoot had involved the use of dozens of beaters and the installation of a tree stand with seats. We were out for smaller game: Asian deer and antelope, called nelghai and chinkara. The nelghai, or blue bull, is a large gray, cow-like creature with short antlers, a face like a horse, and a little tuft of white hair under his chin. The chinkara is a tiny spotted gazelle with coiled antlers and a white belly; fleet of foot, he runs like the proverbial greased lightning— a challenging target for the expert gunner.

Our first hunt was organized for Colonel Gilmore, but the rest of us went along hoping to get a shot or two. The shoot was managed in the following manner. We'd drive along until we saw a single animal or a herd. If we were not close enough to make a hit, we'd chase the deer until we got within firing distance, and then the designated gunner would jump down from the car and fire. Under these conditions a deer didn't stand much of a chance in the sights of a good shot.

Colonel Gilmore did all the early shooting. Most of his shots went wild. By the end of the day the colonel had bagged one nelghai. He blamed most of his bad shots on the nawab's gunning piece, a classic Holland and Holland. "This gun shoots too high," he would say, as each little beast scampered away after his fire. "I'm sure I saw hair in my sights."

During the course of the day we saw all sorts of other creatures: jackals, foxes, wild cats, monkeys, pheasant, grouse, wild peacocks, partridge, and quail. Frequently we had to suspend fire because of the many natives who roamed the fields and thickets. Once the colonel had his gun to his shoulder, ready to fire at a nelghai in the brush, when Major Singh suddenly stopped him. The rest of us saw what Major Singh had seen.

"I don't think it's open season on the villagers," Jim said dryly to the colonel, after a loin-clad Indian jumped out of the bushes directly in the line of fire. The colonel turned crimson and said nothing.

As we headed back to the palace at dusk, the colonel complained, for the third time, about the imperfect sighting of the Holland and Holland. J.C. said, "Let me try the nawab's gun. We'll see if the thing is sighted right." Handing Major Singh the gun he had carried all day, J.C. took the nawab's favorite shooting piece. He caressed the carved walnut stock and gently rubbed the engraved steel.

On a distant rise, J.C spotted the silhouette of a tiny chinkara running full speed across the horizon. "Stop the car," he shouted. He stepped out of the Buick and fired a single shot. As the chinkara struggled, then dropped to the ground, J.C. handed the nawab's gun back to the colonel and said, "A sweet little gun if I ever saw one."

Several days later, on a second hunt, the nawabzada announced that things would be arranged differently this time. Everyone, including the memsahib, would have a chance at the game, beginning with the captain and me. I shot and luckily missed a chinkara. The captain and Jim each bagged a nelghai. J.C. also brought down two nelghai, one of which was as big as a Hereford bull.

At dinner that night the nawab promised to have the horns sent to the States for us. But we never received them.

His Highness Leads a Tour

We jumped at the chance for a tour through the countryside when His Highness asked if we would like to see how the farm families lived. Early in the afternoon of our third day, J.C., Jim, the two officers, and I joined His Highness in the Land Rover for a swing through the farmland, past small villages, with a final brief stop at the summer palace in the hills. Along the way the nawab gave us a running commentary on the history, present status, and future possibilities of his beloved little kingdom.

He told us Palanpur's main industry was farming. We drove past fields now greening with rice shoots and emerging vegetables. Because of the aridity of the soil, this monarch twenty years earlier had initiated modern cultivation methods. With irrigation, the little state had managed to supply not only her own food, but enough vegetables and rice to export to other Indian states and China.

Most of the people lived in farm compounds or small villages adjacent to the farming areas. Their homes were two and three room dwellings of sturdy wood and thatch. Outside we saw children playing while mothers cleaned brass pots with water from large terra cotta jugs. Old crones sat in the sunlight and watched the children's games.

"What a change from the mud huts of Assam!" I said. "These people seem prosperous and healthy."

"As indeed they are," the nawab said. "You will understand why when we see the schools and medical facilities."

The colonel was particularly interested in the irrigation. "When did you set up your system? And who helped you get it going?"

"I can thank you Americans for getting us started," the nawab said. "After the first world war, I met the U.S. representatives in Geneva, at the League of Nations where I was India's representative, and it was there that I learned about your modern farming methods. I invited American engineers from your Midwest to put in my system here."

"Looks like they did a good job," the colonel said. "But you need some upgrading and expansion. Perhaps I could help you out with that since water-engineering is my business."

En route to the large village we stopped at the home of a cloth weaver. After farming, weaving was Palanpur's main industry. Under a shanty extension of the roof overhang the owner was busily at work at a handloom, shuttling the white thread back and forth with mechanical precision.

"What's he making?" I asked.

"Probably a dhoti or common sari," was the reply. "Our home weaving industry produces up to 12,000 yards a day. Before the war we sent tons of cotton cloth to North Africa. Even now, with exports cut off, we provide enough extra to relieve the cloth shortages in many Indian cities."

At our approach the weaver jumped to his feet, bowed low before His Highness, cupped his hands in the Indian greeting and remained bent over until the nawab bade him arise. Repeating the welcome to us, he said, "Namaste, burrah sahib! Namaste, memsahib! Namaste sahibs! Please to honor my house. Please to come inside."

The weaver led us into a neat front room lighted by a single window, its clay floor swept clean. Two low wooden benches flanked one wall behind a low round table. Gleaming brass bowls and a pitcher hung over the open floor hearth. No family members were in sight. I wondered if a shy wife and children were hovering in a back room, fearful of such august company.

As we walked back to the car I said to His Highness, "Is this the home of an entrepreneur? What is his caste? He seems fairly well off for a working man."

"Indeed you are right to call him an entrepreneur since he owns his own small business. He employs several cousins to help with the weaving and has a sweeper to help his wife. He's what you might call middle-class, a cut above the mahlis and dhobis, but below the cooks, priests, and local councilmen."

We stopped next in a central village to look at a new mosque in process of construction. For such a small town the mosque seemed out of proportion in size, elegance and cost. Built and financed by the people themselves, its total cost was 300,000 rupees (about $100,000). A large rectangular building, with tall round-topped windows and a flat tiled roof, only the tall thin white spire, etched in blue and surmounted by a crescent weathervane, indicated that it was a Muslim mosque rather than a Methodist church.

The nawab's chauffeur then took us to the primary school, a white modern structure with neat benches for the students and a table with chair for the teacher. Here the Indian "three R's" were taught in Urdu, and then in English, to primary through high school students. As we entered one of the classrooms, a sing-song style mass recitation was in progress. Then two little boys, about ten, showed us how beautifully they spoke English by reading us fairy stories from their English storybooks. We noted that these stories, about kings and princes, extolled the virtues of the monarchical system of government.

Further on, the glaring sunlit white facade of the rural dispensary presaged its equally bright, spotless interior. Rows of bottled drugs, surgical instruments, splints, bandages, and an operating table indicated that minor ailments, cuts and bruises, broken bones, and small operations could adequately be treated here.

"How many patients a day do you care for here?" I inquired of the native doctor standing by.

"About 50 in a normal day and as many as 120 in the malaria season," he said. "Mostly dysentery and worms and skin infections. We send more serious illnesses and surgeries to the large hospital in New Town. They have intensive care there and new equipment for broken bones."

By late afternoon we were ready for the tea awaiting us on the grounds of the nawab's summer palace, now closed for the season. On a grassy knoll overlooking a small artificial lake, we rested awhile in the shadow of the elegant four-story light blue structure. Then we walked around the terraced gardens, breathing in the fresh air of the foothills. Our eyes feasted on the red-gold mohur trees in full bloom and splashes of rainbow hues in exotic tropical blooms.

A short walk into the woods behind the palace brought us to a tiny white marble temple guarded by a keeper. Big gray monkeys chattered at us from the trees surrounding the temple, as though they resented our intrusion into their hallowed ground. The old man told us that just a few hundred yards behind the temple a tiger pair was keeping watch over their three-months-old cubs. We dared penetrate no further into the woods.

Throughout the tour we enjoyed the nawab as a friend and equal, never feeling awed by his status and authority, or strained by our differences in customs or color. He was truly "a prince of a fellow."

Riding High

The next day we had our fill of "beastly" rides; horses before breakfast and camels before tea. The sun was just peeping over the distant hills when Major Singh called for us at the guesthouse. Five caparisoned Arabian horses, in bridle bells and shell-adorned necklaces, whiffled and pawed the ground.

Major Singh cut a fine figure in his trim riding breeches, English boots, tweed riding jacket, and tan topi. A tall handsome man in his late fifties, he was retired from the Indian cavalry, and managed the nawab's stable. He also arranged all rides and hunting for the nawab's guests.

Colonel Gilmore and Captain Charlie, experienced horsemen, were anxious to get going. Jim, a Texan, groggy at the early hour, slumped like a range rider in the saddle. For J.C. and me, though, it was another story. J.C. had never been on a horse before, so of course he drew the one really strange horse in the bunch. His mount had a habit of hanging his tongue sideways out of his mouth.

"What's the matter with this horse?" J.C. said. "Is his bit uncomfortable?"

"No, sahib," said Major Singh. "It's just his way of keeping cool, like a dog."

"But the others aren't doing it " J.C. went on. "This fellow must be an individualist."

In spirit the horse was a also nonconformist. While the rest of us proceeded at a walk because of the excessive heat (100 degrees in the shade), J.C.'s mount cantered throughout most of the ride before breaking into a full gallop. Luckily, by grabbing the horse's mane, J.C. was able to stick on without a spill.

Though I had done a little riding, of the untutored variety, I hadn't been on a horse since an oversized stallion ran away with me eight years before. But I let it be known that I was semi-skilled and could post with the best of them. The men were frankly skeptical.

"I'll bet you don't even know which side to mount on," Jim said.

"Of course I do," I said tartly. "And I'll just show you guys a thing or two about riding straight and tall, which is more than a certain Texan does."

In deference to my gender, Major Singh helped me first. Approaching the left side of a gorgeous black mare, I put my left foot into the stirrup, gripped the saddle, and tried to hoist my right leg up over the horse's rump. But she was one tall mare. I kicked her in the flank instead. Jim coughed audibly and remarked under his breath, "Looks like age is catching up with Lib."

Then Major Singh led the horse over to the guesthouse steps and I tried again. With a healthy lunge I heaved my body upwards, completely missed the saddle, and landed heavily on the horse's rump. As I pulled myself forward into the saddle, Jim said, "Well, I guess we're ready to proceed, now that the duchess has found a comfortable seat."

Apparently that mare didn't like other females. As though to prove the truth of Jim's statement, she tried everything in her repertoire to make me fall off. When I tried to rein her in to a gentle walk, she charged into a canter, sneaked in two or three rough trots, then went back to the canter before finally coming to a sudden halt that nearly catapulted me over her head. I wondered if Jim had had a private conversation with my mount.

As we rode along the desert road, beyond the palace compound, we saw camels carrying great sheaves of wheat tied across their humps. Major Singh called our attention to two newborn camels, tiny spindly-legged creatures with innocent expressions, not yet besmirched by the supercilious look of the full-grown beasts. Long-horned bullocks, prodded by half-naked coolies, pulled two-wheeled ox carts loaded with branches for braziers in the city. In the distance, jagged hills were silhouetted against a sapphire sky.

It had been a long ride. My back ached and I was hungry. After two hours I was frustrated with my mount, and the offhand comments of my fellow riders, and I just wanted to get back to the guesthouse.

Jim spoke for all of us when he said, "Let's hope there's good American scrambled eggs and hot buttered toast waiting for us." There was, plus fresh cut pineapple, bananas, and steaming coffee.

In the afternoon Major Singh was at our door again, this time for a short camel canter around the palace grounds. Three turbaned drivers helped J.C., Jim, and me onto double saddles, with the drivers practically on the animals' necks and us riders behind the hump, practically on the switching tails. The colonel and the captain pleaded other plans to avoid this afternoon entertainment.

The camel is a very strange beast, his facial expression not unlike that of some prim old maids I have known. He is averse to taking orders. He hates to kneel down or get up again. He knows his job is to carry burdens, not fearful females, so he makes every effort to scare them off. And he loves to stretch his long legs running across the countryside at breakneck speed.

Before my mount condescended to let me get on him, he snarled, showed his teeth, and spat a regurgitated gob of his last meal at me. When I climbed on his back he thrust his head into the air, then jumped up on his forefeet with a thrust that nearly catapulted me over his rump. Once astride, I clutched the driver in front and enjoyed the loping gallop, as gentle as that of a pacing horse. But when the camel knelt down to unload me, he seemed to take pleasure in spilling me quickly off his rump.

The camels I had seen in other parts of India appeared to like their regular jobs. They seemed to smile as they pulled long flatbed wagons loaded with lumber or balanced bulging sacks slung across their humps. I loved to watch them in Karachi as we bicycled to the wharf for a day at Sandspit. And once from the air north of Lahore I saw a camel caravan, the mica-embroidered load-covers sparkling in the sunlight.

On the return trip atop our camel perches, we caught a glimpse of the red, yellow, and green silk Palanpur flag, fluttering in the breeze on a palace parapet. A soft haze bathed the imposing structure in glamour straight out of the Mogul era. But by dusk we were too worn out to appreciate its beauty. We wanted only to settle down in comfortable chairs with two-ounce bourbons in our hands.

His Highness and His Kingdom

In 1945 the little state of Palanpur, one of the 560 principalities in India still ruled by a native monarch, was a prosperous agrarian area in the large western province of Rajputana, about 150 miles north of Baroda. At one time it had been a substantial part of the great Mogul Empire, but had now shrunk to a neat little forty square miles. Its mostly rural population, of about 300,000, was predominantly Muslim. Its reigning monarch was His Highness, Taley Mohammed Khan, last of a long line of rulers of Mogul ancestry.

Brought up in the royal tradition of his Mogul ancestors, His Highness was proficient in the elements of warfare, hunting, and governing. But he modified the old ways to meeting changing social and environmental needs. Most of the pomp and ceremony of the past was discarded. Fluent in several languages and impeccable in English, he entertained world diplomats with panache and authority. His training and talents thus enabled him to be India's representative in the 1920s to the League of Nations.

Though a "modern" ruler, the nawab of Palanpur maintained some of the old social practices. Among those taught to his sons was respect for the prince. The Indian tradition for the ordinary man, regardless of age, is to rise in the presence of royalty. This was demonstrated one afternoon as seven of us: the nawab, his younger son, his councilors, the nawabzada, and I were watching a volleyball game between our American soldiers and five young members of the extended royal family. The five-year-old son, usually well behaved, entertained himself by testing this custom on the aged council members. Several times he deliberately walked in front of these old men, comfortably seated in wicker chairs, just to see them hoist their creaky bodies to a standing position, then bow low to their future ruler.

In his marital adventures the nawab departed from custom in his later life. Like all Muslim princes, as a very young man he married a Mohammedan girl of noble blood who gave him an heir, the present nawabzada. He then married another Indian woman, probably hoping for a back-up heir in case their first son could not serve. These early wives were in purdah, living in the palace in their own apartments, isolated from the outside world. Nine years before our visit, His Highness took a third wife, a young, beautiful Australian girl, thirty years his junior, who provided him with a second heir. Their son was five when we saw him in 1945.

Despite the differences in their age and backgrounds, the nawab and his third begum appeared to be very compatible. A fine sportswoman, Her Highness accompanied the nawab on many safarais, bagging tigers, panthers, and leopards, as the photographs in the game room attested. Full of life and gaiety, she also was a good companion on summer trips to the hill stations of India—Missouri, Mt. Abu, Simla, and Naini Tal. As the nawab's official hostess, she presided over state dinners, planned the décor and menus, and charmed his guests with her elegance and wit.

The begum was well read and a good conversationalist. Unlike the traditional Indian wife, she not only had ideas, but she freely expressed them. Even the nawab deferred to her opinion. He pointed out that she was the motivating force behind the new boys high school and was largely responsible for the construction of the women's nursing home, where she established classes for mothers in pre-natal care and birth control.

The begum's concern for the welfare of all her adopted people continued even in her childbearing years. A case in point was the conversation that followed one of the dinners at the palace we attended. We asked her about the chained men we had seen the day before. On hearing the clank of chains as we sat on the guesthouse porch having tea, we thought it to be a passing ox-cart. Instead, a line of twenty handcuffed, nearly naked men, their feet in heavy chains, passed by us. We were shocked at this feudal display within the very gates of the palace.

Her Highness explained that the men were prisoners who had committed petty crimes and were serving their sentences at work in the palace gardens. The chains were to prevent escape and saved the hiring of a guard with a gun.

"It's one of those things that I don't like," she said apologetically, "and it's one of the things that some day will be changed. But changes come very slowly in India and we have to work persistently and patiently."

Palanpur was a prosperous agrarian state. Its countryside presented a gently rolling aspect, with bare rocky crags rising to 5,000 feet on it's northern border. The well-irrigated, arid soil produced vegetables and rice. Cactus in abundance fenced off farm plots. By late March the thermometer regularly registered 105–107. The heat was broken only by occasional cooling sandstorms and monsoon rains. From April to October the wives and children of the rich moved to their summer homes in the hill stations of Simla, Mt. Abu, and Kashmir.

Palanpur Old Town, with a population of about 3,000, had grown up around the old palace, a centuries-old rambling wooden structure now used for offices and shops. Within the city walls most of the inhabitants lived in ancient two-story wooden structures above their places of business. The streets of the town, winding picturesquely in and out and around the rambling old palace, were cleaner than those of the larger Indian cities. Outside the city walls several new schools, with comfortable classrooms, looked not unlike some of our American country day schools. The new town of Palanpur, closer to the railway station and the present palace, boasted modern government buildings, a large general hospital, a public library, several mosques, and a hospital for women, the result of the young begum's interest and effort.

The people of Palanpur appeared to be healthier and more prosperous than those I had seen in other parts of India. I saw no beggars or ragged children in the streets. The present nawab had broadened the education and health opportunities for all castes with new schools, dispensaries, and public clinics. The small compact size of Palanpur made it easier to implement health, education, and farming programs than in the larger provinces where transport, distribution, and communication problems abounded.

In governing Palanpur His Highness embraced the best of feudal and modern concepts. His first responsibility was to his people, to see to their welfare and respond to their needs. In an effort to awaken interest in at least partial self-government he appointed a prime minister, four lesser ministers, a customs officer, and a carefully chosen advisory council. But these "helpers" seemed devoid of a sense of civic duty, so the nawab was obliged to go directly to the people for information.

The aloofness of the feudal lord discarded, the nawab made frequent visits to the homes of farmers and weavers, which his councilors had been unwilling to do. In his younger days he regularly rode on horseback into all corners of his domain, substituting real concern in lieu of the ancient practice of instilling fear. In emergencies he often personally attended to the welfare of his subjects. Thus he was able to build rapport with all castes, breaking down barriers between serf and lord.

Their Highnesses had many plans for Palanpur's future. They hoped to extend the education system eventually to include all castes, at least through elementary school. Plans were already underway to build a whole system of rural dispensaries similar to the one we saw. Just before we arrived in Palanpur, the nawab had conferred with an Austrian physician, brought to the palace for a month's business visit. The two men had set up a plan for the construction of additional dispensaries right after the war. As a result of economic development, coupled with education, the nawab hoped that someday, representative government might prove feasible for Palanpur.

In 1948, with the partition of India into three separate countries of Pakistan, Bangladesh, and India, hundreds of small states were swallowed up by larger ones, and their princes were deprived of their lands, power, and wealth. What happened to Taley Mohammed Khan in that shake-up, I do not know. The last I heard from him was in the summer of 1945, when he sent my parents a cable of congratulation in response to my marriage announcement. Then at Christmas he sent an elegant card, engraved in gold, with the royal crest.

On a map of India printed in the 1960's, Palanpur is shown as just one of a thousand towns and cities in the large Central Provinces, no longer a separate state. Recent books on modern India do not even list Palanpur in the Index.

The Nawab's Special Glasses

On our last scorching night in Palanpur we once again dined at the palace, only this time in the cool of the begum's private quarters. Her Highness thought we would be more comfortable in her upstairs air-conditioned living room.

Spending a few hours with the nawab and begum as "one of the family" felt almost as though we had been invited to our own president's private White House quarters for Sunday supper. The nawab told us that we were the first guests outside the family to share the intimacy of the royal home. Even the nawab's nephew, who had lived all his thirty years in the palace, dined there with us for the first time.

Forewarned that the dinner would be informal, we all changed to clean uniforms. Jim and J.C. shined their GI clodhoppers. I dressed up my dark slacks and white shirt with multicolored dangly earrings.

The nawab's Buick delivered us to the palace. A bearer led us upstairs to the end of a long hall, beyond the closed doors of other apartments where the two older begums lived in purdah. At the last door the nawab and the nawabzada greeted us with warm handshakes.

"Come on in and relax," he said. "I'm sure you'd like a cool drink after your hot tiring day."

As we entered the small American-style living room, His Highness unbuttoned his tight tunic collar and said, "Take off your ties, gentlemen. We don't stand on ceremony here at home."

The nawab joined us bourbon drinkers with a Coke. Toasts were offered all around. We chatted informally for a quarter-hour about world affairs, the war, and our families back home. A few minutes before supper, Her Highness joined us. She was anything but casual in a striking yellow lace sari, with pearls at her ears, neck, and wrists.

Our hostess ushered us into an anteroom adjacent to the living room, where we sat at a round table to dine.

Bearers brought the three courses from a buffet table set along one wall. The first course was a salad of tropical fruits with cilantro, other local greens, ginger, and topped with olive-oil dressing. The second course consisted of cold roast beef and lightly seasoned lamb curry with rice, a dozen sweet and sour savories in small bowls, plus bringal and other local vegetables. Though sweets and cheeses were offered as a third course, none of us could find tummy space for them.

After supper His Highness sat down on the living room floor, took off his shoes, and said to us, "Do take off your shoes and make yourselves comfortable. Your feet must be hurting after your long day in those heavy boots."

This was not a household where one removed his footwear before entering. As a modern Muslim the nawab eschewed that practice. He removed his Italian-made shoes simply to make us feel at home. We happily peeled down to our socks and sat cross-legged in a circle on the Persian carpet. Only our hostess, sitting in a chair, kept her open-toed gold sandals on, revealing red lacquered toenails beneath her beige nylons. We chatted for the next half hour. Then Her Highness abruptly arose, bade us goodnight, and urged us to return again some day. We jumped to our feet to say our thanks.

For another few minutes we stood there discussing politics, health, and the history and present status of Palanpur state. Then the nawab said, "Please sit down and make yourselves more comfortable. Excuse me a moment while I fetch something to show you that I'm sure you've never seen before."

Of course we were intrigued. Moments later our curiosity was satisfied when he brought back a pair of eyeglasses with a strange contrivance over the lenses. The nawab sat down, placed a book in his lap, put on the glasses, looked straight ahead, and started to read without looking down. Then he rose awkwardly to his feet, hindered by injuries from a long-ago polo accident, and walked across the room still looking ahead, not missing a step. What a boon for a man who could not bend at neck or waist!

"Try them out," he said, handing the glasses over to us.

For the next few minutes we bent over in laughter as we watched J.C. and Jim stumble across the floor, and saw Jim thrown to the rug when he looked down. I couldn't even get up from my chair without removing the glasses, but did manage to take a few upright steps after I got the hang of the gadget.

On our departure, the nawab and the two young men accompanied us downstairs to the palace door. "You must come again before you leave India," our host said, embracing each of us warmly. "Maybe I can arrange a leopard shoot for you then. In the meantime I'll mail the chinkara horns to your home in the States."

As we said goodnight, the nawabzada held on to J.C.'s hand as he whispered in his ear. I saw lifted eyebrows and heard snatches of provocative dialogue about a moonlight ride. The men were apparently concocting a late-night rendezvous of a nature that had me worried.

"What goes on here?" I whispered to a nonplussed J.C., steering him toward the waiting car. Jim conferred with the Indian men a few seconds longer before he joined us in the Buick.

"What was that all about?" I said, as we sped back to our quarters. "Was the nawabzada trying to lure you back to his apartment? Why all the hand-holding?"

Once inside the guesthouse, Jim and J.C. quickly cleared up the matter. The nawabzada had offered to show the boys the nightlife of Palanpur. Not knowing this, I had misinterpreted the suggestion as a different kind of moonlight ride. Seeing the strange expression on my face, the nawabzada had pursued the suggestion no further and the boys missed out on their tour of Palanpur's red light section. How was I to know?

At noon the next day we boarded the train for the hill station of Mt. Abu. An hour later a taxi took us up to the village on a jagged mountain, with rocky crags, old castles on faraway hills, and picturesque temples nestled among the trees. The setting was perfect for our planned event, but the off-season accommodations in this summertime resort were not conducive to a long stay.

After an almost inedible supper and a dismal night at the single shabby hotel, we sought out a resident parson who, for a sizeable consideration performed a simple double-ring ceremony for J.C. and me. Jim was our witness and best man.

The Double Knot

Coming back down to earth after a heavenly leave was a letdown. But, with body refreshed and spirit eager, I was ready to tackle the ongoing job problems. In early April, 1945, I wrote my parents:

> *We arrived here [Karachi] at three in the morning, after a long, hot, dirty train ride during which I did not remove my dress for two days and two nights. It took another hour to find a taxi to get me home, and then I had to knock on the door to get in, only to discover that I had no bed to sleep in.*
>
> *Returning a week earlier than planned, I had not foreseen that another worker would come in during my absence and be sound asleep in my bed. But that's just what happened. I was obliged to finish out the night in fitful slumber, while noisy little mice ran around the floor and threatened to crawl into the love seat where I finally curled up.*

Lou was out on a date when I arrived back from my leave. Though I could hardly wait to tell her my exciting news, I stretched out on the love seat and fell asleep from sheer exhaustion.

Around midnight Lou tugged at my sleeve. "Wake up, you lazy lummox," she said, giving me a big hug. "Gee, it's good to see you, Lib. The place has been like a morgue while you've been gone."

"An unusually busy morgue, I'll wager," I responded wearily.

"Did you have a perfectly marvelous time? I'm dying to hear all about it."

"We couldn't have had more fun, even in paradise," I said, now wide-awake. "Our stay at the palace was fabulous, but Mt. Abu was a big disappointment. One thing was lacking."

"What was lacking? Did you run out of money?"

"Oh, yes, that too. But we missed something else more important."

"What do you mean? Don't make me guess all morning."

"I didn't have a maid of honor," I said as calmly as I could.

"A maid of honor? What are you talking about, Lib?"

"Just that. I needed someone to stand up with me. Jim was J.C.'s best man, but I had to stand alone."

"Good gosh, Lib! Surely you didn't elope. It's against theatre rules."

"I know it is," I said with a shrug. "But the US Army can't rule out love. And neither could we."

"Wow! Can't say I'm really surprised though. I just hope J.C. doesn't get busted. I'll keep my fingers crossed."

"Me too," I mumbled. "But let's wait 'til tomorrow for all the details. Right now I just want to get a little shut-eye."

"Sweet dreams, chum."

"Same to you."

A double knot, I'm told, is much stronger and harder to untie or break than a single one. Such was the case with J.C. and me. To satisfy the military and to forestall a dishonorable discharge for J.C. after our elopement in Mt. Abu, we had a second ceremony in Karachi in late May 1945.

What a wedding it was! No flowers, no music, no spectators throwing rice. Jim stood up for J.C. again. I hummed my own wedding march, the traditional Lohengrin. I wore the simple polka-dotted pique that J.C. had designed for the occasion and stuck a sprig of jasmine in my hair. A dark-skinned local Methodist minister raced through the double-ring service, now pronouncing us man and wife. Then J.C. enfolded me in strong khaki-clad arms and planted a long keeper-kiss on my eager lips.

J.C.'s best buddy, Jim Peden, an "old married man" in his late thirties, stood by with tears in his eyes. Jim provided three important items: $20 cash to the preacher, who spared us a sermon, and two silver wedding rings, lovingly pounded out of Australian florins, each engraved "Souvenir CBI." Then the three of us drove, in a borrowed jeep, to a Karachi hotel for extended libations and dinner in the dining room.

Jim took the jeep back to the airbase. After a two-day stay in less than sumptuous quarters, J.C. and I returned to our respective jobs and the "Oh's" and "Ah's" of our co-workers.

It was not the wedding I had dreamed of for years: the big affair with heirloom veil, bridesmaids galore, and a hope chest long ago filled with Stieff silver and embroidered linens. I dared not let myself ponder my family's shock upon learning about my sudden life commitment to a man so unlike their expectations for their only daughter.

But J.C. was the man I wanted.

After a later extended honeymoon in the fall of 1945, at J.C.'s hunting cabin in Michigan, we began our glorious life adventure in the wild that lasted for forty-seven years, until his death in 1992.

The Man I Married

$\mathcal{I}$n May, 1945 I wrote this account of my new husband and our nuptials to my Wisconsin U. friend, Dorothy Wirtz:

> Well, after years of making up my mind and un-making it, I finally took the bull by the horns and made the final plunge. (Excuse mixed metaphors.) Yep, the corporal, now a sergeant finally convinced me, so we were secretly married on that famous leave two months ago. We had a three-day honey-moon at that time and a two-day one just recently, when a second ceremony was performed, this time with the army's permission. It's all very compli-cated.
>
> Marriage without permission is a court-martial offence and permission is very hard to get in this theatre. If we had waited for it in the first place, we wouldn't have had any time together at all. So we got married on leave and just kept it quiet until the military permission came through and the second ceremony was performed.
>
> This is the first time I've ever felt that my life had any meaning or my personality had any integration. I feel settled, secure and complete at last. Gosh, it's such a wonderful feeling! I hate people who get com-placent and change after marriage, but I can almost understand it now. It's like groping in the dark for years, then suddenly finding what you've been grop-ing for. Oh well, enough of such drivel. Hope to see you soon. I'm now Mrs. J.C. Appel.

To somewhat ease the shock for my family, I wrote them in early May:

> I suppose it must be hard for you to think of your daughter getting married away from home to some-one you've never seen, just as I feel kinda funny about not knowing J.C.'s family.

> *But this is war, and we just can't bend circum-*
> *stances to our will as we can in peace times. J.C. is*
> *the man I wanted to marry—the only one I haven't*
> *been down deep afraid to marry. He suits me to a T."*

Because of our different social and educational back-grounds, personalities, and philosophies of life, our friends didn't give us six months. Realizing this early on, J.C. said to me, "This is it. There isn't ever going to be a di-vorce."

Mom and Dad must have been amazed to see how quickly J.C. was able to dominate their willful, headstrong daughter, as shown in these letter-excerpts:

> *It's fun having a new boss. J.C. is so staunch and*
> *sturdy and dependable. Yesterday he told me about*
> *reassigning his insurance to me and how much he's*
> *allotting for my living. The gov't. automatically takes*
> *out $50 for the wife, but J.C. is adding $25 to that*
> *out of his pay. I didn't think this necessary, but he*
> *doesn't want me to have to eat into my savings, or to*
> *borrow from the family. If, and when, we have any*
> *children, I will get $25 more. J.C. expects to save a*
> *little from the $35, which will be left in his salary.*

> *J.C. says I must write to his parents, to his grand-*
> *mother, and to his favorite aunt and uncle once a*
> *week after I get home. Said I, "If that's the case, you*
> *can write to my parents and to Gram and Aunt Wib."*
> *Incidentally, J.C. told me the kind of letter he was*
> *going to write you soon. It was of a type that could*
> *be misinterpreted, so I bet him he wouldn't send it.*
> *He bet me a Lily Daché hat to a light fly-rod that he*
> *would send it. Knowing him as I do, I guess he will*
> *send it, so don't be surprised when you get a strange*
> *letter from your new son-in-law.*

J.C.'s Letter

J.C. did send that letter. I found it years later tucked away in Dad's filing cabinet, along with the 200 letters I had sent from India. It tells more about the man I married than anything I can now add after forty-seven adventurous years with J.C. Appel: hunter, fly-fisherman, archer, mechanic, jack-of-all-trades, wildlife refuge manager, devoted father of two sons, and exciting, caring husband.

Here's the letter, copied from the handwritten original:

United States Army

Dear Mr. and Mrs. Chitwood,

I have married your daughter. This may or may not meet with your approval. Frankly I hope it does, on the other hand I suppose there is no good reason why it should. Personally I am quite happy about the whole thing.

I don't know what Libby has told you about me but I expect, since we have had no serious differences as yet, that it has been highly colored in my favor. While you may have taken this with a grain of salt, since you have known her a good deal longer than I, let me assure you that I have at least a normal collection of faults and vices. Not that Libby would be deliberately misleading, it is just that she is not constitutionally impartial and I notice a lamentable tendency to use just those facts that suit her cause.

Before the war I worked for money so that I could eventually lead a preferred way of life. After the war I intend to live that way of life and make it eventually provide money comforts. I sometimes wonder if Libby married me because of or in spite of this idea. In either case I'll try not to disappoint her.

It is unfortunate that we do not know each other. I would have wished it otherwise but these days a whole lot of wishes find themselves back logged. Time always seems to clean up backlogs and perhaps it will not be too long before it will take care of this one.

Before I sat down to do this I kept saying to myself: "It will be simple. Just write two or three pages, put them in an envelope and mail it." Nothing could be simpler than that except that I didn't pay attention to what I was going to say on those two or three pages I so blithely mentioned. So far I find myself trying to make an impression. Looking over what I've written, I can't figure out whether it is good or bad I'm trying for.

Just what do you write to newly acquired Father and Mother-in-laws? Especially when they had nothing to say in the matter. When I first thought of it I was a bit surprised that anyone except Libby and I were involved. Must be a rather uneasy feeling to just sit back and rely on your daughter's judgment as to what she brings into the family. Let's hope it was good.

I think I'll end this by giving you my opinion of your new son-in-law. To begin with I'm tall, slim, if you want to be kind, if not, skinny will do, brown hair, blue eyes, a Roman nose and a few crooked teeth. Proud of my hands and spend a lot of time keeping them up. Your daughter thinks I'm good looking but every time I shave I get the idea that she is prejudiced. High School education, traded college to learn a trade. Have two: electrician and elevator constructor. Worked at a number of things before going into the contracting business, from lumbering to training bird dogs. Labor under the fixed delusion that I could do anything if I wanted to do it badly enough. No great ambitions except to live comfortably and to be as independent as possible. Like Shakespeare because he said a number of things I should have liked to have said first. Hunting and fishing have been my hobbies. Conservative politically, I distinctly dislike government interference with the individual and realize that it is going to more and more. I love my wife.

Sincerely,

J.C. Appel

Mounting the camel
with Major Singh,
Nawab's aide de camp.
Libby in back.
Palanpur, March 1945.

Taley Mohammed Khan,
Nawab of Palanpur,
1945, with his oldest
son, the heir apparent
(nawabzada).

Zorowar Palace, Palanpur, March 1945.

Zorowar Palace,
Palanpur, March 1945.

J.C. with his nelghai
at Palanpur, 1945.

J.C. and Libby at the
guest house steps.
Palanpur, March 1945.

The members of the
shoot. Palanpur, 1945.

Mr. and Mrs. Oliver Perry Chitwood

announce the marriage of their daughter

Elizabeth Anne

to

Sergeant J. C. Appel

United States Army Air Force

on Tuesday, March the twenty-seventh

Nineteen hundred and forty-five

India

Wedding
Announcement.

Newlyweds in wedding finery.
Karachi, 1945.

Second wedding.
Karachi, 1945.

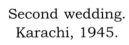

AMERICAN RED CROSS

APO 886, Local
March 8, 1945.

Cpl. J. C. Appel
AACS, 176th Det., 126 Sqd.
APO 882, Local

Dear Cpl. Appel:

In reply to your query concerning the possibility of spending some time in the state of Palanpur as the guest of His Highness, the Maharajah, we wish to state that arrangements are now being made for your sojourn there and that an official invitation will be forthcoming shortly. The invitation is extended for two weeks beginning Tuesday, March 20, or as soon thereafter as train travel can be arranged. You will be met at the station by His Highness' social secretary, who will instruct you in procedures which will be helpful to the enjoyment of your stay in Palanpur.

You may be interested to know that this is the first time that an enlisted man has been invited to the palace. There will be other American military and Red Cross guests there at the same time. You should bring with you whatever uniform is considered as formal dress for enlisted men in the U.S. Army.

It is probable that big-game hunting will be arranged during your stay in Palanpur. All such arrangements for this, as well as for smaller hunting trips, will be made upon your arrival there. Guns and ammunition will be supplied by His Highness. There will be no expense attached to these hunting trips.

Will you please let us know as soon as possible just what your train schedule will be, so that we may notify His Highness exactly when to expect you.

We hope that your stay in Palanpur will be pleasant and exciting in every way.

Yours sincerely,

American Red Cross, APO 886

Acknowledgments

Many friends and family helped me get this book together. Julia Chitwood and Barbara Lawing, my editors, shepherded me through six rewrites. Cathy Brophy, my publisher, and Pace Clem, graphic designer, worked hard to produce a final product to my specifications. Eileen Marshall, Shirley Morrow, John Monahan, and Taylor Blackwell read early editions, pen in hand, and made thoughtful comments and corrections. My thanks to you all.

I am grateful too to Brenda Barger, Ann Lee Cook, Pat Sailstad, Patrick Conner, Joy Adiletta, Sarah Almond, Henry Chitwood, and Rudy and Helen Almasy, who waded through early editions and encouraged me to "keep at it." The two Jim's (Webb and Dunlap), early fans, listened and laughed and cheered me on through the three years to production. And to all my friends at The Pines, who waited so patiently for the final product, I offer my deep appreciation and love.

Libby